THE NIGGER IN YOU

THE NIGGER IN YOU

Challenging Dysfunctional Language,
Engaging Leadership Moments

DR. J. W. WILEY

STERLING, VIRGINIA

Published by Stylus Publishing, LLC
22883 Quicksilver Drive
Sterling, Virginia 20166-2102

Library of Congress Cataloging-in-Publication Data
Wiley, J. W., 1958-
The nigger in you : challenging dysfunctional language, engaging leadership moments / J.W. Wiley.
    pages   cm
Includes bibliographical references and index.
ISBN 978-1-57922-985-6 (cloth : alk. paper)
ISBN 978-1-57922-986-3 (pbk. : alk. paper)
ISBN 978-1-57922-987-0 (library networkable e-edition)
ISBN 978-1-57922-988-7 (consumer e-edition)
    1. Cultural pluralism—United States.   2. Invective—
United States.   3. Racism—United States.
4. Discrimination—United States.   I. Title.
E184.A1W487   2013
303.3'85—dc23   2012049636

13-digit ISBN: 978-1-57922-985-6 (cloth)
13-digit ISBN: 978-1-57922-986-3 (paper)
13-digit ISBN: 978-1-57922-987-0 (library networkable e-edition)
13-digit ISBN: 978-1-57922-988-7 (consumer e-edition)

Printed in the United States of America

All first editions printed on acid-free paper that meets the American National Standards Institute Z39-48 Standard.

Bulk Purchases

Quantity discounts are available for use in workshops and for staff development.
Call 1-800-232-0223

First Edition, 2013

10   9   8   7   6   5   4

This book is dedicated to all the people who have suffered at the hands of others' inconsiderate word choices as well as all those who have had the courage to engage in a leadership moment and make a difference by challenging dysfunctional language.

CONTENTS

ACKNOWLEDGMENTS

As with most significant accomplishments, it was quite a journey arriving at this point in my life. My overriding desire to leave a legacy, validated by accomplishing specific goals, was well under way, with the only thing left being the writing of my own book, which is now complete. Sigh! What is undeniable, though, about my journey is all the people who played a pivotal role in my embracing my leadership moment to challenge dysfunctional language.

Mom, your never-ending encouragement along with you writing your own book convinced me that I had a book in me. Ivory (Dad), your wisdom, patience, love, and ever attentive ear during our morning walks when I visit you two, especially during those visits this last summer when I was actually writing this book, as always were invaluable. Mikki, big sis, I actually created the front cover of the book during our ride from Redondo Beach to your new place in Torrance. Sayyid, your alter ego (Terry James) may have been the one who introduced me to some of the language I am addressing in this book. Derek, you and Lovell were probably my road dogs through the early days of using the dysfunctional language I engage within this book. Evelyn, I can still hear you admonishing me for much of that type of language. Pauline, I can still hear you trying to resist laughing at how clever we were in dispensing it.

Thanks to Adrienne Boyd, the most superb ex-wife/co-parent/best friend a man could possibly have. On so many levels none of this happens without you, your love, mentoring, insights, humor, and patience.

Thanks to my brothers and sisters: Julius Bedford, George Jackson, Maurice McGlothern, Alva and Zack Stewart, Byron Mobley, Alan Zinsmeister, Bernard (Buford) Ferguson, Dr. Al Sargent, Dr. Abe Recio, Deb Light, Kristie Gonyea, Michael Thompson, Monte Prather, Dr. Eddie Moore Jr., Dr. Ken Palm, Butch Turgeon, Wayne and Stacy Kneussel, Glen Huber, James Collins, Shalonda Thompson, and Joseph Aesquivel.

Thanks to some of my current students—Edmund Adjapong and Aaron Schwartz, my YBs for life, Robyn Edghill, Lauren Gonyea, Jill Mann, and Alyssa Velsey—for the roles they played in helping me research my book as well as for conversations that we had that directly contributed to its message.

Thanks to what I refer to as some of my top-shelf students (students who are personal friends and both protégés/mentors for me): Angel Acosta, Nick Horgan, Nick Tubbs, Derek Hess, Anna Epshteyn, Tim Sarrantonio, Marvelle Roberts, Erica Bohlen, Heather Wright, Shanah Krug, Yslane M'Sahi, Cecille LeGalles, Charlie Peppers, James Goosey, Derek Rosenbaum, Krystle Furioso, Art Graves, Kevin Pearson, Sean Matthews, Kristen Saheim, Katie Murphy, Gabrielle Equale, Sara AbiBoutros, and Raquel Matthews. All of you were extremely influential in keeping me academically upright as teaching assistants, top-notch students who intellectually challenged me to grow or shrink before your greatness and now are personal friends. Oh, and thanks to the four infamous SUNY Plattsburgh students whom I won't mention by name, but know who they are and that without their contribution a certain chapter would have had a very different flavor.

Thanks to my colleagues who contributed to different opportunities for me to develop and polish my ability to engage leadership moments: Deborah Walsh, Nicole DiDomenico, Kent Eldridge, Amy Valentine, Martha Swan, Shanelle Henry Robinson, Mike Harrington, Lorraine Seidel, Crystal Shipp, Kevin Smith, Dr. Melissa Paradee, Robert Parks, Bob Grady, Elise Rock, Dr. Michelle Kavanaugh, Richard Allen, Garth Frechette, A. Paul Scott, Chris Mazella, Shelley Nielsen, Gerry Goldman, Lois Clermont, Robin Caudell, Ron Brady, Steve Bartlett, Robert Smith, Dr. Richard Johnson, and Russell Banks. Each of you directly contributed to the book in some way or another that you can ask me about when next we talk if it isn't obvious to you.

Thanks to my academic crew: Dr. Thomas Keith, Dr. Robert Golden, Dr. Joel Smith, Dr. Tom Moran, Dr. Mike Morgan, Dr. Kathie LaVoie, Dr. Doug Skopp, Dr. Richard Robbins, Dr. Marc Cohen, William Laundry, Dr. Pat Higgins, Cerise Oberman, Jean Mockry, Dr. Darrell Cleveland, Dr. Daryl Smith, Dr. Al Spangler, Ana Torres-Bower, Dr. Halford Fairchild, Dr. Ed Bloomfield, Mark Mastrean, Dr. Murray Schwartz, Dr. Larry Soroka, Holly Heller-Ross, Dr. Dan Lake, Dr. Judith Aiken, Dr. David Shiman, Dr. Michele Carpentier, Brian Hartmann, Dr. Beth Dixon, Dr. James Armstrong, Dr. Dave Mowry, Dr. Tracie Guzzio, Dr. David Stone, Dr. Lisa Lax, Dr. John Etling, and Dr. Jean Ann Hunt, whose peer mentoring, political posturing, and various conversations assisted me in weathering certain storms until I discovered the necessary perspective to remain dry.

Thanks to "my" publisher and now friend, John von Knorring, who after hearing my ideas for the book followed up with an e-mail two days later asking me if I had started it. We went after it and, at times, one another in our uniquely different ways, but stayed the course.

And last but not least, thanks to my children, Justin and Autumn, whose lives colored-in many of my anecdotes, whose friendship and energy always inspire me and fill me with hope, and whose sometimes daunting experiences armed me with the passion to challenge dysfunctional language. Thanks to Dr. Helene Fournier, my personal psychologist, unpaid researcher, and love-Her; and Vanessa White, my soul mate/daughter—two of the most amazing women I've ever known—for holding my hand throughout the short but all-out sprint to write this book. Your encouragement and feedback as the primary readers of the manuscript gave me the confidence I needed to keep going.

PREFACE

R andall Kennedy (2002), in the introduction to his book *Nigger: The Strange Career of a Troublesome Word*, states,

> Contrary to what some detractors suggest, *nigger* does not appear on the cover of my book absent a context for its presentation. The book's subtitle . . . immediately signals an intention to highlight the problematic status of the term—an intention that is advanced by over 100 pages of text, most of which focuses on the reprehensible ways in which Euro-Americans have deployed language to stigmatize African Americans. (p. 144)

Similar to Kennedy's intention/efforts I decided to write this book not to glamorize the word *nigger*, nor to capitalize on it beyond the reality of getting out a viable message, but to focus "on the reprehensible ways in which" all Americans "have deployed language to stigmatize" all Americans. *Nigger* is often considered by many to be the most deplorable word in the English language. While I understand that sentiment—and as a Black man appreciate the concern—the word doesn't impact every person and isn't the worst thing that could be said to insult different people with unique realities. In other words, calling a person with little confidence in her social skills outside of the context of her expertise in technology a "nigger" might have that person looking at you as if you have lost your mind. However, calling that same person a "nerd" or "geek" might completely ruin her day.

The purpose of this book is to discuss "the nigger in you." The conversation I am endeavoring to have with my readers is quite a different one from the conversations of others who have explored the term. Dick Gregory discussed it in the context of an autobiography. Randall Kennedy discussed it from the perspective of the term *nigger*'s journey through American society, with an occasional glimpse of its global implications. My intent is to engage it specifically as they both have done, but to a much lesser extent. *Nigger* in the context in which I'm using it is more a point of departure for discussion of other problematic terms that are known to dehumanize others. Because *nigger* has obtained the reputation of being the worst of all dysfunctional terms that can be used to denigrate another, we often sanctify it as the ultimate insult. However, it has been my experience, as a university diversity director and educational/business consultant, that the ultimate disparagement is at best contextually derived. Terms such as *bitch, fag, sissy,* and *retard* when aimed at those who consider themselves "cool" can and more often than not do cut like a knife.

In this book I invite my readers to travel with me for a while. As a Black man in American society, my way of seeing—my lens, my indoctrination, my socialization—is one that is steeped heavily in African American culture. Traveling with me through this book my readers will find many if not most of our examinations of dysfunctional language engaged on some level from an African American perspective. However, because I am fully aware that no one operates solely from one identity, throughout this book you will also get glimpses of my perspective that are tempered and shaped as a result of my other identities. Ultimately, though, our final destination is an elevation of consciousness that is best obtained by first making nine distinct stops along the way. Each one of those stops is articulated thoroughly within a chapter that frames it. I use personal stories, scholarship, film and television excerpts, and song lyrics to provide my readers with a variety of different stimuli as a point of departure for the discussions. In some chapters, I also use poetry, blog excerpts, and revisited newspaper op-ed pieces I have written. Our journey will have us first, in chapter 1, reflecting upon diversity's relationship to social justice, and how diversity and social justice contribute to the consideration of our multiple identities. In chapter 2, I engage what is arguably the most problematic term in American society—*retard*—as a result of its general acceptance and usage as an awkward but not necessarily profane term. I then, in chapter 3, explore some of the problematic tensions of the language that surrounds sexual orientation.

In chapter 4, through some personal and professional anecdotes, I challenge my readers to consider gender and many of its sexist overtones. In chapter 5, as a result of a class I designed and teach, titled "Examining Dimensions of Cool: A Study of Social Class," I explore the notion of "cool" within a context of social class. Chapter 6 is where the term *nigger* is engaged from a historical context to its current-day impact and implications. Chapter 7 challenges readers to consider how the social injustices that are articulated within the other chapters often result in unearned privileges for unaware recipients as well as those who would unashamedly accept and leverage that privilege in their favor. Chapter 8 articulates bullying as a diversity concern, with an explication of respect, hypocrisy, and consideration as germane to the discussion. And chapter 9 challenges readers to avoid hating the hater while taking responsibility for defining themselves.

My objective in writing *The Nigger in You* is not just to engage/unpack the dysfunctional language we inconsiderately use with one another. I endeavor to create a revolution, an army of allies that will assist us in understanding how ridiculous, as well as how socially and psychologically damaging, it is for us to refer to one another so inhumanely, so disrespectfully, so inconsiderately.

As someone heavily invested in diversity and social justice education, in all the work I do I emphasize the intrinsic link between diversity and leadership. I also suggest that all my students, workshop participants, and readers take ownership of how they affect their community/world and how they allow their community/world to affect them. I unrelentingly attempt to convey the necessity of respect within a diversity context by assessing disrespect. I also unflinchingly examine diversity by examining the notions of responsibility, sanctuary, adversity, consideration, hypocrisy, privilege (earned and unearned), perspective, illusion, "isms," moral obligations, courageous defiance, success, influence, the benefit of the doubt, and humanity.

The reason we use dysfunctional language is that we don't examine our problems with language in detail. Instead, what is often done is just telling people that they shouldn't use it, with no rhyme or reason attached to our sometimes not adamant enough condemnation. Language's power, especially when dysfunctional, can be debilitating. The cure to the type of communication cancer that dysfunctional language causes within a community begins with consideration of the Other.

I imagine this book could be invaluable to scholars, students, parents, and people in general who could benefit from exploring some of the reasons why people choose to use dysfunctional language. They could all benefit from considering what the language actually does for them and what the language says about them as perpetrator, as well as from rethinking what their intended purpose was in using it. I wrote this book to provide a point of departure for difficult conversations on dysfunctional language. I wrote this book to assist others in unpacking societal situations that enable if not promote hate speak. I wrote this book to serve as a resonating resource if not repository of rhetorical wrongdoing. I unabashedly endeavored to write a book with more than just many-chapter appeal. I wrote this book in hopes that it might offer, to varying degrees, an enticing every-individual's story filled with as much intrigue as insight. I wrote this book for parents, friends, and book club members so that they can begin a dialogue about dysfunctional language. I wrote this book to challenge anyone with an interest in promoting an appreciation for diversity and social justice to take a step further into an always available but not always engaged opportunity for leadership that I frame as a "leadership moment." I wrote this book to inspire hesitation before hypocrisy, respect over disrespect, and consideration of the importance of consideration.

So, inspired by W. E. B. Du Bois's efforts to provide insight into "the souls of Black folk," bell hooks's efforts to engage why it is that "we real cool," Cornel West's articulation of why "race matters," along with Michael Eric Dyson's explication of "race rules," I am presenting for your consideration if not edification an opportunity to become better situated in conversation around words like *nigger/nigga, bitch* and *ho, girl* and *you guys, retard* and *handicap, wetback, cracker, fag* and *sissy, trailer trash,* and other problematic language that dehumanizes, insults, hurts, embarrasses, humiliates, and essentially makes no sense when we really consider it. So yes, this is my attempt to coexamine dysfunctional language with you, the reader, while also providing you an opportunity to explore "the nigger in you."

INTRODUCTION

This is a revolution. It started long before I came into it, and I may die before it's over, but we'll bust this thing and cut out this cancer. America will be as strong and beautiful as it should be, for black folks and white folks. We'll all be free then, free from a system that makes a man less than a man, that teaches hate and fear and ignorance.

You didn't die a slave for nothing, Momma. . . . Those of us who weren't destroyed got stronger, got calluses on our souls. And now we're ready to change a system, a system where a white man can destroy a black man with a single word, Nigger.

When we're through, Momma, there won't be any niggers any more.

—Gregory (1964, p. 209)

My mother once recounted a story in which I must have been about six years old when I approached her and confidently offered her what was perhaps one of my earliest theories. She said I proffered to her—after examining a world map—that Negroes must originate from Niger while niggers must come from Nigeria. She said it was the only way I could rationalize the different usages of the terms from my limited exposure and experiences.

Many years later, my then six-year-old son, Justin, walked into the house after exiting his school bus the way any first grader with high energy and a natural zest for life does: smiling. Our eyes met as he approached me. My energy was also good in that moment and I anticipated some fun moments with him on the horizon. He then said to me, "Hey, Dad, this fifth-grade girl on the school bus keeps calling me names." I replied, "What types of names, son?" Justin responded, "Oh, she calls me fathead, meathead, and boxhead." I looked at him as earnestly as I could and replied, "Come on, man, I call you those names as well as rockhead, so what's your point? Get over it." After a moment of him smiling and shaking his head at me in amusement, I further chimed in, "Listen, Justin, here's what you do. The next time this fifth-grade girl calls you those names you say to her, as seriously as you can, 'Hey, I'm a first grader! You're a fifth grader! Grow up!' " Laughing and seeming impressed with me, Justin turned to walk away. It was in that moment that I knew, somehow sensed, I needed to inquire further. "Hey, son, I was just wondering, has anyone else called you names?" He turned around and said, "Actually, Dad, there is another kid on the bus, another fifth grader, who kind of whispers something to me as I pass him." My heart sank and yet, at the same time, I attempted to steel my emotions for what I thought might be coming next. Begrudgingly I asked my innocent little man, "What is it that boy whispers?" Justin responded, "Dad, I think he was saying something like 'nigger.' " As I write this now I am emotional. I can still never successfully stifle the emotion I feel when I reflect back on the pain I felt having to tell my little boy that he would be hearing that word the rest of his life, why he would hear it, and what people meant by it. In one swift instant, a part of his innocence that he would not have lost if he were a little White boy was gone forever. How I wish it just meant that he was from Nigeria.

How many incidents like mine have shaped other Black parents' realities I'll never know, but I have no doubt that such incidents have occurred to others with the impact being huge. On so many levels there is no story more powerful that I can tell that doesn't involve a homicide or rape, though this tale itself reflects an untimely death (in terms of the murder of my child's sense of fair play, equality, and justice) and blatant violation of someone's personhood against his will. When we consider all of this, is it an overstatement when people consider the far-too-often-called "*N*-word," as so many people assert, to be the most biting insult in the English language? Is it because *nigger* has a history associated with it that no other socially unjust terms reflect? Is it because it has also been applied to Native Americans (red niggers), Arabs (sand niggers), and even Whites (wiggers)? Is it because it's a term that only one U.S. president has probably ever had to consider as an insult toward him?

The fact that people's words and actions can be affected by the use of a term they really don't have much knowledge about is as perplexing as anything I've encountered in my lifetime. However, it is no less perplexing than the old adage of the pot calling the kettle black. The kid who whispered "nigger" to my son did so in a covertly, stealthily manner. As he said it, each time he said it, he knew he was wrong. He said it with complete disregard for my son's sense of self, aiming it at my son to gauge his reaction, to assert his fifth-grade power over a first grader, perhaps even to amuse himself at someone else's expense. There was a time in my life when I would have easily said that the nigger isn't the one being called the term, but the one affixing the label on others. That was before I realized that in redirecting that label, I'm only creating the possibility of transferring the dysfunction, essentially becoming, albeit subconsciously, poised to hate the hater. My position is that the person receiving the word isn't a nigger. A nigger isn't a person, but a societal problem created through society's inability to educationally engage, to successfully integrate our differences. As a result, when we label someone a nigger, beyond referring to him or her as a problem, we also disrespectfully imply an expectation of behavior that at the very least borders on criminal activity, both elements of someone whom society deems as a conundrum of sorts. We also imply that the person is a societal misfit but in the context of society's inability to have better engaged all of its citizens. This is how *nigger* is framed within our society, yet not actually articulated, if we closely consider it, and how I attempt to specifically define it within this book. However, I emphatically do not condone labeling others with dysfunctional language. I do not call those who use dysfunctional language to disparage others names, nor do I encourage others to do that.

Within this book the use of the phrase "the nigger in you" has multiple meanings and purposes for the reader's edification. My appropriating what arguably is the most contentious word in the American vocabulary is to provocatively declare that the reader is about to depart upon one of the edgiest intellectual journeys she or he may have ever embarked upon. As a Black man and Black father, the term *nigger* is the one I am most familiar with. Hence, it is my point of departure, and although it will make many uncomfortable, there is no gain without pain. As an educator, though, I have come to realize that *nigger* is not the term that adversely affects all others. I endeavor for my readers to recognize that *nigger* is really only another equally wounding and dysfunctional epithet among a plethora of problematic, dehumanizing language that is in common daily usage. I endeavor for my readers to recognize the impact that all these hateful terms have on those to whom they are applied. To the extent that you let words such as *bitch* and *retard* cut you like knives, there is a nigger in you. When we are that affected by this type of language we've given someone the power to define us. This book is about unmasking those perpetrators, which, to our chagrin, are often many of us, inadvertently. To the extent that we realize that we are using dysfunctional terms to define others, we need to unpack that insipid indoctrination for what it is worth, and undertake whatever measures necessary to ensure we cease and desist. This book is about a necessary conversation that is long overdue.

The nigger in you, the retard in you, the bitch, fag, sissy, chink, wetback, nerd, cracker in you are all nonsensical terms given far too much agency. These words abound in our society and are the reasons why diversity initiatives are taking on new dimensions that transcend a monolithic conception of diversity as predominantly a racial initiative.

Dictionary definitions of diversity often define it as "noticeable heterogeneity" or "the condition or result of being variable." If we were to get inside of these definitions where would we ultimately arrive? In defining diversity as "noticeable heterogeneity" most appropriators of this definition would focus more on the "heterogeneity" than the noticeable. They then would be comfortable peering into a room full of people that may all belong to a certain racial category and conclude that due to the homogeneity of race present in that room, the room is devoid of diverse racial representation, the room lacks noticeable heterogeneity, and therefore the room lacks diversity. Conversely, someone peers into a room where many races are represented and the "noticeable heterogeneity" that is characterized in other terms transcending race provides the viewer with a perspective that diversity is in full effect. However, in the first case the room has quite a bit of diversity present because while everyone isn't necessarily of noticeable "racial" heterogeneity, there does exist "the condition or result of being variable." And if we can allow for the possibility to exist that in a room where there doesn't appear to be diversity there actually is, then in a situation where there appears to be quite a bit of diversity or "noticeable heterogeneity," there can be quite a limited perspective.

Just as the definition itself is problematic, the D-word is often wielded about as a tool of manipulation. For far too long it was synonymous with race. What this actually meant was that when people were prepared to discuss diversity they were prepared to discuss race and racism. Imbedded within that conversation was primarily a discussion about blacks and whites. Then society progressed a bit and diversity conversations began to be more inclusive, featuring many non-black disenfranchised groups like Latinos, Asians, and Native Americans. Now finally, in this new millennium, agents of diversity have discovered its new meaning. Diversity is still reflective of a noticeable heterogeneity, but has also become inclusive of an invisible heterogeneity. Social and economic class, disability, homosexuality, ageism, sexism, heterosexism, and disenfranchisement in many contexts are all integral and indistinguishable outside of conversations about diversity. If they are all not a part of diversity discussions, then the discussions are limited and stagnant. But diversity doesn't advance because it just happens. Diversity advances because individuals, colleges, companies, and corporations begin to understand how counterproductive and counterintuitive it is to have any mission, strategic plan or initiative that doesn't engage others' perspectives. In other words, actions that advance diversity don't just happen and conversations about diversity that inspire action don't just occur. (Wiley, 2009, p. 255)

1

OF DIVERSITY, SOCIAL JUSTICE, AND MULTIPLE IDENTITIES

The question I asked of the seventh graders at the beginning of the Diversity Enlightenment (DE) session I was presenting for a middle school in the North Country of New York was simple. When you hear the word *diversity* what comes to mind? The responses were quite intriguing, especially considering the students' range in age from 11 to 13. So, when they responded with "differences," "sameness," "variety," "equality," "justice," "many," "race," "everyone," and "people," their responses were about what I expected. However, the response I didn't expect to hear was "nigger." I was completely thrown off balance. And as if that wasn't peculiar enough, after having presented more than 100 DE workshops at that time all across the North Country of New York, two weeks later an eighth grader at another North Country middle school also responded with "nigger" when asked what comes to mind upon hearing the word *diversity*. Yes, "nigger."

Now, of course they could have been saying the word to shock their teachers, or me the presenter. Nonetheless, there is no doubt that those two young White boys had somehow been socialized to associate the word *nigger* with the word *diversity*. Possibly both words symbolized for the two boys two negatives with a commonality that suggests some type of oncoming and/or required White guilt. Perhaps in their lives any conversation about diversity always resulted in a race conversation, which usually resulted in a conversation about Black and White tensions, which coupled with a synonymous usage of *Blacks* with *niggers* made it impossible to disassociate the two terms. Perhaps the absence of any Black presence in either of their grades created a dynamic whereby words like *nigger* flowed more freely.

7

Perhaps the two White boys from different schools said it to titillate the other students and paint themselves as students capturing the moment, being cool, edgy, or rebellious. Perhaps the boys had been consistently privy to conversations like the one between the father and son at the dinner table in the film *American History X* in which the father warns the son to be leery of "nigger bullshit," when apprised of his son's Black teacher with two PhDs.

What type of an environment is necessary for the word *nigger* to come to the mind of a seventh and an eighth grader when they are asked to respond to the word *diversity?* Not *poor person, retard, queer, bitch, sissy, trailer trash,* etc., but *nigger.* Well, upon accepting a job in the largest city of northeastern New York, Plattsburgh, I was immediately informed by many people that my job was going to be quite difficult. Curious, I inquired why this would be the case. I was then informed of the bottom line in terms of the impending difficulty, if not impossibility, of my new job. I was going to have a difficult time doing my job because there is no longer diversity in the North Country due to the Plattsburgh Air Force base closing. In response to this sentiment I sought a smile, albeit not an amused one. I also endeavored to take a very, very deep breath. I knew the man I spoke with was correct about the difficulties of my job, but incorrect as to the reason. My job was going to be difficult not because of the purported lack of "racial" diversity (because diversity in the truest sense of the word was and always is in abundance), but because of people's misinterpretation of what diversity is, and their lack of understanding exactly how pertinent it actually is and can be to them, and for them.

In conversations I've had all over America people continue to express a sentiment that they have no problem and little hesitation in articulating. With certainty they unapologetically assert that in their communities they have no diversity. This comment often arises from people who are about to participate in the earlier mentioned educational session I present to various audiences called Diversity Enlightenment (DE). It is a strategically conceived interactive session that frames diversity as relative to us all. DE also frames diversity as oftentimes problematic for us all, depending upon the context of our perceived differences. No matter where I present the DE session, the audience itself always comprises a wide array of people of different ages, genders, socioeconomic class, ability, sexual orientation, religion, and privilege within these different groups. However, somehow it is nonetheless believed by many in attendance that their community doesn't have diversity. With all the diversity within any and every community, how is it possible that anyone could articulate such a position? It is because, as W. E. B. Du Bois (1990) accurately framed in *The Souls of Black Folk*, "the problem of the 20th Century is the problem of the color line" (p. 16).

Conversations about race/racism, or the lack of such necessary discourse, have dominated the American landscape from the early beginning of dialogues and discourses on differences. The problem of what to do about the so-called Negro dominated America throughout slavery and especially during the post-emancipation period, even eclipsing the early days of the women's liberation movement. As a result, it makes sense that America would become preoccupied with its racial representation at a level that would somewhat blind Americans to the other differences that exist among them. More so, it makes sense that Americans would default to race-speak whenever they attempted to engage their lack of sophistication and/or their communal growing pains. After all, while women and people with disabling conditions were being denied access to equal opportunity and prevented from voicing their sociopolitical reality, no towns were ever decimated in response to their very existence in those towns. Lies that result in mass murders and lynching never occurred in America as a result of someone's lack of mobility, ability, and/or reliability. Women, or more precisely, White women, were far too often the catalyst for the wanton destruction of townships and cities as a result of an already disenfranchised second-class citizen (women themselves) crying wolf, claiming foul to get their oppressors' (men's) feet off their neck. Let us not forget, though, the White man's xenophobia toward the Black man. Or let's not forget the paranoia about an angry Black man's response to White men's legacy of ownership of Black bodies, an ownership that consequently left him predisposed to a predilection of emasculating this often seen as soulless creature. While Ugly Laws (also known as the unsightly beggar ordinances—laws established from the 1860s until the 1970s in several American cities that made it illegal for persons with "unsightly or disgusting" disabilities to appear in public) and other problematic policies contributed to the marginalization and/or ostracism of people often inconsiderately referred to as retards or handicapped, there are no records of mass murders because of community collusion to systematically eradicate those not seen as temporarily able-bodied.

It is no accident that my response to statements like "There is no diversity in my town" is initially met with surprise and intellectual curiosity, if not disdain. When I respond with my series of questions to challenge any notion of a racially monolithic, one-dimensional culture within any community, it takes citizens a moment to gather themselves. Hence, when I respond by saying, "So Plattsburgh is a city of all men, or a city where everyone is the same height, or weight, age, socioeconomic class, sexual orientation, and religion," for a moment they are quite bewildered. Then it becomes apparent that what they meant to say is that there is no "racial diversity" in their community. Is this a big deal? Yes, it is. If people can see diversity as relative to someone other than themselves, or more so, relative to "the Other," then they have an excuse not to lean into that conversation, not to genuinely care about it, and to comfortably not consider it. However, diversity and social justice educators, initiatives, workshops, and programs that are truly worth their weight don't allow their students and/or clients to escape that easily. A necessary yet challenging method to emotionally cultivate a passion for diversity and social justice is to inform them that they themselves are "the Other." By doing this it is possible to frame the notion even tighter by establishing their inability to disassociate from diversity because of their multiple identities. This is significant because if they have any predisposition toward adhering to the golden rule—doing the right thing, loving thy neighbor, representing properly, handling their business, etc.—then they would want to avoid scenarios that frame them as oppressive to others. Obviously it would be paramount to a socially conscious person to not be committing social injustices deliberately. That type of personal transgression would make it hard for that person to sleep at night, let alone get through his or her day. But once we have knowledge about the myriad ways we disrespect others, once we start to cultivate insights about how we might be unknowingly deflating someone due largely just to our ignorance of that person's reality, we no longer have legitimate excuses to continue on with that behavior. It was Albert Camus who, in his provocative essay "The Myth of Sisyphus," eloquently stated, "Beginning to think is beginning to be undermined" (p. 617). Once someone has discussed with you, in detail, significant underlying reasons for how/why we inadequately relate to or treat one another, or more so, once someone has challenged you about the way you engage others, it is quite a bit of work to distance yourself from those lessons. As a matter of fact, eventually many, if not most, people realize it is far more work to fight the change to a more productive behavior than it is to continue to succumb to our inconsiderate whims.

Camus's "Beginning to think is beginning to be undermined" is one of those quotes that allows you to step deeply into a conversation with students about their authenticity and/or lack of sufficient consideration of others. It forces you to either *step up* to being an ally once you've achieved a level of consciousness about exactly what that entails, or own the fact that you may be a hypocrite. For example, one of the phrases many of us say without hesitation is "deal with." Administrators declare without batting an eye that they had to "deal with" this employee. Professors explain how they had to "deal with" a student over a grade. Parents share how they must go home and "deal with" their children, or spouse, or neighbor. What are we really saying when we say "deal with"? Well, if you consider that "deal with" actually has a negative connotation to it, along the lines of "dealing with" a problem, or an adverse situation, why would we be using it in regard to people we should be valuing? What we are really saying when we are about to "deal with" someone is that we are about to "tolerate" our employee, student, children, spouse, or neighbor. What we really mean to say if our goal is to positively affirm an encounter is that we are about to "engage" our employee, student, children, spouse, or neighbor. After all, we tolerate babies crying on an airplane and headaches, but not interactions with people, right? Or, at the very least, we don't want to exclaim to the world inadvertently that we are about to go tolerate an employee, student, children, spouse, or neighbor, even if that is how we feel. It's just not a sophisticated thing to say to someone we may not know quite well who is really listening, possibly trying to figure us out.

Often, though, we are *repulsed* by differences that we have seldom if ever encountered and even then not fully. We then have an *experience* that leaves us with a modicum of *discomfort* to unpack. Upon reflection we realize that we are capable of *tolerating* (dealing with) the difference, eventually moving toward *acceptance* of the difference. We then realize our growth and are more ready to *celebrate* whatever the difference was that had us once upon a time repulsed. It is sometime within or after the moments of celebration that some of us *consider* the path we've traveled as well as what we've achieved, which then contributes to our *enlightenment.* We now know that we can make a difference in the struggle that others have with achieving growth relative to diversity. The passion for *engagement,* becoming an ally and working as a change agent actively engaging others, is the most significant level we can attain on this *elevation of consciousness.*

Elevation of Consciousness

Engagement
Enlightenment
Consideration
Celebration

Acceptance
Toleration
Discomfort
Experience
Repulsion

This new level of consciousness changes our way of seeing. It then has those of us invested in diversity and social justice seeing the person who unwittingly uses the word *retard* in a crowd of people, or the word *nigger*, or the phrase *trailer trash*, as less a perpetrator and more a victim. We see the person who uses dysfunctional language as naively somehow unaware that *someone* in the crowd probably loves the so-called retard, so-called nigger, or so-called trailer trash and may now be offended. We then try to create an environment whereby the person who knowingly uses it, knowing it is hurtful, has to wrestle with her or his demons in terms of her or his living outside of the context of the world's slow evolution toward a more considerate person on a more socially just planet. It will take tremendous effort to knowingly/willingly continue to operate in ignorance.

However, the ability to operate in ignorance has always been accessible, albeit subconsciously. Many people, if not most, who are the targets of inconsiderate language inadvertently default into some dimension of "double consciousness" when incessantly faced with stressful identity situations that have no easily apparent resolutions. An example of *double consciousness*—as originally articulated by Du Bois—can be ascertained in most racial encounters in which a racially underrepresented person feels as if she or he must conform to some dimension of the dominant culture's overvalued normality. I emphasize overvalued because it is precisely the adorning of certain aspects of a dominant culture's reality at the expense of the underrepresented culture that contributes to the dominant culture not considering the perspective of the underrepresented. Conversely, it is the overvaluing of the dominant culture's perspective that often finds the underrepresented doubting the significance, if not validity, of their reality. This is easily seen when Black people who originate from predominantly White neighborhoods are not comfortable with other Black people. Perhaps this is more a phenomenon of the '70s and '80s when positive Black role models were severely lacking anywhere/everywhere in mainstream American culture. Black people being acclimated to a racially dominant culture of Whiteness would find it quite a challenge not to succumb to some of the racial stereotypes/negative assumptions about them being bandied about. And being disassociated from their Blackness, living in predominantly White enclaves, it would be easy to buy into the misguided hype of how problematic Blackness could be when not leveraged against Whiteness. In other words, Blacks from all Black neighborhoods are seen as more apt toward exhibiting criminal behavior because they are too Black, not resembling seemingly safer Blacks like Lenny Kravitz, Raven Simone, Will Smith, Tia and Tamera Mowry, Drake, and the ultimate safer Black, Barack Obama, though they also may have originated from predominantly Black neighborhoods that were also economically challenged and racially regulated. Interestingly enough, many of the Blacks who seem safer eventually become armed with an urban edginess due to a cultural awakening regarding how—though racially privileged in seeming less Black than Blacks of darker shading—they somehow gain a perspective that it is how they negotiate the American culture of capitalism that will be the deciding factor.

Double consciousness, though—the Du Boisian articulated response to a racial identity crisis that frames those racially underrepresented as a problem best treated by them devaluing their racial identity—isn't a phenomenon to be considered in response to only racism. Double consciousness is just as applicable within the context of all other identity crises that arise when underrepresented people's voices are at risk of not being heard or, to a varying extent, the people themselves are being marginalized or ostracized. You can see double consciousness in the student who goes silent in a conversation about summer vacations, preferring to defer any articulation of her experiences over the summer due to her or her family's inability to afford travel. You can also see double consciousness in someone who is hesitant to share her experiences traveling across the country with those who she imagines have nothing to share. Or the disabled boy who is convinced he will be thought of as a retard because his body doesn't allow him to run and jump without pain, so he doesn't even try, and instead of entering the Special Olympics for the opportunity to compete, he sits frustrated at an athletic competition once again overvaluing the experiences of unimpaired athletes. Double consciousness—as a response to an identity crisis—had Hilary Swank's character (a boy born in a girl's body) feeling as if he had to hide his femininity while overprojecting his maleness in the film *Boys Don't Cry* (1999). As the title suggests, the answer to Swank's character is to deny himself access to his "one true self," one that might be more or less resistant to crying, or feeling shame over shedding tears. It is in this moment that Swank's character, born Teena Brandon, now self-proclaimed Brandon Teena, can't avoid and must engage *the nigger* in him. But what is this nigger in him, or more so, the nigger in all of us whom we are forced to engage, forced to deal with in American society?

The diversity and social justice implications of engaging "the nigger in you" are as intriguing as considerations of differing people's usage of the word *nigger*. While applying a logic of assessing the social if not psychological implications of dysfunctional language that is similar to the transitive property of equality in mathematics (if $a = b$ and $b = c$, then $a = c$) in which we will examine differing people's usage in later chapters, the social justice implications of engaging "the nigger in you" begin with unpacking some key concepts. What is diversity and social justice? What do I mean when I speak of "the nigger in you"? What, for the purpose of this conversation, does the word *nigger* suggest, imply, or frame?

Defining *Diversity* and *Social Justice*

Diversity and *social justice* for the purposes of this extended conversation mean what exactly? *Diversity* can be defined simplistically as differences unfolding and/or "the differences" existing within a societal space that does not hinder it. More so, diversity initiatives eliminate barriers that restrict differences from being naturally explored if not celebrated and encouraged to beautifully burgeon. So, a very different-looking and/or -acting person (shorter, taller, darker, lighter, smarter, poorer) who isn't hurting anyone by his or her words and/or actions can thrive within a community that appreciates and responds to this description of diversity.

> Diversity on the other hand is an initiative that is sweeping the country not because it is mandatory or federally regulated, but because it is ethically on target, morally on the mark. The factors that mandated Affirmative Action and inclusion of traditionally underrepresented people by race is paralleled to some extent by diversity's outcry for inclusion and participation by those same individuals who desire to see themselves as significant inside the margins. Whereas Affirmative Action was structured to mandate a space for the underrepresented by race and gender, diversity insists that you don't have diversity without pluralism and inclusion. As a matter of fact, the concept of diversity suggests exactly that and a bit more in its implementation. At SUNY Plattsburgh, we unabashedly assert as part of the mantra for the Diversity Center:

DIVERSITY, WITHOUT PLURALISM AND INCLUSION, BECOMES ADVERSITY, SEPARATISM, AND ILLUSION.

In other words, in your diversity efforts you will end up with adversity, separatism, and illusion if you do not find yourself with a plurality of people, thought, and ideas accentuating your diversity efforts. Without creating safe spaces where people can feel included, people will see those non inclusive efforts as limiting and adverse, they will be more apt to separate from the initiative in its entirety, and all that will be left of your initiative is the illusion of diversity, not the diversity that logically replaced affirmative action, stilted notions of toleration, and limiting notions of multiculturalism. (Wiley, 2009, p. 251)

Is there something significant occurring within the conceptual pairing of the concepts diversity and social justice? Is it a necessary pairing? Yes, it is! Diversity without its relationship to social justice is like bread without butter, lunch meat, jelly, or something to add flavor to it. It may be better stated that diversity without social justice considerations attached to it is just two pieces of bread, something that you can eat with nutritional value, but that will become bland rather quickly.

Considering diversity without social justice leaves efforts at teaching, implementing, and/or understanding diversity far less appealing. This can result in diversity initiatives becoming much more vulnerable to those wishing to undercut their significance due to its lack of moral weight or ethical emphasis. Social justice provides that added something-something, that needed/necessary oomph. Social justice situates the concept of diversity as a topic of conversation that can occur safely, that has merit, significance, and worth. So, that difficult conversation that a teacher has about why a student shouldn't be calling another one names like Wop, ugly, or nerd can be better framed as socially unjust, suggesting an action greater than just wrong. It leverages the use of disrespectful and/or dysfunctional language as problematic for the impact such terms leave not just on the individual(s) they are used against, but also on the community of individuals who often must endure those types of terms. Social justice also empowers the community of individuals—aware of the moral decline that terms disparaging of diversity/differences bring—to engage the perpetrators earnestly, sincerely, and patiently.

The concept of social justice conjoined with diversity gives diversity more emphasis, more logical significance. The invaluable marriage of diversity to social justice gives diversity a context for rational engagement and ethical consideration. Without social justice the concept of diversity is somewhat lessened in terms of the emotional reaction dysfunctional language and inconsiderate actions can have on the victim or witnesses to the victimization. It is like my son calling his coach an asshole because his coach made the decision to not play him, when his coach has always been deep in his corner. I cannot logically accept my son's description of his coach without more contexts no matter how much my son would like me to not question his description. Social justice is the context that makes diversity significant.

Defining *Nigger*

The "nigger in you" as a concept comes out of my understanding of the word *nigger*. Africans brought to America were often identified as niggers during a time when they were consistently referred to as Negroes and widely considered as property. Any understanding of *nigger* today not coterminous with Black and/or non-White, oppressed (slaves had no or very limited rights), illiterate (denied the right to read), and property (as legal possession) is inconsistent with its referents at the time of its origin. *Nigger* wasn't necessarily a contemptuous term, though its use often did refer to a person deemed less than others, and more often than not for no reason other than that person's lack of opportunity. However, when used so often over the years it eventually became an exclamation, not too dissimilar to today calling someone *brother*, *dude*, or *man*.

Perhaps the most significant dimension of any attempt to define *nigger* arises when we begin to situate the term within differing time frames. *Nigger* prior to the Emancipation Proclamation was not about personhood, but property. This barely-a-person, so-called Negro was as much a nigger at that time as he or she was a piece of property. I imagine a slave at that time was no more offended by being referred to by *nigger* as he would have been offended if he were called *property*. However, *nigger* wasn't deliberately dehumanizing in ways that it would become after so-called Negroes were so-called emancipated. Calling an enslaved person who was of African descent a nigger meant that he or she belonged to someone, or didn't have control over his or her own body. You were someone's property, and most likely would continue to be. More to the point, it wouldn't have mattered if an enslaved African or born-into-slavery so-called Negro were referred to as a *nigger*, *boy*, *girl*, *dog*, or *tree*. The bottom line, the overriding situation that dominated the dysfunction, was being considered property, not being called a nigger.

However, post-slavery, post-emancipation, so-called Negroes that were called niggers must have been more greatly offended by its usage than their ancestors. Why? The emancipation meant freedom, and with freedom comes access to the American Dream. If some of the intricacies of the notion of the American Dream are equality, access to opportunities, along with the ability to choose, and a newly emancipated person is under the impression that he or she now has equal status with other Americans, being called a nigger would naturally be very much disturbing. If a newly emancipated person has discarded his or her slave name and chosen a name that better frames his or her new reality, and started to develop an identity, being called a nigger would be a disruption to the creation of that identity.

Du Bois (1986) articulates another approach to engaging *nigger* in an article titled "The Name 'Negro'" in the NAACP's magazine, *The Crisis*, wherein he replied to a youngster's concern over the use of the words *Negro* and *nigger*. The boy said, "Why would [the NAACP's magazine] designate, and segregate us as 'Negroes' and not as 'Americans.' . . . The word 'Negro,' or 'nigger,' is a white man's word to make us feel inferior. . . . I hope that by the time I become a man, that this word, 'Negro,' will be abolished" (p. 1219). Du Bois responded,

> Do not . . . make the all too common error of mistaking names for things. Names are only conventional signs for identifying things. . . . If a thing is despised, either because of ignorance or because it is despicable, you will not alter matters by changing its name. If men despise Negroes, they will not despise them less if Negroes are called "colored" or "Afro-Americans." . . . Names are not merely matters of thought and reason; they are growths and habits. . . . Of course it is not historically accurate. No name ever was historically accurate: neither "English," "French," "German," "White," "Jew," "Nordic" nor "Anglo-Saxon." They were all at first nicknames, misnomers, accidents, grown eventually to conventional habits and achieving accuracy because, and simply because, wide and continued usage rendered them accurate. . . .
>
> Historically, of course, your dislike of the word Negro is easily explained: "Negroes" among your grandfathers meant black folk; "Colored" people were mulattoes. The mulattoes hated and despised the blacks and were insulted if called "Negroes." (pp. 1220–1)

> Suppose now we could change the name. . . . Would you be any less ashamed of being descended from a black man. . . ? The feeling of inferiority is in you, not in any name. . . . Exorcise the hateful complex and no name can ever make you hang your head. (p. 1221)

Du Bois's challenge to the young man to put others' disdain and hateful refrain in perspective works not just for engaging *nigger* but all other hateful, dehumanizing terms aimed at implying difference is less-than.

Du Bois's articulation of double consciousness as an inadvertent response by the so-called Negro to her or his being seen as "the problem" is profoundly problematic in itself. It isn't difficult to imagine how much of a problem for American society newly emancipated Black folk must have been. The Civil War had just been fought over them, or for those in denial of that fact, over states' rights to decide sovereignty over racially enslaved people. Many newly emancipated Black people were now homeless, economically powerless, and yet somehow in competition with poor Whites for the same type of jobs in an economy that was recently severely impacted by a devastating war. While all this was their reality, these newly emancipated people still had to provide for themselves and their families. Du Bois (1990) suggested in his essay "Of the Sons of Master and Man" that *the inevitability* of the Black criminal should not have been a surprise to anyone (p. 129). With no resources to rely on, no financially solvent relatives for support, and a society constructed to unfairly critique, systematically deny, and harshly police their every move crime was not just a reasonable alternative but actually probably the only alternative. So, with that consideration, *nigger* became more of a problem for newly emancipated people than it was when they were slaves. In fact, *nigger* for once enslaved as well as newly emancipated people brings to mind this equivalence:

$$P = N$$

in which N means *nigger*, and P prior to the emancipation means *property*, and after the emancipation, *problem*. In either scenario, when called a nigger, it equated to one of these two terms, depending on which of the two contexts the phrasing was leveraged in. The insinuation was either *nigger as property/possession*, or *nigger as problem*.

As well, the equivalence

$$C = N$$

is reflective of a nation of newly emancipated, severely disenfranchised people, now conveniently, or inconveniently, depending on your way of seeing, framed as *criminals* (C in the equation), with far too few options available to them beyond doing whatever was necessary to survive. To varying extents in

America, *criminal* became synonymous with *nigger* in many if not most interpretations, albeit subconsciously. This is why in the film *Rosewood* (Singleton, 1997) the matriarchal Aunt Sarah character would say "nigger, just another word for guilty" to justify the unjust beatings her grandfather received from the slave master who knew his own son had actually perpetrated the crime. This is also why it has been long said that the face of crime in America is Black.

> With the emancipation of the so-called Negro, the problem and criminal was best framed as "nigger." "Nigger" wasn't a term that was problematic before emancipation because all terms addressing so-called Negroes were terms that were legally addressing property, so while they may have offended and definitely dehumanized this once free race of people, being born and bred into slavery had black folk born and bred into a certain degree of oppression, both external and internal. However, emancipation ignited a search for identity, culture, and respect. No longer considered property, an expectation by Black folk of unencumbered opportunity wasn't an outlandish wish. Unfortunately, ultimately you could draw an equation that reflected these equivalences:
>
> $$P = C = N$$
> which symbolizes "Problem = Criminal = Nigger."
>
> This problem and its various manifestations has never ceased plaguing American democracy. Of course, now the American perspective on the Du Boisian existential question, "How does it feel to be a problem?" in many cases, is sophisticated enough not to limit the question to Black folk. At the time Dr. Du Bois posed the question, it was one specifically directed at the so-called Negro and rightfully so. (Wiley, 2009, p. 253)

In the sense that the legal system was/is much more punitive toward Blacks than Whites, *nigger* could now be used as a moniker for a criminal expected to soon commit a crime. Hilary Swank's character Brandon Teena in the film, *Boys Don't Cry* (based upon a true story) was a self-proclaimed male who unfortunately was born Teena Brandon, a female. In his male persona, by simply challenging the prevailing paradigm that mandates restricted gender roles, Brandon Teena boldly addressed the *nigger* in him, a societal assertion that insisted he was both a problem and a criminal and treated him as such for daring to be different.

If we push this thought a bit further, we see that Brandon Teena's desire to be male may have been caused by an array of reasons, including nature or nurture. Unpacking the nurture aspects first, we see there is a chance that life as a female for Brandon Teena was impossible to fully enjoy. Brandon may have seen the second-class status that females are subjected to and refused to accept that role. It actually makes quite a bit of sense that Brandon would want to be male instead of female in a society that undervalues femininity if not females, especially outside of a context of their usefulness to males. This is not too dissimilar to my daughter at the age of four turning her mother and my world upside down/inside out by declaring she wanted to be White. As the only Black child in her day care, and usually anywhere else she went, why would she want to be Black? Why would she want to stand out when all about her Whiteness was being celebrated and Blackness either not being celebrated, being ignored, or being unabashedly denigrated?

On the other hand, in terms of nature, with no reference to Brandon's childhood in the film, Brandon may easily have been the poster child for the gender assignment decisions that are often made by parents when the child's genitalia are ambiguous and parents are pressured to determine gender right then and there. In either case, nature or nurture, the following assertion by Beverly Tatum (2004b) couldn't ring any more profoundly for Brandon Teena personally, and the world that she had no choice in living in: "Dominant groups, by definition, set the parameters within which the subordinates operate" (p. 11). The maleness she desired to access, the dominant identity she desired to not just appropriate but own, was controlled by men who were not going to allow her to just decide she was a male and thereafter become one. If that were to occur, then what value would maleness have? If one person born female can arbitrarily make such a call, what would prevent a mass exodus from one gender to another, especially with significant degrees of privilege available to one, and a life of oppression evident in the other? Albeit overtly, covertly, or inadvertently determined, the protectors of America's identity hegemony nonetheless project the sentiment/rationale that the *nigger* in her must stay in her. They may have feared that if she is able to solve the problem that society insists she is it could/would mean that people actually might be capable of defining themselves.

Multiple Identities

What is also interesting about our identities is that we each have more than one. These multiple identities often find us struggling with which one will have dominion over the other. Within the context of my existence in the predominantly White North Country of New York, I have no viable option if I want to maintain my optimism other than to focus upon my gender, socioeconomic class, heterosexuality, and temporary able-bodiedness. With all these facets of my identity I emerge dominant. Race is the only one in which I more often than not am underrepresented if not a minority. However, my majority/minority status is always context-driven. When I enter a Black community my racial minority status dissipates rapidly, but depending upon the Black community I am entering, I may become the minority because of my economic class status if the average income is $50,000 and I make $175,000. Or if I am visiting Spellman College in Atlanta, Georgia, a historically Black all-women's college, and for the duration I am on its campus, my race is inconsequential and I become a gendered minority. The harsh reality of multiple identities, though, is that most people who haven't taken the time to seriously "engage/unpack" their reality aren't equipped to and/or can't control or easily manage the moment one of their identities suddenly situates them as dominant or oppressed.

> "When we think about our multiple identities, most of us will find that we are both dominant and targeted at the same time. But it is the targeted identities that hold our attention and the dominant identities that go unexamined."
>
> —Tatum (2004b, p. 11)

As Dr. Tatum suggests is the case for most of us, I seldom consider my *ability*, rarely reflect upon my sexual orientation, am more aware of my age, and almost always consider my race. However, as a maturing professor on a college campus, I find myself more invested in staying fit/healthy to avoid my *ability* becoming another one of my more consistently targeted identities.

> "As Audre Lorde said, from her vantage point as a Black Lesbian, 'There is no hierarchy of oppressions.' The thread and threat of violence runs through all of our isms. There is a need to acknowledge each other's pain, even as we attend to our own."
>
> —Tatum (2004b, p. 13)

It is the value inherent within our understanding of the role we play in oppressing others while we grapple with being oppressed that is why those of us who promote diversity and social justice are invaluable to the national conversation. This is a conversation that we all should be invested in. It is a conversation that will benefit all of us even more as other voices contribute to it. John Stuart Mill (1988) once said,

> He who knows only his side of the case, knows little of that. . . . But if he is equally unable to refute the reasons on the opposite side; if he does not so much as know what they are, he has no ground for preferring either opinion. The rational position for him would be suspension of judgment, and unless he contents himself with that, he is either led by authority or adopts, like the generality of the world, the side to which he feels most inclination. (p. 28)

Engaging/unpacking diversity and social justice is about examining our multiple identities to better understand ourselves as we become more adept at considering others. To do this well, we must also engage/unpack the language we use to connect with one another, or the dysfunctional language that keeps us disconnected. So, don't think that we've already covered all the territory that needs to be covered and now there is nothing left for you to engage. Oh, contraire!

> "The task of resisting our own oppression does not relieve us of the responsibility of acknowledging our complicity in the oppression of others."
>
> —Tatum (2004b, p. 14)

2

OF SO-CALLED RETARDS AND LEADERSHIP MOMENTS

For some, being differently able is like walking
a tightrope, skydiving and skinny dipping all at
once.

—Edmund Adjapong

Years ago I was approached by a group of my ex-students who had
been informed that a theme party was being planned that I might
want to know about. These students were visibly upset, and after
listening to their concerns so was I. Before I responded, the students then
informed me they were going to ensure that the "retard party" didn't happen. Yes, you read that correctly; some students were going to throw a
"retard party." My first reaction was an emotional transition from my earlier
sense of dismay to pride in their passion toward social justice. My colleagues
and I obviously had succeeded in our efforts to create students who genuinely cared about social justice. I nonetheless left that conversation with
them with my stomach in knots. Looking back I discovered that I had really
walked around in a fog for a while trying to find a perspective from which
to understand that potential party's chosen theme. Try as I might I was
unable to do it.

Now, if you have never been to a college party, a theme party more
specifically, you don't know what you may have missed or are missing. The
theme parties that I had previously attended were always toga, beach, or
sports gear parties. So, as theme parties go, I know a little something. I also
heard that SUNY Plattsburgh students know how to party as well. So, I was
blown away when I was told that the theme party that they were preparing
to throw was a "retard party." I guess many of you are out there thinking to
yourself, "What is a retard party?" Well, I was informed that it is a party

23

that grants access only to those who portray themselves as retards. In other words, to attend the party you have to dress and/or act like a retard! I can't begin to tell you how disappointed I was to hear this. At the Center for Diversity at SUNY Plattsburgh we work so hard to educate our students about social justice and respect for diversity. It was heartbreaking to discover that there could be a population of students on our campus that could even believe other students would want to attend a party with such an insensitive theme. It was apparent that none of these students throwing the party had a disabled family member, because if they did how could they begin to even conceptualize such a party?

Years ago the hip-hop group the Black Eyed Peas released a song titled "Let's Get It Started." The original name of the song was "Let's Get Retarded." You may be curious as to why they would have changed the name. However, the more pertinent question is, How could they originally have been comfortable naming a song "Let's Get Retarded"? It's hard to imagine that someone in the group wasn't sophisticated enough to tell the others how uncool it would be to have such a title affixed to their song. I have no doubt that will.i.am and Fergie, two of the more prominent members of the group, do not have close family members who are severely disabled. It would also be a mistake on my part to not consider the fact that the Black Eyed Peas may have chosen that song name specifically for the sensationalism, anticipating a buzz around the name. But somehow I still struggle with the fact that their sense of privilege was so extreme that neither one of them or anyone else in the group was savvy enough to put a halt to the idea of giving a song such a title.

Well, fortunately the ex-students who came to me handled their business better than the Black Eyed Peas did initially. The party didn't occur, largely in part because they and a large number of other Examining Diversity Through Film students (both past and present) decided they were going to take action to make sure that it didn't. This group of students knew it was wrong for anyone to host such a theme party and were adamantly invested in making sure it didn't occur. I then moved into concern mode because I didn't want this group of students invested in diversity and social justice to be seen as a diversity gang overreacting to someone's dysfunction by themselves becoming dysfunctional. However, they assuaged my concerns with heightened diplomatic aplomb. They created such a fuss about the party that they may have shamed the students who were planning the party. When asked why they would even host a "retard party" some of the students planning the party laughed and claimed it was not that serious. However, there are questions that I feel need to be addressed about this "retard party":

1. Was their desire to host a "retard party" something that others—upon discovering their intentions—should take seriously? Why?
2. What is it that could even make students host such a theme party?
3. How is it possible that not one of those students would emerge as an *ally* or *voice of reason* to end such a horrific idea for a party theme?
4. Is the desire to host a "retard party" truly a social injustice or just others imparting their value systems?
5. Are there other moments that you have encountered that mirror or resemble the basic level of inconsideration about to be exemplified by these students as they planned to host their "retard party"?
6. What would you tell your children as they grow up to better ensure that they will never participate in such a party?

While there are never, necessarily, definitive answers to questions like these, here are my thoughts:

1. **Was their desire to host a "retard party" something that others—upon discovering their intentions—should take seriously?** Yes! First of all, they may seriously have been innocent (or clueless) about the pain that might be visited upon people attached to the disabled community. As a result, upon receiving feedback on the insensitivity of hosting such a party, many of the students might have been embarrassed about almost participating in it, with it later becoming a life-changing experience. Those students easily might become allies. Of course, there are always people who have no interest in being told what they should and should not do. When we encounter them we must be strong in our position that the only upside of hosting such a party for them is a few really cheap, self-centered laughs at the expense of people who are not as privileged in terms of their ability. The downside for them is the fact that they are possibly hurting individuals as well as a community of people who don't deserve to be hurt. Another negative is that students hosting such a party reveal to all aware of the students' actions that they are insensitive. Yet another negative is that years later when by "six degrees of separation" they are connected to someone from the differently able community, they will have to manage their emotion around a moment where they could have done the right thing. The last negative is that, in the given moment, once they were informed of the consequences of what they were poised to do, they chose to do the wrong thing for no reason other than to placate their own egos.

2. **What is it that could even make students host such a theme party?** Most people, students in this case, want to do the right thing but often aren't as clear as to what the right thing is. So, peer pressure, cheap laughs, and lack of creativity can all contribute to the bad decision for students to do the wrong thing.

3. **How is it possible that not one of those students would emerge as an *ally* or *voice of reason* to end such a horrific idea for a party theme?** Often we challenge our children to be leaders without concrete examples of exactly what actions are required in the crucible that defines/inspires a leadership moment. Often we don't take the time to define what "cool" is, and therefore because of its lack of definition, cool becomes something many if not most would deem uncool upon deeper reflection. Unfortunately, the deeper reflection required within the actual moment wasn't available. This is why conversations about differences and how we respect and unfortunately disrespect them are so germane. As well, it isn't difficult to frame the actions of the students who desired to host such a party as bullying and a result of their unearned privilege of being born able bodied and able minded, though the latter unearned privilege could be questioned because of the fact that they desired to host such a party.

4. **Is the desire to host a "retard party" truly a social injustice or just others imparting their value systems?** Well, it no doubt is the case of others imparting their value systems, but if others don't communicate their value systems to us we often don't acquire better or new values. In terms of whether or not hosting a "retard party" is a social injustice, would any of these students appreciate such a party if they were mentally and/or physically disabled? Ten to 15 years later, how would they process such a party hosted in their community if their child was physically or mentally challenged? Dr. Martin Luther King Jr.'s assertion that "injustice anywhere is a threat to justice everywhere" is quite appropriate here.

5. **Are there other moments that you have encountered that mirror or resemble the basic level of inconsideration about to be exemplified by these students as they planned to host their "retard party"?** Yes, some of those moments were the many times I was hanging out/kicking it with some of the boys in my youth, or hanging with other men and a discussion about girls/women ensued. Within those moments often one of the boys or men referred to girls/women in disrespectful ways, and as a boy I sat silently and allowed it. As a man who had matured and finally found my voice, I challenged them by asking them why they were referring to these women as

"bitches," "sluts," or "tricks." By engaging them to unpack their language I was facilitating a leadership moment.

6. **What would you tell your children as they grow up to better ensure that they will never participate in such a party?** I know that I have told my children how ashamed I am of myself that it took me as long as it did to do the right thing. I could have come into *a sense of consciousness* and *consideration* about the level of disrespect I was condoning much earlier if I had actually stopped myself and considered what I was doing and its larger consequences/implications. I have told my children how much we inadvertently scar others when we succumb to peer pressure and don't overcome our propensity to be inconsiderate. More so, I have told my children that if they don't like to be called disparaging names, then they should never contribute to anyone else experiencing it. Last but not least, I have told my children that the most important thing is they know the difference between right and wrong and that when they are doing things secretively, or in the shadows, whispering, hoping not to be discovered, then they know it is wrong. At that point they should check themselves, before they wreck themselves!

Also, considering the equation I use to define the term *nigger*, $P = C = N$, it can unfortunately be applied to someone differently able. The person labeled a retard is a problem for those who have used the term comfortably and have no interest in changing their language. Someone differently able may present a problem for those who may be uncomfortable imagining another physical reality awaiting them. Interacting with or simply seeing someone physically challenged may have them feeling vulnerable. Disability or being differently able is not considered a criminal activity legally but does carry with it a social stigma of inadequacy, of limited access if not abnormality in the minds of most people who haven't unpacked their ability privilege. So while not legally ostracized—if people don't consider or willfully ignore the unequal access to full citizenship that people with disabilities must endure—they lack respect and as a result are marginalized when not forgotten. This means most people with disabilities have been and will be experiencing life as outcasts, not too dissimilar to criminals in enough people's minds as to be seen as denigrating. When the "problem" is too easily seen as "criminal" it is more easily seen as "nigger." So why aren't all people who are differently able and all other people who have also felt like a "problem," a "criminal," a "nigger" all on the same page?

Retard as Profanity

The word *retard* is arguably one of the more problematic terms in the English language. I say this because of how it is often used to describe someone's behavior as dysfunctional, peculiar, and/or abnormal, yet it isn't necessarily considered profane. People even use the term *retard* to describe themselves as odd or awkward when they find themselves doing something inexplicable. Ironically, the fragility of ability is another one of those reasons we should be cognizant of our actions. A colleague of mine, sociologist Dr. Lynn Schlesinger, once told me that the one community that we are all apt to join is the disabled community. As I heard this, my perspective on the disabled community became forever altered. It is sad that it took me realizing that I was mindlessly disrespecting a community that either I or others I love would one day be a part of, in order for me to make this shift in perspective. It also taught me that I wasn't as forward thinking as I wanted to be, or subconsciously thought I was. Most of us aren't, though. For example, in the New Student Orientations that I present every summer at SUNY Plattsburgh—as well as for quite a few other colleges that lack adequate diversity initiatives, but desire to challenge their incoming students to be more cognizant of diversity and social justice—I present a dysfunctional language chart for the students to consider. Before they see the chart, though, I ask them to anticipate the words that they will see on my dehumanizing language chart, keeping in mind that what I'm looking for are the words that they may have heard an hour or two prior to the presentation. What ensues as they offer the words that adversely dominate their campus conversations is a room full of energy punctuated by laughter, frivolity, and gross inconsideration of how they are actually demonstrating a heightened sense of insensitivity. The chart that they will ultimately see has a plethora of hurtful terms on it, ranging from the all too familiar words that cut like a knife (*bitch, ho, fag, sissy, Spic, nigger, cracker*) to the words that we dismiss as not that serious (*nerd, geek, strange, weird, odd, stupid, dork, freak, ugly, loser*) to the words that are creative yet nonetheless damaging (*terrorist, tramp, bum, raghead, mutant*).

It never fails that when these words first hit the screen students find them quite entertaining, and many if not most are laughing as the terms individually appear one after another. It isn't until we go deeper that they experience a profound awakening, perhaps their first real wake-up call for social justice. For many, when I reveal to them some images of children on social networking sites being ridiculed with no compunction whatsoever, they have their first personal epiphany relative to diversity and social justice. More specifically, I show them a poster found through research done by my colleague (Kristie Gonyea) revealing a college student having posted upon her or his Facebook page, in an attempt to be witty, a picture of a young man with Down syndrome breaking the winner's tape after concluding a race with a caption above that reads, "What is better than winning the Special Olympics?" After a moment of letting the students ponder the question and thereafter become poised to answer, I reveal to them below the picture the answer, which is "Not Being Retarded." At that point, there is a daunting and even eerie silence in the room, probably as a result of shame. Occasionally a few students laugh, but then they are ostracized so intensely by the seriousness of their peers' self-reflection that it shuts them down immediately. I then admonish all the students for their previous cavalier attitudes toward these same words, informing them that I understand it is because no one had probably systematically challenged them to unpack these words in a context of the pain they cause others, and the hypocrisy that visits their usage. Not one of these young men and women wants to be called something disparaging, or wants their friends or loved ones to be verbally accosted, but they far too often silently assent to that exact behavior.

To further accentuate the experience for them, I share with them the story of a young couple excited about the birth of their first child. I know this story firsthand because I have the pleasure of being close friends with this family and godfather to their second child. This couple, in the late stages of their pregnancy, traveled across Southern California in heavy traffic for a checkup due to labor pains. After being told the mother was experiencing false labor, they attempted to return home, only to realize that what she was experiencing was quite real. Of course, they attempted to reach the hospital in time to avoid any problems. Unfortunately, though, by the time they arrived, their unborn child's umbilical cord was wrapped around his neck, adversely affecting his birth, contributing if not causing him to have cerebral palsy.

After this anecdote the students are uncomfortable in their seats, pensive, reticent, and attentive. Challenging them to leave in their rearview mirrors the mindless, inconsiderate, hypocritical behaviors that they exhibited as middle school and/or high school students is not difficult at this point. It is not necessary for me to further assert that any poor behavior resembling that previously discussed will not be tolerated, especially by those students who now fully understand how immature, juvenile, self-centered, and dysfunctional they were at one time. Their quiet assent occurs on a major level. For the students in my new student presentations, the professionals in attendance at my Diversity Enlightenment sessions, and the mixture of both in my leadership retreats, I am now confident they are ready to lean into their upcoming and unavoidable leadership moment.

> "Without knowing a leader's values, those in the leader's group have no way of knowing or predicting what he or she will do. Without a clear set of values, clearly expressed and lived, a leader can only ask others to follow blindly, something most people rightly hesitate to do."
>
> —Halpern & Lubar (1998, p. 198)

There are times when certain battles that may not seem so significant at the time still need to be waged, if for no other reason than to establish your values, so that, as Halpern and Lubar (1998) assert in the preceding quote, others will not feel like they are blindly following when a leader exerts himself or herself or so that others will not be confused about the leader's value system.

However, the scenarios that require people to step into leadership moments vary. When we realize this, it doesn't hurt to offer poignant vignettes for consideration, as I do here with this scene from the hit television show *Seinfeld*. I believe the necessity for stepping into leadership moments is made quite clear by Elaine Benes in this excerpt from the episode "The Handicap Spot" (David, Seinfeld, & Cherones, 1993a).

Seinfeld: "The Handicap Spot"

Scene: (*George is driving through a parking lot, looking for a spot with Jerry, Elaine, and Kramer as passengers.*)

Elaine: So what are we gonna get him?
Jerry: Anything we want, we're chippin' in.
George: I like this area. I could live out here.
Kramer: Yeah, we oughta all get a house together and live out here.
Jerry: Yeah, that's a good idea. I'll tell you what, Chuckles, I'll give you permission to sublet my room right now.
George: Look at this. There's no spaces here.
(*To a man outside his window*) Excuse me, are you gettin' out? (*Man shouts, "No!"*)

Kramer: Why don't you take that handicapped spot?

George: You think?

Elaine: No! No. We'll find a space. There's spaces in the other lot.

George: Oh, I don't wanna walk that far.

Elaine: What if a handicapped person needs it?

Kramer: No, come on, they don't drive?

Jerry: Yes, they do.

Kramer: Have you ever seen a handicapped person pull into a space and park?

Jerry: Well, there's spaces there. They must drive.

Kramer: No, they don't. If they could drive, they wouldn't be handicapped.

Elaine: So if you can drive, you're not handicapped?

George: We're not gonna be here that long anyway, we gotta get to the party.

Kramer: I got news for you, handicapped people, they don't even wanna park there. They wanna be treated just like everybody else. That's why those spaces are always empty.

George: He's right. It's the same thing with the feminists. You know, they want everything to be equal. Everything. But when the check comes, where are they?

Elaine: What does that mean?

George: Yeah. Alright, I'm pullin' in.

Kramer: Go ahead, George.

Elaine: George!

George: Oh, come on. It's five minutes.

(*Scene ends as George pulls into the handicapped spot.*)

Emotion is one of the essential reasons I use film and television to tightly frame the message I'm attempting to impart. The emotional impact of this scene comes from those of us who drive having experienced at some time or another the situation that George is in. Emotion also visits those of us who have been passengers in a situation similar to the one that Elaine, Jerry, and Kramer are in. There is probably also among viewers of this scene emotional impact on behalf of our empathy toward people who are differently able who are often not considered or are disrespected in ways that are too easily dismissed.

Leadership Moments

As we try to "understand leadership" we must also understand ourselves as humans. We are not necessarily comfortable speaking in a language that we are unaccustomed to articulating, especially in awkward moments. Elaine is the only one in the group who hesitates to pull into the handicap parking spot and for some reason does not mount enough of an argument to dissuade the others. Yet, when George makes an offhanded comment about feminism, Elaine finds her voice and challenges him to further clarify his point. Did Elaine go silent on her friends because they were taking advantage of their unearned privilege (having unimpaired health) while violating one of the few societal privileges afforded to differently able people because she was the only woman in the group? Did Elaine go silent because she did not know enough about the reality of "the Other"—in this case people with disabling conditions—to effectively engage her friends? Or did Elaine go silent because she simply did not focus on the fact that she had the power to change the situation by adamantly stating she did not want to park in the space?

If Elaine had exerted herself with her friends on behalf of respecting designated parking spots for underprivileged people, she might have established herself with them as someone who will protect the rights of others. She might also have redefined herself in a powerful leadership moment. Instead, she did not, which allowed Kramer to position himself as an authority on the reality of people with disabling conditions. It should also be noted that Jerry most likely was sitting on the fence, unsure what to do in this situation. An assertive Elaine might have pulled Jerry over toward her position that it was wrong, instead of contributing to him remaining silent due to his uncertainty.

What do you do when someone innocently uses the term *retard* or refers to something as "that's gay" and honestly doesn't understand the ramifications of his actions? What do you do when you are in a conversation with someone who actually believes it is okay to tell a sexist, heterosexist, racist, or classist joke because no one has ever challenged him about it? Once you finally understand the deleterious consequences of unearned privilege not being considered by the individual(s) who has it, how do you communicate it to others? These are some of the questions that considerate people struggle with every day in their lives.

My dissertation was essentially on what I refer to as "leadership moments." I researched and ultimately used film to paint a vivid and emotional picture of the leadership moments that we all face and respond to so differently. Then, coincidentally, I saw the *Seinfeld* episode "The Handicap Spot," of which I incorporated an excerpt into my dissertation, as well as in many presentations I do. I recently used that and another similar *Seinfeld* clip for presentations at Norwich University, Bombardier Corporation, and a New York State Nurses Association retreat I co-facilitated. Participants' responses to these film excerpts always take me a few intriguing places. In essence, I wandered into reflecting on how many of us might process these leadership moments so differently. In a scene from "The Handicap Spot," Jerry, Elaine, George, and Kramer are attempting to decide whether to park in a parking spot designated for the physically challenged. George rationalizes that it is only for a moment, and Kramer, in a disturbingly philosophical manner, suggests, among other things, that "the handicapped" don't even want to park there themselves. Elaine flirts with stopping them but acquiesces when Kramer confidently reasserts himself. Jerry, for the most part, is silent. The scene is ripe with intriguing opportunities for considering how we choose to engage, or not engage, leadership moments.

My concept of a leadership moment is situated and predicated within a context of diversity and social justice. It is the moment when someone can step up and challenge problematic prevailing paradigms that exist solely to undermine a person because of a unique dimension of her personality. So, in the case of the *Seinfeld* episode, the very thought of inconsiderately parking in a parking spot specifically identified as off limits is a leadership moment. It is as blatantly ablest as it is classist and an instance of leveraging unearned privilege. What is provocative about that scene is that it challenges people to articulate which of the *Seinfeld* characters best reflect how they see themselves handling a similar situation. All of us want to see ourselves as the ideal person always making ideal decisions. Honestly, though, how realistic is that? So, are we George, inconsiderately doing whatever he feels is appropriate without considering not only consequences, but why he would even think it is okay for him to do it? Are we Kramer, running with sound bites (stereotypes) to fuel or legitimate his desire to do what he wants, let the chips fall where they may? Are we Elaine, prepared to challenge dysfunction, but only to the extent it doesn't require major work? Or are we Jerry, not sure what to do and silently waiting for a compelling argument for motivation to act?

Other instances of leadership moments that are or aren't accessed can be found anywhere. In the film *Mona Lisa Smile*, Julia Roberts's character is both a visionary and a transformative leader who challenges the young women she is hired to teach to not succumb to outdated notions associated with their identity as women. Throughout the film, Julia Roberts's character and others are faced with leadership moments that they either step fully into, or sidestep, for an array of reasons.

As parents we encounter leadership moments constantly. Whether to allow our sons to fit the description of "boys will be boys" when they disrespect their sisters or a friend is probably a recurring issue. Whether to act as if it is okay for us to not practice what we preach simply because we are the adults is always an odd moment to be in. Whether to act as if we are not role models—when we display hypocritical behavior in comparison to what we expect from our children—is conveying a heightened level of absurdity. Do you recall some of the leadership moments your parents stepped into, or sidestepped, from your childhood? Do you recall some of the leadership moments wherein you had the opportunity to make a difference and instead chose not to?

I recently did some work with an organization that comprised many leaders who appeared to be prepared to lead but didn't seem to be prepared to lead outside of the context of a fixed result that they were expected to achieve. Sometimes leadership is finding the way to have a difficult conversation that you really don't want to have, or can't imagine having. Sometimes, like a racial incident (involving harassment of a young Black girl with the word *nigger*) that occurred within a North Country school, leadership moments avail themselves to many constituencies that arguably are all linked in potentially changing the game, but are not communicating that fact. At that school, or any educational institution, for that matter, the fact that underrepresented students were suffering because of the differences in their identities is a failed leadership moment for teachers, principals, and, yes, superintendents of any school district that has instances of this occurring with nothing "real" in place to combat it. Seriously, you aren't fooling anyone who is seriously discerning how sophisticated a leader you actually are. It wasn't an accident that Obama won and Hillary was in the hunt for the presidency. Times, they are a-changing, and those of us who aren't changing with them flirt with becoming irrelevant, with becoming dinosaurs. Yes, an incident of racist activities toward someone grossly in the minority could happen anyway, but probably far less often if adequate structures are put in place.

The fact that law enforcement investigative units and community organizations aren't responding to a member of the community being ostracized, vilified, and demonized makes a statement about the entire community, whether people want to own that fact or not. It also makes a statement about the hypocrisy of every individual who could make a difference, and doesn't, but would be ready to tar and feather a person for her or his bias toward someone connected to the hypocrite. And it is hard to argue that knowingly and willingly succumbing to your own hypocrisy isn't the epitome of stupid acts. I know. I may be a diversity director, but I've done my share. Nonetheless, as a Black man, a member of an underrepresented group, and as a North Country resident who wants to believe that many of us are committed to changing the game, I was outraged by what transpired within that North Country school district. It only takes an incident like this to reinforce that everyone is not in the game.

We see leadership moments in film and so-called real life all the time. The Black lieutenant in the film *Crash* who doesn't want to deal with the racism of one of his White police officers because of its threat to his pension is facing a leadership moment. The father of Charlize Theron's character in the film *North Country* faces a leadership moment when he attempts to come to her rescue when she is undertaking a leadership moment herself as she speaks to a heavily misogynistic male-dominated union membership. In his moment he reveals his failures at previous leadership opportunities even while he is attempting to redeem himself on this one occasion. In essence, he speaks up only because it is his daughter at risk, not realizing that in the grand scheme of things every woman is someone's daughter, sister, mother, if not his.

I am always curious how often people actually reflect upon some of the leadership moments they have encountered that challenged them to become change agents or that made them shy, introspective, or perhaps left to reflect upon their cowardice. I know that leaders aren't made in a day, though they can experience a personal epiphany that can serve as the catalyst for their evolution. But more often than not a leader is shaped in the crucible of life. I take quite a bit of pride in seeing that my daughter Autumn is on her way to becoming a leader. A while back this precocious preteen of mine shared with me that she was quite smitten with a boy who is very intelligent, handsome, witty, and protective of her among their friends. As a father I am not really interested in having extended dialogue with my daughter about a crush she has over some boy who will eventually grow up naturally endeavoring to respond to his hormones. For months Autumn had told me stories about this boy and what a class act he is. It wasn't until recently that she shared with me that he is differently able. Her interest in him may be aided by the fact that her father and mother have done a good job developing her worldview. Her worldview may also be favorably tweaked by her having a godbrother with cerebral palsy. But her lack of hesitation to enter a burgeoning relationship with a boy who is differently able gives me a sense of pride in her ability to look toward someone's soul as much as the person's exterior.

It brings to mind this quote from Eli Clare's article, "Gawking, Gaping, Staring" (p. 496):

cripples, queers, gimps, freaks:
we are looking for lovers and teachers
—teachers to stand with us against the gawking;
lovers to reach beneath our clothing,
beneath the words that attempt to name us,
beneath our shame and armor,
their eyes and hands helping return us
to grace, beauty, passion

My bottom-line take on leadership is that if we teach our kids how to bravely step into leadership moments when they are confronted with one, and then another, after habitually replicating this behavior, how can they not be leaders? Aristotle taught that it is through good habits that we acquire virtue. My precocious daughter exhibits virtuous behavior every day in an array of ways. She is becoming the teacher that Clare talks about in the preceding quote by unhesitatingly standing against the gawkers. And I have no doubt that she is well on her journey toward being quite the love interest for someone temporarily able-bodied, or differently able. Since we all fit into one of these two categories it is nice that she is receptive to both. Her mind is open to all her possible choices. I do expect that journey to not be fully under way, though, anytime soon.

3

OF SAME SEX, STRAIGHT, AND GAY

In terms of diversity and social justice
considering the language acquisition of children
when I use the word STRAIGHT
and know that if I had an identical twin
who was GAY
while I identified as straight
my children possibly could
SUBCONSCIOUSLY
see their uncle (my twin) as crooked
Which is why as an ALLY,
I can no longer refer to myself
as STRAIGHT . . .

It was a warm summer day. I had gone running around Fox Hills Park in Culver City, a park favored by joggers. On this specific day I had decided to run with my shirt off. I had confidence in my physique and figured I might get some attention from the preponderance of beautiful women who jogged around the park on any given day. Well, to my chagrin my running was uneventful. At no point did any young woman evince any interest in me. Soon after, while walking toward home a car slowed as it passed me. Because this was Los Angeles, known for its drive-by shootings, I paid close attention to the car, whose driver seemed to be taking an interest in me. When it passed I breathed a sigh of relief. A couple of minutes later, though, it appeared as if the same car that had passed by me moments earlier had only gone around the block and was now again passing closely by me,

37

only slowing down even more. This time, though, the window opened and the driver, a man, said in a softly measured voice, "Do you want a ride?"

I was in shock. His invitation felt as if it were a pass at me. Within that pass I was forced to struggle with the fact that something about me gave him the impression I was gay, gay-curious, or bisexual. Unable to suppress my anger I lashed out verbally. I put together an extremely profanity-laced tirade that lasted probably 10 of the longest seconds in this man's life. I lashed out at the driver of the car with venom I did not know I had in me. You will have to use some of your imagination to get inside of the profanity-laced tirade I leveled at him as a result of his proposition. I said, "No, #$%&, I don't want a #$%&* ride. Take your #$%&* away from here before I kick your #$%&."

It wasn't until I had finished and watched him recoil in surprise—only to roll his window up and screech off from the curb—that I actually processed what it was I had said. In essence, I told him I wasn't interested and the fact that he suggested I might be was enough for me to physically harm him. When I did catch my breath I realized that all this man had done was offer me a ride in his car, probably because he saw me as attractive, possibly because he imagined a signal that wasn't there. It is possible that within the Fox Hills community gay men had some method of connecting that was unbeknownst to me, a heterosexual man. Perhaps gay men jogged shirtless to attract other gay men. If so, how would I have known?

As he pulled off, totally caught off guard by my extreme reaction to his simple invitation, I was so physically angry I could feel the tension in my body. I felt it so much that it made me ask myself the question that began my epiphany. Why was I so upset? First, why did I believe that he was flirting with me? Second, I was looking for attention that day, and had gotten it. So, assuming he might have found me attractive, was that a good enough reason for me to threaten him with bodily harm? If it had been one of the beautiful women running around the park just moments before who offered me a ride I would have jumped in that car with no hesitation, and no expectation of affection either. So who was I kidding? I had just taken my first psychology course and only recently been introduced to the ideas of Sigmund Freud. What would Freud have said about me, in some larger context? When I look back on the experience, I see that there was no way I could have distanced myself from my homophobia in that moment.

In less than five minutes I experienced pride, confusion, anger, introspection, shame, and pride all over again. Without getting too detailed, the final sense of pride I felt was in realizing that a compliment is a compliment and no one, and I truly mean no one, deserves to be treated rudely simply because he or she said something to you that you may have preferred not to hear but that was genuinely meant as a compliment.

My response to him is something that I wished I could take back, but on another level, I value it as the first step to my becoming more enlightened about the differences in the ways we treat one another and some of the intriguing ways we respond to one another. For example, would a woman jogging around a park looking for attention from men have reacted that way to another woman propositioning her for a ride? I know I am speaking in generalities, but would the average woman be as hostile in her response? Men's egos get so threatened when their masculinity is challenged or questioned. Michael Kimmel, in his 2000 essay, "Masculinity as Homophobia," stated, "Homophobia is the fear that other men will unmask us, emasculate us, reveal to us and the world that we do not measure up, that we are not real men" (p. 214). I was not familiar with Kimmel's theory back then, but something similar to his assertion did cross my mind once I regained my composure. Why was I so upset? All the man had done was offer me a ride. He validated my desire to be noticed for what I deemed was my attractive body. If a woman had approached me with a similar proposition, even one whom I may not have been physically attracted to, I would not have tried to dehumanize her with my language. My response to the man's proposition was embarrassingly over the top, even though there was no one present to hear it. At some point that evening I was wishing I could take back my comments.

Kimmel (2000) further asserts that "being seen as manly is a fear that propels American men to deny manhood to others, as a way of proving the unprovable—that one is fully manly" (p. 217). I now recognize that I was insulted more about the fact that the masculinity I believed I projected wasn't at the level I thought it was. Or perhaps I was projecting hypermasculinity that was alluring to him. Somehow, ridiculing this man, who on one level was giving me a compliment in that he found me attractive—or at least attractive enough to ride with him—was my way of regaining the masculinity I had lost with his proposition. Of course, I had not lost any of my masculinity. That's impossible! Masculinity and femininity are social constructs on the same continuum, which comprises far too many gradations to truly assess anyone consistently, especially in ever-changing contexts. It would not be hard to make an argument that my receiving his flirting solicitation with aplomb would have made more of a statement about my masculinity remaining intact, instead of the way I projected fragility. Warren Blumenfeld (2000), in his essay "How Homophobia Hurts Everyone," states, "Homophobic conditioning (and indeed all forms of oppression) compromises the integrity of heterosexual people by pressuring them into treating others badly, actions contrary to their basic humanity" (p. 271). Blumenfeld is so correct in his assertion. I seldom in my life have blown my cool like I did in that situation. I haven't felt self-imposed pressure to disrespect anyone like that since. So, why did I do it that time? I'll answer that question by taking the long route home.

Consideration of Others

Often, when I do diversity and social justice retreats, after the requisite introductions and icebreakers I start the retreat weekend off with the participants all sharing what are the top three holidays that they believe all Americans should have no problem celebrating. It never fails that among the three that are chosen there is one consistent answer, the Fourth of July. After this fact is revealed to each group by tabulating their responses, we then unpack some things that most people just don't know and, more so, don't even consider.

Frederick Douglass, the once-enslaved Black abolitionist, gave a speech in 1852, titled "What to the Slave Is the Fourth of July?" From that speech I share an excerpt that challenges all participants' *way of seeing* profoundly. Douglass asks what should be an obvious question, but an overwhelming majority of people who celebrate Independence Day admit to never registering a thought anywhere near Douglass's question. Now, before you read further, ponder that question for a moment! Seriously! Indulge me for a moment and truly reflect on that question.

In the speech Douglass says: "As a people, Americans are remarkably familiar with all facts which make in their own favor. This is esteemed by some as a national trait—perhaps a national weakness" (p. 111). So, Douglass began his speech with an insult-laced preface about American self-absorption. Douglass further proclaimed:

> I am not included within the pale of this glorious anniversary! Your high independence only reveals the immeasurable distance between us. The blessings in which you, this day, rejoice, are not enjoyed in common. . . . The sunlight that brought light and healing to you, has brought stripes and death to me. This Fourth of July is yours, not mine. You may rejoice, I must mourn. To drag a man in [chains] into the grand illuminated temple of liberty, and call upon him to join you in joyous anthems, were inhuman mockery and sacrilegious irony. Do you mean, citizens, to mock me, by asking me to speak to-day? (p. 112)

Undoubtedly there are some current-day societal implications still reflective of Douglass's question about the perpetuation of this historical inconsideration. Additionally, there are other aspects of so-called American culture, or the so-called American Way, that still remain a bit awkward, and/or somewhat inconsiderate, or downright offensive to other groups in the United States as framed by the Fourth of July holiday. I use this example to frame the fact that some of the reasons we succumb to homophobia, heterosexism, and other "isms" is our inability to consider the Other without being prompted to do it. Even my prompt of asking participants at a diversity and social justice retreat to share the three holidays that they imagine most Americans would have no problem celebrating doesn't effectively ignite enough philosophical consideration to take the Fourth of July out of the top three choices. I have done this exercise numerous times and have yet to have one participant articulate the hypocrisy of an Independence Day being celebrated when social injustices permeate the societal landscape. Dysfunctional language such as *retard* continues to be used to casually frame behavior deemed as somewhat odd, though it further exacerbates the marginalizing of and contributes to the ostracizing of individuals and communities that are physically and/or mentally challenged. Women are often unfairly painted as sluts if they enjoy sex too much and/or appear to have multiple lovers, and whores if it is somehow confirmed that they have had multiple lovers, in contrast to men, who receive fist pumps and verbal praise as players or pimps. But in the context of heterosexism and its far-too-often resulting homophobia, the inconsideration feels more culturally pathological. Same-sex marriage is still not sanctioned everywhere throughout the United States. Phrases like "no homo" are used/overused to qualify an expression of physical or verbal affection between two men, implying that affection between two men is not only wrong, but something that must be addressed. The irony is that every time I have ever heard a man state "no homo" I have struggled with either not viewing him as a mindless minion of society's socialization or seeing him as someone whose insecurities could benefit from intestinal fortitude push-ups.

I remember while pledging my fraternity during my undergraduate college days an oddity within the process. For years I had thought about the merits of joining an all-men organization and dismissed it as inconsequential due to the lack of necessity from having played team sports most of my adolescence. But when I considered the need to learn how to work with other men, it was a no-brainer that it was time for me to explore what an all-Black male fraternity and I might offer one another. The intake process was one of the more provocative experiences I had ever undertaken in my efforts to become an adult. Learning how to work proactively within the framework of a wide array of very different men was intensely daunting at times. Learning how to remain proactive and productive was quite the challenge when many of the lessons being taught amounted to humbling and intimidating the prospective brother. The pledge program, be it by design or happenstance, generated quite a bit of introspection. As a "pledge," if I was not self-reflecting I was not reflecting at all. However, in my self-reflection I continued to rediscover how much there was to know about people who truly considered me for my depth and breadth, and responded to me accordingly. I started to care about what I projected to others because now it wasn't just a statement about me, or my family, but also one about my fraternity, Alpha Phi Alpha.

Ironically, there was a gay brother in our chapter who was in the closet. At that time in the early '80s, some of the most so-called "enlightened" Alpha Men were profoundly homophobic. Beyond the hypocrisy of not wanting to endure racism from racists, many of my Alpha brothers didn't hesitate to discriminate toward him and other gay men, usually indirectly, discussing gay men's worth to the organization as essentially more problematic than worthwhile, prejudging their rights to even be members of Alpha Phi Alpha. After a probing conversation with this brother of Alpha who loved and worked as hard if not harder for our fraternity than many shirt-wearing (brothers who had joined the fraternity only to don its colors), overtly opinionated heterosexual brothers, I became committed to making sure this brother of mine/ours knew that it was possible for him to have the type of brothers who would judge him by the content of his character.

Upon joining Alpha Phi Alpha, with all of this questionable brotherhood activity in the backdrop, I was inspired to write a poem within a week of becoming an Alpha. I had the good fortune of seeing it published numerous times since then in the national magazine, *The Sphinx*. I even had the pleasure of the Fraternity's 33rd General President, Herman "Skip" Mason, reciting it as he concluded his keynote address at the 2011 Eastern Regional Convention in Bermuda. I recited the poem three months later at the 2011 National Convention in Chicago, during the College Brothers Luncheon.

Interestingly enough, when brothers read and celebrate the poem today most wouldn't know that it was greatly inspired by the hypocrisy of Alpha Men, and other heterosexist practices existing in most nongay fraternities. This excerpt from the poem "Dare to Be an Alpha Man" reveals how I actually wrote it as a call to arms of sorts:

For brotherhood is what we have dared
In a world that is frankly scared
To express feelings of love and care
Due to society's image laden game of chess
But we know images are to project,
not to hide nor to protect.
So we try to always reflect
exactly who we are and nothing less

True to ourselves we will always be
For success in life is not guaranteed
So we will most assuredly
Conduct ourselves with the utmost taste.
For we are men that all should know
when cast as extras
can steal the show
for unlike the wind which dies and grows
our aura remains constant to state our case.

We are men of colors, Black and Gold.
Men who won't be bought and sold.
With Alpha Phi Alpha dwelling in our soul
In a world that can't understand
That men of destiny from birth we are
Men that shine bright as a star
Men who have dared to have gone so far
As to have dared to be
Alpha men.

—Brother J. W. Wiley, May 1983

"Dare to Be an Alpha Man" was written as a challenge to incoming and current men of Alpha Phi Alpha to truly build an organization that is about changing the game when that game is dysfunctional, and working diligently to not succumb to it. That is why it talks about authentic "brotherhood," "projecting images" instead of "protecting images," and "men who won't be bought and sold" in terms of their ideals. Most of us, men especially, often don't realize that our *way of seeing* has been packaged and sold to us through the culture of capitalism. We have bought into the marketing of our machismo the same way Americans have blindly purchased the celebration of certain holidays, how we unthinkingly romance one another, and why men ironically can go topless at beaches without a second thought while women, generally speaking, don't, but instead wear bikini tops rather than their brassieres.

I firmly believed in the principles I articulated when I wrote the poem back then but without the academic insights to define them, which I now have to truly frame them. Now I know that before we could/can be Alpha Men, we must dare to be a new type of Alpha Man, one who has wrestled with his homophobic insecurities and heterosexual privilege, one who strives for an ideal that isn't easily attainable. This progressive mind-set would benefit not just my fraternity, but all male organizations that operate under the unstated premise that loving another man makes you less of a man.

> "Homophobia is a central organizing principle of our cultural definition of manhood."
>
> —Kimmel (2000, p. 214)

I fully understand now that if being an Alpha Man or, more apropos perhaps, an enlightened man was easily attainable everyone would be an Alpha Man, everyone would be enlightened, and therefore no one would be. Perhaps that wouldn't be so bad after all.

The Snapshot Syndrome

When Warren Blumenfeld (2000) stated that "homophobia inhibits the ability of heterosexuals to form close, intimate relationships with members of their own sex" (p. 271), he brought to mind a concept I call "the snapshot" (I will discuss this shortly). I remember as a high school student my first exposure to a gay male. Upon arriving at a new school in Tulsa in my junior year, I connected with a group of young men who were all fairly cool. By that I mean not necessarily judgmental, not obnoxious toward others who had a different "flavor" or "flow." I remember more distinctly attending the high school after-prom party with this group of guys and all night long rapping about how hot a particular girl was, or how nice it would be to have some romantic time with certain girls. The semester ended and summer passed. That following fall, on the first day of school I recall people running up to me asking, "Have you seen Kerry?" When I answered, "No," their response was almost uniformly, "Wait till you see him." Well, within 10 to 15 minutes of this warning I encountered Kerry. This handsome, smart, engaging guy who was checking out the young women with me and the other boys just three months ago was now dressing like a girl. Without a doubt it rocked the school, but it rocked me even more. What could have happened to him over the summer to inspire him to change his identity to such a degree? What could have happened to him to motivate him to put forth an identity that would have him become the butt of a thousand jokes? What was it that made him decide it was okay for him to basically accept the fact that he was not only becoming a leper of sorts, but also possibly suggesting that others like me may belong in the colony as well? Kerry's exiting the closet was one of the bravest things I had witnessed in my young life up to that point, though it took me a minute or two, figuratively speaking, to fully engage it and, more so, to appreciate it.

After Kerry came out, he was like a man with no country. Some of the girls made a space for him, but others went out of their way to avoid him. The boys at school, though, either were hostile toward him or pretended he didn't exist. It almost became a sin to even look at Kerry. Somehow, through our homophobia we all contributed to somewhat incarcerating Kerry for just being Kerry. As I reflect back upon it now, an excerpt from a poem by Oscar Wilde comes to my mind:

> *This too I know—and wise it were*
> *If each could know the same—*
> *That every prison that men built*
> *Is built with bricks of shame,*
> *And bound with bars lest Christ should see*
> *How men their brothers maim.*

—Oscar Wilde, The Ballad of Reading Gaol

I *feel* this poem more than I can even begin to communicate. For every moment that I contributed to Kerry's imprisonment I feel an hour of shame. That shame forces me to further relive those moments that feel as if they morph into days, weeks, months, years, and an eternity when I wonder what scars he may be wearing from those high school episodes.

Thinking again of Kerry, I recall one day rounding a corner and almost bumping into him. It was my first opportunity, more so my first "moment," to engage him verbally since he had exited the closet. He said hello, and my response was a shocked, indiscernible mumbling, barely worthy of uttering. After I escaped that awkward moment, I couldn't shake the feeling of shame I had. Somehow I left that moment knowing that the next time I saw Kerry would be different. In retrospect, I realize now that even then, when we fortuitously encountered one another, it was a defining moment for me. Within that moment I had succumbed to the *snapshot* syndrome. I couldn't relax while talking to Kerry for all of five seconds because I was too worried about someone passing by and taking a mental snapshot of Kerry and I talking, or even seeming to talk, which was actually more the case. I was overtly preoccupied that with a passing glance someone might think I was gay, perhaps even situating myself for a moment with Kerry. In fact, to be more frank, I was horrified about the possibility that someone might think I was gay.

The snapshot syndrome isn't limited to our homophobia alone. As a college professor in any extended one-on-one interaction with a young woman who might be deemed as attractive by onlookers I experience the snapshot syndrome. As a Black man who has dated White women, when seen by Black women with a non-Black woman I have sometimes experienced the snapshot syndrome. I even remember experiencing it when as an older man I started to obtain some socioeconomic class status and felt uncomfortable in conversations with others whose socioeconomic class status paralleled mine if those conversations were being heard or viewed by friends of mine who were still financially struggling.

Possibly one of my first real leadership moments occurred when I decided not to succumb to the snapshot syndrome and instead care enough about the person before me to give him or her my undivided attention, impervious to the gossiping and whispering of others. As a college professor engaging an array of students with different identities, it is important for me to not project negative energy around students who may be somewhat fragile to begin with. When the old adage "Just because you are paranoid doesn't mean you aren't being chased" is more the rule than the exception, it is important to tread lightly. However, there will still be those times when no matter how lightly we tread we are going to step in shit.

Defining *Straight*, Implying *Crooked*

Once in my early years as a university administrator I was invited to speak to a gay and lesbian organization. Before I embarked upon sharing my thoughts, I prefaced my thoughts by declaring that though I wasn't gay, this is my perspective. I had always done this type of caveat when addressing a diverse group that had experiences that I cared to know but was limited in accessing. On this occasion, after extending my preface to those assembled, I gave my talk. I essentially was informing them of the support the unit I directed was prepared to provide them. Upon finishing I left. The next morning when I got to work a colleague of mine who was in attendance at the talk informed me that the woman who had invited me to give the talk informed the students that I must be homophobic since I found it necessary to proclaim my heterosexuality. The majority of the students in attendance, who were very much attuned to the librarian and her leadership role as their advisor, from that day forward were uncomfortable with me, distanced themselves from me, and probably upheld the legacy of my homophobia toward them by communicating it with new members over the next few semesters. It took years for me to be able to once again situate myself as an ally to the gay, lesbian, bisexual, and transgender students. More importantly, it taught me an invaluable lesson as to how vulnerable people are who are paranoid about how others see them.

In response to that incident I started thinking deeply about how I projected my sexual orientation. I then really processed the term I used to define my sexual orientation. After cogitating about it for an extended amount of time, I sat down and wrote an "In My Opinion" on the topic that was published in the *Press-Republican* newspaper, which I share with you here:

STRAIGHT TALK CAN LEAD TO CROOKED THOUGHTS

I often find assertions that God chose to make some people "straight" and some people "gay" quite interesting. *Straight* is a popular reference to a colloquialism about heterosexuals. I have no knowledge of who coined the phrase. I have heard it used by so many others and must acknowledge that I used it myself quite some time ago, without recognizing what I was implying by the usage. What is implied when we compare or contrast heterosexuals with homosexuals by using the terms *straight* and *gay*? Well, if heterosexuals are straight, and gayness is the alternative lifestyle being considered, aren't we insinuating that homosexuals are crooked? Furthermore, aren't we suggesting that it would be better for gays to be straight because who wants to be crooked when there aren't many, if any, redeeming qualities associated with crookedness?

Am I creating a mountain out of a molehill by offering these thoughts up for public consumption? Not if you understand and take language seriously. Non-vitriolic insinuations of crookedness can do as much damage as over generalizing or irrationally labeling any community of individuals worthless, deviant, ignorant, racist or privileged. For years scholarship has revealed that cavalier assertions of character assignments can contribute to the devaluing of one's history, a self-hatred of one's identity, and an institutionalized cruelty that may persist for hundreds of years. That is why battles over the usage of terms like *cripple* for individuals with disabling conditions, *girl* for women, *boy* for Black men, *gypped* for someone feeling ripped off, *jewed* for someone feeling they were taken advantage of in some financial transaction, *Asian* as if all people in that category really have something in common and it is okay blurring their uniqueness, and *people of color* as if White people don't have color, are being waged all across the country with a fervor that clearly endorses this type of language as problematic.

Unpacking language is an interesting exercise. Notions of "traditional family values" finds us often interpreting those who are comfortable or cavalier authenticating such values as oppressors inconsiderately assisting people who are in dire need of holding onto their privilege. As well, abhorrent attempts to link pedophilia with homosexuality are about as sophisticated as rationally justifying a woman who was raped as asking for it because of her attire. That logic works until it is your mother, daughter, wife or sister that is the victim and/or your child, grandchild, or great grandchild that is gay or lesbian. Then all of a sudden it becomes a different matter! While these are extreme examples, the point is, reading between the lines is often necessary.

I have had members of the gay, lesbian, bisexual and trans-gendered community say to me that they refer to heterosexuals as straight and don't feel as if it is a reflection on them in any way. I can respect that and consider it a healthy attitude to not be actively dodging bullets from guns that haven't been fired. However, I know that many Blacks use the term nigger fairly loosely, often as a term of endearment, and don't realize how they may be further perpetuating a slave mentality within themselves, not to mention further contributing to an inferior perspective that many may have of them already as a result of the word nigger and all its complex meanings. In other words, just because we don't have a problem with the use of certain terms doesn't mean they aren't problematic. It brings to mind the story of the boy who was severely beaten by his father for years and beyond the pain of that moment didn't realize it was paternally problematic if not downright deviant until adult conversations revealed that those physical admonishments by his father were not socially acceptable.

Language is a powerful tool. If you refer to a person as crazy long enough, the possibility of them second-guessing their sanity increases as opposed to if the reference to their sanity had never been levied against them. That isn't a fact that needs any more discussion, as it seems fairly prima facie. It is time that we "straighten" the meaning out of terms that contribute to the disenfranchisement of any members of our community and not be too quick to dismiss the use of these terms as potentially dangerous.

A postscript to this "In My Opinion" is the fact that now, in all my classes, when discussing sexual orientation we challenge all of our students to no longer refer to themselves as "straight." After discussing it at length and reinforcing it throughout the semester, I am confident that many if not most of our students who get bitten by the social justice bug are no longer able to reconcile using the term. Yes, it does require a bit more work to stay vigilant regarding our language usage. However, those of us committed to the struggle do what we must do.

I remember a female student of mine I was very close with who identified herself as straight until she realized she might not be, and then shared with me that she might be gay. Months later, she told me she was bisexual, and over an array of conversations eventually opened up to share with me some of the names of the young women she had been involved with. I noticed that the women this exceptionally fit, well-conditioned young woman had mentioned she had dated were only women who would be considered overweight if not obese. Yet I recalled when she dated she seemed to always date men who were athletically built, or at least as fit as she was. It was only a matter of time before I asked her why the different romantic expectations. Why fit, athletic men in her heterosexual dating but out-of-shape women when homosexually dating. I challenged her to ask herself did she think less of herself as a lesbian and/or bisexual, or homosexual, than she did as a heterosexual. Did she now see herself as crooked because of her same-sex interest in women and, therefore, less straight, incapable of involvement with women whom she actually found more attractive? She went deep into self-analysis and returned to our conversation with an understanding that she actually lacked the courage to initiate romance with lesbians she deemed extraordinarily beautiful, hot, or even cute. The women she had enjoyed relationships with were limited to sexual relationships. Somehow she saw herself as less attractive as a lesbian and subsequently lacked the courage to go after the type of women whom she really desired.

Was this lack of self-esteem connected to the "straight" label she carried, and then when she became not straight, perhaps subconsciously seeing herself as crooked, her romantic expectations lessened since she had become less-than in her own mind? If we know the potential impact of words like *retard, bitch, sissy*, etc., on people's psyches, then we should not underestimate *straight's* weight as a dysfunctional term, only one giving too much energy to a socialized identity while implying deviance to all others.

Leadership Moments

There are many ways we can model leadership while engaging sexual orientation. One of my ways is by often writing "In My Opinion" pieces, such as the previous one, to create conversations and consideration of others' realities. Leaders, knowing they are onstage at all times, in terms of those who are apt to follow them, should be cognizant of the fact that often it is the little things that make the largest statements. Our humor or lack thereof at times makes statements about our worldviews. This is poignantly present in this scene from the television series *Seinfeld* (David, Seinfeld, Cherones, 1994b), which we use and thoroughly engage in the Examining Diversity Through Film course.

Seinfeld: "The Outing"

Scene: (*Elaine and George are sitting across from each other at a table in a restaurant, eating breakfast. Jerry is on the pay phone near the restrooms.*)

Jerry: (*Away from the table where Elaine and George are seated, Jerry is speaking into the phone.*) I'm trying to get in touch with Sharon Leonard. She works for the NYU paper. This is Jerry Seinfeld. She was supposed to meet me at a coffee shop to do an interview.
Elaine: (*To George*) Oh, what are you gonna get Jerry for his birthday?
George: I got him a great gift.
Elaine: Really? What?
George: I got two tickets to see *Guys and Dolls*.
Elaine: Oh, that is a good gift. Maybe he'll take me.
George: No, I'm gonna go with him. (*Jerry begins walking to the table.*) What did you get him?
Elaine: I got him a two-line phone.
George: Really? That's good.

Jerry: (*Jerry reaches the table.*) Unbelievable! She's not there. (*He sits down next to George.*)

George: What paper does she write for?

Jerry: She works for the NYU school newspaper. She's a grad student in journalism. Never been to a comedy club, never even seen me, has no idea who I am.

Elaine: Never even seen you? I gotta envy that.

Jerry: You know, you've been developing quite the acid tongue lately.

Elaine: Really? Who do you think is the most unattractive world leader? (*A woman in the booth behind Jerry and George perks up to listen to Elaine's conversation.*)

Jerry: Living or all time?

Elaine: All time.

Jerry: Well, if it's all time, there's no contest. It begins and ends with Brezhnev.

Elaine: I don't know. Did you ever get a good look at De Gaulle?

George: Lyndon Johnson was uglier than De Gaulle.

Elaine: I got news for you. Golda Meir could make 'em all run up a tree.

Jerry: (*The woman in the booth behind Jerry and George shakes her head and smiles to her friend in the booth with her.*) Golda Meir. Good one, babe.

Elaine: Hey, come here. (*Jerry and George lean in.*) Those two girls behind you, they're eavesdropping.

George: Really?

Elaine: (*Louder than normal tone*) You know, uh, just because you two are homosexuals, so what? (*Jerry leans back and the woman behind him smiles.*) I mean, you should just come outta the closet and be openly gay already.

George: (*To Jerry*) So what do ya say? (*The women behind him lean closer together.*) You know you'll always be the only man I'll ever love.

Jerry: What's the matter with you?

Elaine: Come on.

George: Go along.

Jerry: I'm not goin' along. I could just see you in Berlin in 1939, goose-stepping past me, "Come on, Jerry. Go along. Go along."

Elaine: You're no fun. (*The woman behind Jerry and George gets up to use the pay phone.*)

Jerry: You know, I hear that all the time.

Elaine: Hear what?

Jerry: That I'm gay. People think I'm gay.

Elaine: Yeah, you know, people ask me that about you too.

Jerry: Yeah, because I'm single, I'm thin, and I'm neat.

Elaine: And you get along well with women.

George: I guess that leaves me in the clear.

Eavesdropping Woman: (*On pay phone, but away from the tables*) Hi, Jerry, it's Sharon Leonard from the paper. I'm here at the coffee shop and I was a little late. I guess we must have missed each other.

Jerry: I'm goin' to the bathroom.

George: Oh, me too. (*They get up to use the restroom.*)

Eavesdropping Woman: (*On phone still*) I'll be here for a little while longer and I'll try to hook up with you later. (*She hangs up the phone as Jerry and George walk into the men's restroom.*)

(*Scene ends with Sharon walking away smiling.*)

I seriously hope that most gays, allies of the gay community, or anyone socially conscious—in response to Elaine's insinuating that Jerry and George are gay—would not see this scenario as funny. This scene speaks specifically to the subtlety of homophobia and heterosexism. Elaine's attempt to entertain the eavesdroppers through humor came at the expense of a far-too-often disparaged group. It was evidenced earlier in their conversation that they are comfortable being inconsiderate of others if it suits their purposes. First, Elaine refers to the two women as "girls" in the typical manner that infantilizes women but is far too often rationalized away by the perpetrator as not that serious. On some level we can situate Elaine's inability to recognize how she, as a feminist, undermines her own agenda by contributing to keeping alive the sexist use of terms like *girl* inconsiderately applied to grown women. Then Elaine questions Jerry and George regarding the attractiveness of different world leaders as if it is safe for them to do so. They most likely did not need to be concerned with one of the world leaders they were discussing overhearing them. They could somewhat disregard or expect no reaction to their conversation by most people apt to overhear them. They also appear to not have given a single thought to the level of unearned privilege they were born with, if they seldom if ever were called "ugly." Beauty privilege is as real as any privilege we could count as unearned. However, if Elaine had chosen the Jewish community for her attempt at wit instead of the gay community, both Jerry and George may have found her anti-Semitism unattractive. Conversely, Elaine herself may not have appreciated jokes about women that implied being a woman was problematic in some significant manner, though not explicated. But since no one was gay at their table, Elaine felt comfortable making a mockery of a lifestyle that is already under siege.

Jerry does attempt to embrace his leadership moment when he admonishes both Elaine and George for being insensitive. He even likens their encouragement of him to "go along" with their prank as unacceptable, to the point of paralleling their attempt to enlist him in their inadequate attempt at humor as similar to people "going along" with the Nazis. The entire situation may have been better served if Jerry had explicitly insisted that they cease the feeble attempts at wit at a socially oppressed group's expense. Instead, by not being crystal clear in his admonition for them to stop, they appear to have interpreted his urging them to end their prank as a light-hearted resistance to their prank, not a passionate response to a social injustice.

There is a scene in the television show *Glee* (Murphy, 2010) that is one of the most powerful leadership moments involving homophobia I've ever seen on film. It centers upon the expectations of two male high school students from different families on the verge of becoming part of a blended family. Within the scene one of the two young men, Kurt, is gay. His father has given him money to redo his room, and in the scene he is showing his soon-to-be stepbrother the results of his renovating what will soon be their room, the room they will share as brothers.

Glee: "Theatricality"

The scene is downstairs in the basement of Kurt's home, where Kurt, Burt's son, and Finn, Burt's fiancée's son, will be sharing a room.

Kurt: I had to skip school to finish it, but I think you are really going to like it. Consider it a peace offering after all the yelling we have been doing. I used Marlene Dietrich and Gary Cooper in *Morocco* as my inspiration. It's a perfect blend of the masculine and the preeminent and the muted and the theatrical.

Finn: Are you freaking insane? I can't live here, I'm a dude. What the hell is that supposed to be?

Kurt: It's a privacy partition. It's the only one I could find on such short notice. Why are you getting angry about everything? I worked hard on this.

Finn: That's not a privacy partition. Why is this so hard for you to understand? I don't want to get dressed in front of you. You know that I put my underwear on in the shower before I come out when you're around? It's just, I don't want to have to worry about that kind of stuff in my own room, man.

Kurt: And what stuff are you referring to?

Finn: You know, you know what I'm talking about, don't play dumb. Why can't you just accept that I am not like you?

Kurt: I have accepted that.

Finn: No you haven't. You think I don't see the way you stare at me? How flirty you get? You think I don't know why you got so excited when you found out we were going to be moving in together?

Kurt: IT'S JUST A ROOM, FINN! WE CAN REDECORATE IT IF YOU WANT TO!

Finn: OKAY, GOOD! THEN THE FIRST THING THAT NEEDS TO GO IS THAT FAGGY LAMP, THEN GET RID OF THIS FAGGY COUCH—

Burt: HEY! What did you just call him?

Finn: Oh no, no, I didn't call him anything, I was just talking about the blanket.

Burt: When you use that word you are talking about him.

Kurt: Relax Dad, I didn't take it that way.

Burt: Yeah, that is because you are 16 and still assume the best in people. You live a few years, you start seeing the hate in people's hearts, even the best people. You use the *N*-word?

Finn: Of course not.

Burt: Yeah how 'bout retard? You call that nice girl on Cheerios with Kurt, you call her a retard?

Finn: Whaaa, uhh no, she's my friend. She's got Down syndrome, that's cruel.

Burt: But you think it's ok, to come in my house and say faggy?

Finn: But that's not what I meant.

Burt: I KNOW WHAT YOU MEANT. What you think I didn't use that word when I was your age? You know, some kid gets clocked in practice, starts crying, we tell him to stop being such a fag. Shake it off. We meant it, exactly the way you meant it. That being gay is wrong. It's some kind of punishable offense. I really thought you were different Finn. You know, I thought that being in Glee Club, and being raised by *your* mom, meant that you were some new generation of dude, who saw things differently, who just kind of came into the world, knowing what has taken YEARS of struggling for me to figure out. I guess I was wrong. I'm sorry Finn but you cannot stay here.

Kurt: Dad?

Burt: (*Still talking to Finn*) I love your mom, and maybe this is going to cost me her. But my family comes first. I can't have that kind of poison around. (*Burt then turns and talks to Kurt for a moment.*) This is our home, Kurt. (*Burt then turns back to Finn.*) He is my son. Out in the world, you do what you want, not under my roof. (*Finn leaves.*) Place looks great.

What transpires in this scene is a typical form of gay bashing, only perpetrated by someone we are surprised to find doing it. Finn, not under-standing of Kurt's homosexuality—combined with his own paranoia around being seen in close proximity to differing sexual orientations—articulates what sadly many boys his age may feel but would never dare say out of respect, or political correctness. He indirectly bashes Kurt by using the term *faggy* to describe the pillow and blanket. Instead of directly calling Kurt a "fag," Finn leaves himself an escape from painting himself as a gay-basher consistent with phrases like "no homo" that many young men use today to rationalize/justify any affection they may show toward one another.

The scene is also intriguing in the moment that Burt asks Finn if he uses the *N*-word or *retard*. When Finn attempts to spin the fact that he was implying something is wrong with Kurt, he is essentially calling him the equivalent of both terms, and Burt realizes it. By insinuating Kurt prefers "faggy" items to adorn his room, he is indirectly calling him a fag. And like the equation I use for *nigger*, $P = C = N$ equates to homosexuality as well. Kurt is a problem for those who are ill at ease being around someone differ-ent. Homosexuality is still considered a criminal activity morally if not legally in the minds of some extremist groups, which nonetheless leaves the image of gay-as-criminal in enough people's minds as to be a dangerous reality for same-sex love.

> "If a man also lie with mankind, as he lieth with a woman, both of them have committed an abomination: they shall surely be put to death; their blood shall be upon them."
>
> —*Leviticus* 20:13

What makes the scene from *Glee* so powerful is the ally Kurt's father reveals himself to be. He owns the fact that he struggled with his son's sexual orientation, which is powerful in that it reveals to others that any journey that is perspective altering requires a bit of time. He also subtly challenges Finn to step into the new millennium. There are many young men out there who have no hang-ups about other people's lifestyles. Ultimately, Burt reveals that he is prepared to sacrifice his own loving relationship to ensure a respectful environment for his children.

Far too many parents have a tendency to want their kids to be extensions of their lives instead of their own person. If more parents like Kurt's father got over themselves, understanding that their sons' and daughters' sexual orientation are their own business, we would have a world full of more love and respect. However, when we recognize the hatred that still exists surrounding same-sex relationships, promoting love and respect for differences needs to be taken to a completely different level when lives are at risk. I often remind my students, if not myself, that abolitionist John Brown risked his life and eventually died in his efforts to assist once so-called Negroes/often-called niggers in achieving freedom. The words he used to rationalize his actions still ring powerfully today (Du Bois, 1909, pp. 361–362):

> Had I so interfered in behalf of the rich, the powerful, the intelligent, the so-called great, or in behalf of any of their friends . . . and suffered and sacrificed what I have in this interference . . . every man in this court would have deemed it an act worthy of reward rather than punishment.
>
> —John Brown (November 2, 1859, during his sentencing)

> If it is deemed necessary that I should forfeit my life for the furtherance of the ends of justice, and mingle my blood further with the blood of my children and with the blood of millions in this slave country whose rights are disregarded by wicked, cruel, and unjust enactments—I submit; so let it be done.
>
> —John Brown (November 2, 1859, during his sentencing where after he would be hanged)

Those of us who consider ourselves committed to diversity and social justice and are appreciative of the depths of Brown's actions must contend with the conundrum of asking ourselves to what extent are we prepared to step into our leadership moments. As a Black man I recognize that John Brown, a White man, exemplified the epitome of an ally when he died for me to be free. As someone who is committed to changing the game, I can't avoid the self-imposed question, "To what extent is my commitment to the freedom of others, to the rights of every person to romance, love, and/or marry whom they want?" Have you asked yourself what is your commitment to others' freedom? Do you ignore others' struggles, or fight with the same fervor you would want others to put forth in assisting you in fighting for yours?

Also, if $P = C = N$ (*problem = criminal = nigger*), and we equate heterosexuality as nonproblematic, any person experiencing relationships outside of heteronormality is a problem for those who feel their relationships are or may be devalued by allowing same-sex love to culminate in what has always been considered traditional marriage. When same-sex love is such a problem that it must be monitored if not managed, while not felonious it is also more than just a misdemeanor to those who must navigate the haughtiness of heterosexism if not the hate often accompanying homophobia. Even within the gay community, $P = C = N$ applies, in terms of internalized oppression. When someone realizes she or he is bisexual and has no interest in hiding it, that person becomes a problem for many in her or his community. We don't live in a society that is comfortable with people doing duality. Biracial people are made to choose a community. While we see all–Native American, all-White, all-Asian, all-Black, and all-Hispanic communities, we don't see all-biracial neighborhoods. $P = C = N$ is no different for bisexuals, only their oppressor when not himself or herself is someone already oppressed, a should-be-an-ally monosexually gay (but not bisexual) friend.

Homosexuals present a problem to men who are insecure about their identity. Homosexuality is a problem for those who have bought into the hype about its deviance. While bisexuality is not considered a criminal activity within the gay community, it does carry with it the social stigma of conformity, of a lack of courage to fully embrace homosexuality. And for many people any sign of nonconformity to heterosexuality, while not legally policed, is demonized by some religions, treated as deviant by some people, and denied full rights and privileges by the prevailing government, all reflective of how the United States treats its criminals. When the "problem" is too easily seen as "criminal," it is more easily seen as "nigger." So why aren't all gays and all people who have felt like a "problem," a "criminal," a "nigger" all on the same page?

4

OF GENDER, BITCHES, SISSIES, GIRLS, AND GUYS

> Just like that, you see the fruit of the confusion
> He's caught in a reality, she's caught in an illusion
> Bad means good to her, she's really nice and smart
> But bad means bad to him, bitch don't play your part
> But bitch's still bad to her if you say it the wrong way
> But she think she's a bitch, what a double entendre
>
> —Lupe Fiasco, "Bitch Bad"

Lupe Fiasco's intimation of the double entendre that visits gender in terms of language is worthy of the type of mention he gives it in his song "Bitch Bad." The mixed messages that we send/receive involving gender are profoundly troubling, far too often culminating in dire circumstances, and are taught/learned early. *Bitch*, as a lesson to be learned that features different forms of oppression, stands on the shoulders of other dysfunctional moments.

This is evidenced clearly when I remember years ago watching my five-year-old son watch me kiss my two-year-old daughter on the lips. Wasn't there any truth in the line "You must remember this, a kiss is just a kiss" from "As Time Goes By," the classic song from *Casablanca*? Well, I knew something was amiss, because my son had this look in his eyes as if to say, "I know Daddy didn't just do something to my sister that he doesn't do to me." Wow! What was I to do? What would you have done? I mean, my two-year-old daughter, having seen me kiss my then-wife on the lips all of her young life, had been puckering up for months with me to say hello or good-bye. My son must have never truly focused on what was going down, until now. So, with no further ado, this was the moment of truth. What was a brotha, or in this case, father, to do?

I teach a philosophy course called Moral Problems. In it I challenge my students to unpack moral dilemmas. Well, what could be more dilemmatic than my conundrum of whether or not to kiss my son on the lips? After all, his puckering up to emulate his sister's receipt of a kiss from Daddy was long overdue. He may have subconsciously spied it before, but today, he was calling me to the carpet. And it wasn't like I could bookmark the moment and come back to it when I felt like it. No, no, no! It wasn't going to be that type of a party. So, I needed to *Stand and Deliver* for *Something New* or I would be *Unfaithful* to *The Mission* of not succumbing to *The War Within*. Sometimes when I am really stressed I speak in movie titles, so bear with me through those moments. Essentially my dilemma was this:

1. If I don't kiss my son on the lips, then a positive consequence of not kissing him is that I can maintain my macho image. Like most men, I have worked diligently over the years to be seen as "cool" and "tough." I couldn't run the risk of losing that image by responding to my son with too much affection, could I?
2. If I don't kiss my son on the lips, my daughter might continue to feel special.
3. If I don't kiss my son on the lips, I don't have to feel the sensation of ever kissing another male on the lips. After all, my dad never kissed me on the lips when I was young, did he? I'm still not sure about that! I wonder how many men's fathers kissed them on the lips when they were young!

Anyway, if I don't kiss my son on the lips, then a negative consequence of not kissing him is that I send a message to him and any other father-and-son tandem that might be caught in a similar situation that there is a double standard that fathers must adhere to if they don't want to be seen as different, or worse, less than the average guy. If I don't kiss my son, then he learns that Daddy is going to treat his daughter very different from the way he treats his son, and really for no certain reason except some ridiculous dysfunctional peer pressure that men respond to. Additionally, I may be inadvertently telling him that he means less to me than the other two members of our household, his mother and sister, simply because I won't give him the affection he desires at that moment. Now remember, I have a career as a diversity director, which only compounds this problem. I'm supposed to be somewhat enlightened. Another negative consequence is that my daughter might find a way to tease my son about the fact that Daddy kissed her, but not him. Though she was only two at that time, she already had game!

If I kiss my son on the lips, a positive consequence could be that he feels as valued as his sister does. His kissing me might be undercutting his sister's game by taking away her sole proprietorship of Dad's lips. It could eliminate in my son any thoughts that there are limits to our affection that don't exist between his sister and me. Another positive consequence would be the statement I would make about my ability to not succumb to certain aspects of my socialization that truly are somewhat irrational. What is the big deal about a man kissing his son on the lips? Didn't I see the very chic Michael Douglas, the Michael Douglas who is married to Catherine Zeta-Jones, kiss the extremely Spartan Kirk Douglas, his father, on the lips once? If the man who portrayed the film *Wall Street*'s Gordon Gecko could do it, why can't I?

If I kiss my son on the lips, a negative consequence might be that he develops an expectation of it occurring more, which could lead to others possibly seeing it, which could contribute to them seeing me differently. Some might even say that it could even contribute to him being more comfortable kissing other males on the lips. Just because I am a diversity director doesn't mean I don't succumb to my socialization at times. The fear of people projecting to others who we are and what we are about is something that intimidates many of us.

So, I took a deep breath, puckered up, and went lip to lip with my Youngblood. It was a very strange sensation, this double consciousness, this feeling. . . . Okay, let me say it another way. Even though I was extremely proud of myself for having stepped up, I was just as relieved about the fact that somehow my son never puckered up to me again after that day. That tells you exactly how deep-seated heterosexism is in our psyches. Or, that unlike my daughter and wife, my son thought either that the experience was overrated or, worse, that I was a lousy kisser. More importantly, though, it framed the fact that we are all victims of a male hegemony that insists we conform to a dysfunctional norm. This norm is the same one that Lupe Fiasco suggests (in "Bitch Bad") exists around the word *bitch*, except he appears to imply that it is women who could/should change the game.

Engaging *Bitch*

For years I have worked with Dr. Eddie Moore Jr., founder and president of the White Privilege Conference, presenting the *N*-word at the various venues often made available through the National Conference on Race and Ethnicity. After a year of Eddie presenting the *N*-word solo, he brought me in on this dynamic conversation he created. During the planning of those workshops we discovered something quite intriguing. In general, women seldom refer to other women as niggers, if at all. Even in films that feature predominantly Black female leads, like the movie *Set It Off,* when the women are getting raucous and/or raunchy, *nigger* is not the term they use to offend or endear. Of course that should not be interpreted as Black women are not offensive to one another.

Bitch or *ho* seem to be more the terms chosen to disparage or dehumanize another woman. Just like the rules of engagement surrounding the use of the word *nigger*, where a "nigger pass" is given to Black folks' usage of the word, usage of the term *bitch* seems to get the same rationalization. It's the in-group dialogue argument. Arguably it's okay for people within groups to have *their own language* to which others don't have access. Fortunately, I was smart enough to figure out this in-group dialogue code on my own, though I was tested. Once upon visiting a female friend, I was asked to answer the phone if it rang while she was upstairs taking a shower. About 10 minutes later I went to answer her ringing phone, hearing an all too familiar inner-city female salutation as I picked up the phone. "What's up, bitch?" the female caller asked. Before I could even attempt an answer, I was rescued by my female friend, who, apparently done with her shower, answered the phone, replying, "Everything, bitch, what's up with you?" Somewhat surprised at the exchange, I didn't suddenly feel empowered with insight into the women's struggle to the point that I felt it was okay for me to bound up the stairs and exclaim, "Are you bitches still on the phone?"

I recognized that these two women would have chastised me with no hesitation had I attempted to emulate their conversation at that level. But hadn't they just engaged one another with a term they both deemed appropriate? Yes! So then it must have been okay for me to use it too, especially since one of them would have known my intentions were not to disrespect. Of course not! But this is the rationale that is often used by non-Blacks to legitimate their use of the word *nigger*. The old "If they can use it, why can't I?" argument. Could that argument be any more fallacious?

Michael Eric Dyson (1996) refers to the word *bitch* as a one-word thesaurus for male supremacy (p. 178) and rightfully so. However, as a one-word thesaurus its definition would also include, ironically, the corollary that its use brands the user with a mark of stupidity for not being aware of the word's other connotations. Thinking about the term *bitch* deeper, though, requires consideration of its application toward men. Could there be any more male supremacy than labeling a so-called man a bitch?

It is also a major statement of exactly how sophisticated or dysfunctional a man's perspective on this gendered dimension of social justice actually is. If a man is hesitant to refer to another man as a bitch in a stereotypical situation in which *bitch* would be applied, then he probably understands how problematic it is to not just avoid referring to women as "bitches" but that referring to other men by this term is just as deep a cut. For example, a man who would hold no tears back at a wedding could/would be seen by some as comfortable with his sensitivity. That same man, though, being assessed by old-school brothers with a sexist mentality, would be considered a "bitch" or "bitchlike" for not holding those tears back and for making a spectacle of himself.

When a man is called a bitch out of anger/resentment or disdain by another man, he is being told he is less than a woman, or womanlike if the man attaching the label sees all or most women as bitches. Even in jest, referring to another man as a bitch is an offhanded comment about the commenter's respect for women, and how, again, even in jest, something was done by some man that could be questioned in terms of what educational filmmaker Dr. Thomas Keith refers to as The Bro Code.

And then there is the conversation as to why *bitch* is problematic in itself. I usually answer that concern with a hypothetical anecdote. Immanuel Kant, the German philosopher, in his articulation of an ethical concept he calls the *categorical imperative*, states as one of his formulations that people should act as if their actions could be willed a universal law. So, if this is the case, then consider this hypothetical scenario. We have 18-year-old Humphrey who enters a parking lot and finds a wallet with $3,000 in it. Humphrey, not fully invested in the consequences of how he handles this possible financial windfall, will nonetheless establish a template for behavior in similar situations, per Kant's categorical imperative, when he acts as if his actions can be willed a universal law. Knowing this, but strapped for cash, Humphrey attempts to do the right thing for both himself and the owner of the wallet. He rationalizes that the person who lost the wallet must be hurting, and that others who might have found the wallet may have not only kept all of the money, but also possibly thrown it in the trash. So Humphrey feels quite validated by taking one third of the money and sending the wallet back with $2,000 in it. Of course, the person who lost the wallet will be happy with receiving something instead of nothing. However, if we apply the categorical imperative to this situation, and then project forward to sometime in the future, what happens when Humphrey, a successful businessman now 38 years old, loses a briefcase with $3 million of investors' money in it on his way to a business transaction that requires cash? How much money can he expect to recover? When the briefcase is returned to him, how much should he expect in it, $3 million, $2 million, or $1 million? Well, considering that upon finding the wallet years ago he acted as if his actions could be willed a universal law, Humphrey can expect back what he established 20 years earlier when he took one third of the money he found in the wallet. He will lose $1 million, but get $2 million back. What does it do for him? Perhaps not much when we consider how his business partners may respond to his losing $1 million. Who knows, beyond not being able to facilitate the business he was empowered to handle, his life could be in danger depending upon who the investors were in the project.

How this story relates to the word *bitch* is in the application of the categorical imperative to its usage. If men would "act as if their actions could be willed a universal law," they would never again use the word *bitch* to describe or address a woman. If men love the women in their lives, why would they leverage such a term at a woman fully knowing that they would be opening the floodgates, a metaphorical Pandora's box, on its usage toward other women? No logical, thinking man would be cool with his mother, daughter, sister, aunt, wife/best friend, or lover being referred to as such. So it is the epitome of hypocrisy for men to do such a thing, and yet monthly, weekly, daily, hourly, this very second some boy, or man acting like a boy, is labeling a woman a bitch. However, call a girl/woman in the perpetrator's life a bitch and he'd be ready to maim you if not kill you.

I specifically draw a distinction between a boy and a man acting like a boy in terms of this problematic word *bitch* because one sign of maturity is understanding the consequences of your actions. Every time we unthinkingly or unwittingly label one of our sisters in this way we contribute to the moral decay of our society. Seriously! As men we inadvertently green-light this language and behavior that supports it. Whether we want to admit it, we overtly model for boys who look to us as role models that in some instances our women deserve this moniker. Covertly, we also suggest that it is okay for us to be inconsiderate and hypocrites because we are men and we have some type of right, perhaps stemming from simply being birthed men, to act as if our actions aren't willed as universal law. So, on some level, for men in our society who choose to speak this way to other people's daughters, sisters, mothers, lovers, aunts, and friends, they have created their own imperative that trumps the categorical imperative. I imagine they are comfortable operating under a *hypocritical imperative.*

This hypocritical imperative rears its contradictory head with men in an array of ways. We claim to want to raise our girls to be fully participating citizens in an egalitarian society, and claim to want to love and support our women in having equal opportunities/voices, but we green-light dysfunctional language that undercuts such an agenda. For example, when a man is with other men and one cavalierly refers to women as bitches, we give him a pass. We don't process the fact that today's "bitch" is someone else's daughter, but tomorrow's "bitch" may be ours. However, that is not the overriding reason we should speak up. The same reason most men would never use such language in the presence of their mothers is the reason they should not only not use it, but not allow its usage in their presence. Most of us were taught it is wrong and understand that lesson well. However, peer pressure is something that often overwhelms us and prevents us from stepping into a leadership moment. Men must fully understand that every time they step into a leadership moment by challenging the profane conversant in a dysfunctional conversation they model socially just behavior for all present to witness. This is the type of behavior within a dysfunctional moment that changes the game.

Another example of men succumbing to our socialization is the time I recall my son at a very young age falling and skinning his knee to the point that he began to cry. Upon recognition of him doing this my immediate reaction was to pick him up, dust him off, and lightly admonish him to not be a "sissy." As the first *s* began to roll off of my tongue, I caught myself on the verge of being a walking contradiction to everything I teach and reeled that language in. I recognized that if my daughter had fallen and hurt herself I would have been totally comfortable with her crying. So, either I needed to reassure him that tears are okay, or the next time simply tell my daughter to toughen up.

Girl Talk

Our casual references to grown women as girls is one way we (both men and women) contribute to the dysfunction of men valuing themselves above women. Over and over again you can hear grown men referring to grown women as girls, but seldom are grown men called boys. Like much dysfunctional language that we use daily, *girl* isn't necessarily meant to disparage women. However, when men are challenged about it, forced to consider what it means, their responses can be quite vitriolic. Throughout the course of a semester it never fails that initially many men (and, interestingly enough, some women) in our diversity course think we are overreacting by challenging them to cease referring to grown women as girls. They dismiss it as simply another somewhat acceptable, not really harmful social norm, like the word *retard* or phrases "that's retarded," "that's gay," and "no homo." By the end of the semester, though, most of the young men who really want to do the right thing are conscious of *girl*'s weight and influence.

Once I sat down to grade papers for the diversity class I teach and was surprised like you wouldn't believe. One of the students' papers began by informing me that he was in a local business and overheard two people discussing Dr. J. W. Wiley's take on the word *girl*. The main reason for the student informing me of the business owner's comments in the paper was that the student couldn't understand how the business owner didn't agree that the use of the term *girl* is usually inappropriate when designating an adult woman, unless coming from a parent aimed at his or her female child of any age, and even then it is about context unless understood as a term of endearment. Perhaps Jackson Katz's (2004) insight into women's self-hatred explains her behavior: "Women inevitably internalize the culture's misogyny, which then contributes to all sorts of problems in their relationships with men" (p. 249). Now, this business owner has a reputation for gossiping. In this case, though, what motivated this gossip was a conversation I actually had one night at a bar with the business owner's husband. During the evening he had repeatedly referred to women as "girls." Now, I don't mean young women under the age of 18—which we actually can feel comfortable referring to as girls because legally they aren't considered women yet—even though their intellectual engagement and responsibility levels may transcend those of many women older than them. The business owner's husband must have referred to at least four different women as girls in a span of about 45 minutes. His references were so casual and inconsiderate, vocal, comfortable, and perhaps unconscious that finally I felt I had no choice but to engage him about it. And, believe me, I don't enjoy being seen or thought of as the diversity police. Nonetheless, after years of encountering him and having to sit by and watch him toss around "girl," I wouldn't have been able to sleep that night if I hadn't challenged him.

I tried tactfully to point out to him that he might be undercutting his social image and framing his respect for women and/or his understanding of women's struggle in a very negative manner. I was attempting to give him an assist, perhaps challenge him to think beyond his own socialized and inconsiderate perspective. Hence, I didn't attack him nor belittle him for referring to adult women in a manner he wouldn't refer to adult men. Yes, at no point in the evening did he refer to any man as a boy. Rather than tackling him head-on, I took a roundabout approach and asked him whether he loved his 13-year-old daughter. He answered yes, with no hesitation. I then asked him if he loved his wife, mother, sisters, aunts, etc. His answer was an unequivocal—albeit suspicious of my motives—yes to all these questions. I then asked him if he had little patience for men who disrespect women. He answered yes to this as well. I then politely pointed out to him that his references to adult women as girls contribute to the infantilizing of women.

If most of the problems with social injustice are a result of the way we are socialized or a result of our inadequate unpacking of how we were inappropriately indoctrinated in terms of how we engage differences, then while we don't want to disparage each other for our inconsideration, we still do want to improve our environment by challenging one another to consider the consequences of those actions we exhibit that are problematic. In essence, that is what I was doing with him, trying to get him to "consider" the statements he might be making about women and the sexist world he was further adversely perpetuating for his daughter to grow up in. I pointed out that his blindly spewing language that he himself had been basically introduced to in his ascent to adulthood wasn't necessarily his fault until the error of his ways was pointed out to him, but from that point forward it would be his fault. (Yes, once again Camus's consideration "Beginning to think is beginning to be undermined" was in full effect.) He took offense at my suggestion and objected loudly. He implemented what I jokingly and arbitrarily often refer to as "protection-of-unearned-privilege move number 14" and immediately went into a spiel about how it isn't that serious. He followed that rationale with what I now will jokingly refer to as move number 29, the argument that "he had always spoken that way" (the fallacy referred to as "the argument to tradition"). Both of these arguments are extremely spurious, especially for a Black man to use (yes, he was Black), because they are the same arguments that people used back in the day to justify calling people that look like him and me "boy" (and other disparaging terms) before so-called civil rights were *inadequately* distributed in our society. When I pointed out the hypocrisy of his position, he only got louder and more annoyed. Go figure!

Ultimately, his voice became louder and edgier. Ironically, the edge that eventually arose from me in my exchange with him came from his repeatedly talking over his wife's voice in a very disrespectful way, as if she should know to defer when he was talking. It got so bad that I pointed it out to him a couple of times and he summarily dismissed that as well, as she got silent each time he did it, rolling her eyes in disdain, while nevertheless yielding the conversation to him. Then later, in the student's paper, it was revealed to me that she did not like my style of communicating. I found this so bizarre, because she was visibly disturbed by his dominating the conversation, not allowing her to get a word in most times, and I was advocating on her behalf. I imagine it is easier to scapegoat an outsider than to own the dysfunction in our own lives.

However, there were some questions that arose in my mind from this moment:

1. Why do "some" men get so defensive when you point out the fact that they are hypocritically disrespecting the same women whom they claim to love?
2. Should men (or people) get a pass on possible disrespectful language simply because the language has always been used that way?
3. Is it possible that eliminating "girl talk" might actually contribute to a necessary change in consciousness toward the way we think, speak, and treat women?
4. Should women also stop the "girl talk" or is "girl talk" an accepted "in-group" thing similar to the use of the word *nigger* by some African Americans, *bitch* by some women, *fag* by some gays, *redneck* by some Whites, and *retard* by some people with disabling conditions? In other words, is it okay for adult women to call one another "girl" but inappropriate for men to do it?
5. Should women who consider themselves feminist or socially liberated feel like hypocrites when they further contribute to their marginalization while simultaneously keeping men in the center when an extreme example of this can be seen when they say, "Farewell, you guys" to a group of all women?

These are questions that should be engaged by any and all people who not only claim to love women, but consider themselves allies of women in the social justice movement. I share next some of the responses I have to these questions, influenced by conversations I've had over the years with students in many of my classes, and with audience participants in the Diversity Enlightenment sessions I've presented to professional and business groups.

1. **Why do "some" men get so defensive when you point out the fact that they are hypocritically disrespecting the same women whom they claim to love?** While some men are receptive to being called out on their dysfunctional language or behavior—because they can get over themselves long enough to decenter and own the fact that from the moment they are being called out it isn't about them, but the women they are inadvertently oppressing—others are offended by it. They feel as if they should be given a pass since they "don't really mean anything by it." They fail to understand that whether they mean something by it or not, it is counterproductive to their role in creating a fair and equitable society and even more problematic if they genuinely do love the women in their life. What they dismiss as "nothing serious" could be quite deleterious to many women based upon the various ways they have been oppressed. Because of the power that men have in many societies, they are the master of women's fate and far too often captains of their souls. So, where does that leave girls/women, especially those who are in subordinate positions to boys/men who can't hold a candle to them? How are women supposed to see and feel about a boy/man who has nothing superior to them going for him except his male birthright? Dyson's question, "Do we hate our women?" while provocative and worthy of consideration as well as engagement, does nonetheless beg another question: "Should our women hate us?" We all really need to understand when a woman does.

Friedrich Nietzsche, in his articulation of the Master-Slave morality in his essay *Beyond Good and Evil*, once stated that the Master sees himself as good and his Slave as bad. However, the perspectives of these two are quite different. Like the Master, the Slave sees himself as good, but contrary to the Master's perspective of the other, the Slave's perspective transcends the Master's perspective of the other as bad, and instead the Slave sees the Master as evil, incarnate, resulting from the power differential existing between the two. In American society our male-female dichotomy too often parallels Nietzsche's master-slave morality.

Men in American society, to be specific, are taught that women are inferior. As a result, it becomes quite a task to truly respect this very different, complex being who we are taught is not equal to us. On some level, a person could be easily considered as stupid if that person grants someone framed as unequal egalitarian status. It's like dressing up a pig in a suit and tie and claiming it is no longer a pig. The fact that the person we respect most in life happens to be a woman makes this snafu quite difficult to engage, especially subconsciously. It makes it even more daunting when it is a woman, in my case my mother, who serves as a primary role model for mature adult behavior, as revealed in this poem I wrote to thank her for her lifetime of mentoring me while loving me.

Beautiful coal skinned enchantress
I finally see your objective
Against all odds you are dead set on
Not losing your unique perspective
And to this effect there is no limit
As to how far you'd go to protect
The gains you have made
For to see them all fade
Would be foolish and due to neglect.

Scintillating sable shaded sister
You are the root of the black family tree
And more often than not
From your childhood you were taught
That's the way it sometimes has to be
For your father was never around
And when he was the only sound
You ever did hear
Was a tall can of beer
As it emptily fell to the ground

An exquisite Ethiopian empress
In Africa that's what you may have been
A Queen on the throne
With a culture all your own
To hand down to your next of kin
But as you matured you got better
And you realized there is wisdom in age
For while you have accepted the way
Society says you must live today
To the book of life you'd add a page

It would tell of a proud black woman
Who had to be stronger and bolder

For with the recession on
And your man gone
Your family's survival rests on your shoulders
You had to be a model for your children
And especially make those boys understand
That try as you might
It's one hell of a plight
For a woman to completely replace her man

Ebony woman
In my eyes you are definitely a wonder
As fascinating as any pyramid
And until the end of time
There is no greater crime
Than for someone to forget all you did
So I promise you this Black Woman
If it's the last thing I ever do
I will find some way
To truly say
How very proud I am
Of you!

—J. W. Wiley, "Black Woman"

We love this woman, who not only birthed us, but carried and protected us, washed and waited upon us, often/usually liked and always loved us. However, society did nothing to dissuade us that this woman was still, somehow, a lesser being. Just look at her sports. Women seldom dunk basketballs. Their times in track for similar running events are not as fast as ours. The awards they receive for weight lifting are for weights that aren't as heavy as those in the same category of men's competition. They only play best two out of three in Grand Slam tennis compared to men's best three out of five. Our fathers far too often either speak for them, over them, to them instead of with them, or derogatorily about them. So, while as men we have viewed our women as less-than, subconsciously, with all the drama that has played out in the array of ways our society has been orchestrated to deny their voices and prevent them access, how could they not, albeit subconsciously, see men as necessarily evil? Why should they not hate us?

2. **Should men (or people) get a pass on possible disrespectful language simply because the language has always been used that way?** Some

men use the "argument to tradition" as a defensive response because they struggle with their loss of privilege when it comes to their communication style. Changing their language will require focus, energy they aren't interested in investing, and frankly, they aren't convinced it is necessary since women themselves use *girl*, or don't blink from its usage. Well, like Black people's usage of the word *nigger* as a term of endearment ("What's up, my nigger?"), or women's in-group usage of the word *bitch* or *girl*, both men and women subconsciously may be adding to our inability to take women as seriously as we do men.

3. **Is it possible that eliminating "girl talk" might actually contribute to a necessary change in consciousness toward the way we think, speak, and treat women?** If men are considerate enough to understand that it is problematic to refer to grown women as girls, whether meant to demean or not, then consciously investing in changing their language toward women is taking women more seriously. An effort to take women more seriously, as framed by the language that describes them, can't be anything but a step in the right direction, compared to a continuation of habits that haven't reaped anything positive.

4. **Should women also stop the "girl talk" or is "girl talk" an accepted "in-group" thing similar to the use of the word *nigger* by some African Americans, *bitch* by some women, *fag* by some gays, *redneck* by some Whites, and *retard* by some people with disabling conditions? In other words, is it okay for adult women to call one another "girl" but inappropriate for men to do it?** Even discussing women's rights outside of a woman's presence—or their appropriateness to refer to themselves in certain ways— could get a man into trouble with women. I'm smart enough to know that, even though I went there with the term *bitch* and am going there now with the term *girl*. However, in my personal life with my daughters, female students in our class discussions, and close female confidantes/colleagues, I challenge them to consider how they may be contributing to men, consciously or subconsciously, seeing or thinking of them as less than a man. Like the word *nigger* used privately between two Black men who both fully understand its power and history, two women or a group of women who have thoroughly engaged the topic and understand the consequences of using it can/may choose to use it as creative discourse. However, I firmly believe that we flirt with trouble we really don't want when we model behavior for others ill prepared to process that behavior outside of their limited perspectives. In

other words, I'm from the old school when it comes to the word *nigger*. I would never use it outside of an academic context and/or in the presence of non-Blacks. When I use the word *nigger* I am attempting to impart a lesson of some sort. If I recommended to my daughters the same strategy regarding the usage of *girl*, then I would recommend that strategy to all women who would ask my opinion.

5. **Should women who consider themselves feminist or socially liberated feel like hypocrites when they further contribute to their marginalization while simultaneously keeping men in the center when an extreme example of this can be seen when they say, "Farewell, you guys," to a group of all women?** References to groups of people that have five women and one man, or three women and one man, or four men and one woman (in other words, any combination of mixed gender in a group) as "guys" is problematic as well because it keeps men at the center, even though women say it just as much as men. Now I understand that many things we say are just instances of language usage that are as automatic as men wearing ties and women wearing brassieres. However, it still is worthwhile for us to consider why we use the language we use as much as it doesn't hurt for men to consider why men don't wear dresses and for women to consider why men don't wear brassieres (when we all know that some men should actually have chest support as much as some women really don't need to wear them). Or how about this scenario: If a man turned and walked away from a group of men that he didn't know very well and said, "I'll see you gals later," what would be the response by that group of men? If a server at a restaurant approached her or his table and greeted a group of five people, four men and one woman, with "Are you gals ready to order?" what would be the response? What type of tip could be expected following a parting salutation by the server like, "Thanks, you gals come back soon"?

A significant reason this type of categorization occurs is the phenomenon I call *stereotypical inclusion* and *systematic exclusion*. You can see stereotypical inclusion and systematic exclusion in film quite easily. Because film grants its viewers easier access to examine the lives of others, often its glimpse of what we consider "reel" life is more a slice of real life than the writer and/or director are intending. No matter the level of sophistication that these artists attempt to convey, their biases more often than not end up revealing themselves as well. So, in a scenario when the processing of film clips is orchestrated to accentuate leadership development, this orchestration can occur in various forms. Too often in articles and books that address leadership development, the topics of diversity and social justice are invariably left on the editing floor, if they were ever included beyond a placating sound bite of stereotypical inclusion or systematic exclusion. Stereotypical inclusion occurs when underrepresented people are represented in a (not necessarily deliberate) problematic fashion. That representation features them in limited ways that further exacerbate their various realities as somewhat dysfunctional. Systematic exclusion can be seen in the story lines in film that would logically have various social dynamics unfolding but for some reason the writer/director has made a decision to exclude particular images or social groups. Woody Allen films centered in New York City are prime examples of stereotypical inclusion and systematic exclusion. Woody's usage of the minority presence is often either a caricature or an odd omission.

From Girls to Guys

The cavalier use of *guys* aimed at women is another version of stereotypical inclusion. Women and all the uniqueness they bring to bear are erased when they are categorized as just "one of the boys" or "you guys." When a woman is one of the guys, does she somehow get a message that there is an expectation of a certain type of behavior that accompanies her inclusion as one of "the guys"? Does she lose her guy card if she isn't drinking, isn't into sports, isn't adept at fixing cars, isn't cool with multiple sexual partners, etc.?

Of course, the use of "you guys" is often so casual that it has no conscious overtones. However, no conscious intent for its usage makes it no less dysfunctional. Can anyone be certain that the use of "you guys" doesn't contribute to a subconscious elevation of men over women, especially when contrasted to the lack of usage of the phrase "you girls" toward groups of men or mixed gender groups? When author Judith Lorber (2000) asserted that "gender is such a familiar part of daily life that it usually takes a deliberate disruption of our expectations of how women and men are supposed to act to pay attention to how it is produced" (p. 204), of course she wasn't trying to give anyone a pass. One of the most high-profile perpetrators of "you guys" is President Barack Obama, whom I consider the social justice president. He has always impressed me as someone who would not consciously contribute to any level of oppression toward an underrepresented or marginalized group. It would be quite intriguing to see how long it would take him to change his use of "you guys" when addressing mixed gender groups to a more appropriate, less problematic "you," or "everyone."

The two systemic linguistic devices, "girls" and "you guys," contribute to the problematic perpetuation of male hegemony in ways so subtle that they are far too often dismissed as "no-brainers" or "not that serious." However, for those times when women just aren't taken seriously enough and can't figure out why, perhaps they need to consider other reasons.

> "Social statuses are carefully constructed through prescribed processes of teaching, learning, emulation, and enforcement."
>
> —Lorber (2000, p. 205)

The use of "girl" when referring to adult women exemplifies systematic exclusion. With intent or inadvertently, calling a grown woman a girl contributes to an expectation that her voice is not as pertinent, not as resonant, not deserving of the respect normally afforded a man, or a mature woman. Instead, referring to a woman as a girl accentuates if not demonstrates a preference for the naiveté and/or unqualified innocence of an adolescent female. Unlike the context it may derive from its being bantered about between women ("That's my girl"), it isn't construed as a compliment when rising from a man's mouth ("That's my girl"). When women say it the interpretation may be aligned with a shared struggle, similar to "That's my boy," or "That's my nigger." When men say "That's my girl," it has overtones of "That's my possession," or "This is someone I can control, whose voice is less important compared to mine."

Storytelling and Storytellers

The scars carried from our struggle with gender are many and often more complicated and nuanced than we even realize. With my dual appointment teaching and directing a cultural center, I teach a course that engages the topics of romance, sex, love, and marriage, which, like all my classes, is taught with a strong leaning toward examining diversity. In one of my classes, to create a provocative conversation that bridged the concepts of romance and sex I chose to use an excerpt from the film *Storytelling* (Solondz, 2002). The scenes I used featured an obnoxious Pulitzer Prize–winning Black professor of English and one of his White female graduate students. Their shared experience one night led to a provocative conversation, some intense philosophical disagreements, and some political maneuvers in response to those disagreements that I never could have anticipated.

In the first scene of the excerpt, the graduate student is arguing with her lover, an undergraduate male who has cerebral palsy, over her lack of authentic feedback over a paper he had written that was so unabashedly critiqued by their professor that the young man felt unjustifiably ridiculed. As a result he ends the relationship with his lover, encouraging her in the harshest of terms to go have sex with that very same professor since it is what he thinks all the White women in the college secretly desire. After tearfully recounting this story to her roommate, calling her now ex-lover "juvenile and cripple," she proclaims that she is going "to a bar to get laid."

The next scene shows her at a bar. After purchasing her drink she turns to check out the bar's possibilities when she espies the Black professor sitting in a dark corner all by himself. Oddly, after all the drama with her lover over this Black professor's criticism of her lover's work, she approaches him. During their ensuing conversation he answers questions she asks with prolonged pauses, often inhaling his cigarette, exhaling his smoke, and sometimes even taking a sip of his drink while she patiently awaits his answers. When she asks him if she can join him, it literally takes him 11 seconds to respond to her. He makes it obvious that he doesn't think much of her, even admitting to her when she asks his opinion of her as a writer that he doesn't see much of a future for her with that as a career. After all of this very awkward conversation, he finally compliments her on how beautiful her skin is and follows that by lightly and affectionately touching her hand. She responds to this one and only act of kindness by saying to him "I have so much respect for you." The scene culminates with them walking down the street together.

The next scene has them in his place. It is apparent that they have gone back to his place for sex, and nothing more. In the earlier scene they had established no rhythm beyond a physical one. When this scene starts they have entered his place, a studio apartment, and are therefore standing in his bedroom, slightly apart. When the professor takes her chin in his hand as a romantic gesture, seemingly as a precursor to a kiss, she nervously asks can she "just freshen up a bit." Inside his bathroom she finds an envelope with nude pictures of many young women, all White, some whom she knows from the very class she is in of his. In some of the photos there appears to be some sadomasochism occurring. As she finishes looking at the photos, seeming somewhat disturbed by them, she looks into the mirror and exclaims softly about a dozen times or so, "Don't be a racist." She basically says it as if it were the mantra she would need to get her through the evening after discovering the photos.

The last scene is an extremely provocative one. Upon reentering his bedroom she finds him reclined upon his bed, though still fully dressed with shoes on. With her still standing while he is anything but prone on the bed, she attempts to make small talk, saying, "This is really a nice place you have here. Is the rent high?" He essentially dismisses her banter by saying, "Take off your top." As with his earlier bar conversation with her, his statement is delivered a bit obnoxiously, somewhat matter-of-factly, as if he expects her to just conform to his wishes. While many women would never have entered a moment like this with a man who appears to harbor contempt for them, this young woman complies with his request and removes her purse from her shoulder, then her light sweater, then eventually her blouse, revealing her breasts. After lying there for an extended moment, the professor then says, "Now, take off the rest." Once again she complies, and now she is standing completely nude before him, while he still lies on the bed. It is at this point that he stands up next to her. She takes a step toward him as if to start some physical interaction and he interrupts her momentum by saying, "Turn around." She does, and he then unbuckles his pants and says, "Bend over." She does this as well, and in doing so, she places her hands against the wall for leverage. They begin to have vaginal sex from a rear entry point. After a dozen seconds or so he breaks the silence of nothing but heavy breathing by asking/telling her, "Say, Nigger fuck me." She replies, "I can't say that." He then replies, "Say, Ni . . ." She then says, "Ni . . ." He asks/ tells her to then say "ger," and she says, "ger." While now sexually thrusting he once again urges her to say "Nigger," and she acquiesces, saying, "Nigger." He then asks/tells her to say, "Nigger, fuck me hard." She does, and with every time she says it the sex appears to get much more physical, though it never varies from the one-dimensional thrusts, just more intense with their now impassioned voices getting louder as he asks/tells her to say the phrase and she continually repeats it.

I mention all of this in detail not to titillate, but because of the class's reaction to their interaction. Like so many other things, we don't take the time to engage gender to the extent we should. By not doing this, we also don't engage rape, an often gendered occurrence that is very much related to how we communicate and the context we communicate in.

Our discussion on the interaction between the Black professor and White graduate student had the class divided in their interpretation of what had just occurred. Some students saw the interaction between the professor and the graduate student as rape. Others saw it as consensual sex, albeit provocative, to say the least. The Black professor's insistence on the White graduate student's saying the phrase "Nigger, fuck me" probably contributed to some of the students' interpretation of their sexual encounter as a rape. Her hesitance to say it and his insistence that she say it were probably quite problematic for many of the students. Her "no" to saying it probably became a "no" to having sex with him for many of the students.

The fact that he was her professor also probably greatly influenced an interpretation of rape, but more along the lines of some degree of statutory rape resulting from the power differential between the professor and graduate student. Arguments were made that the young woman never truly had an opportunity to exit the moment once it began because of his authority over her in another context. This argument, although legitimate, isn't without problems. It is problematic because it portrays the young woman solely as a victim, without power, without a voice. It suggests that her choice to enter into a sexual moment with a man whom she knew was quite complicated should not have been made. However, if he hadn't asked her to say and/or repeat such a traumatic phrase, would that moment still have been viewed as a rape, or as an intense sexual experience between two consenting adults? What do you think?

The mitigating factors that could/should come into play to at least add some context to an interpretation of consenting sex versus rape begin with him being her professor, though she is an adult in terms of age. As her professor he was in a position to evaluate her that could have consequences for her, so he had a leverage that gave him an unfair advantage as he entered a sexual moment with her. Perhaps the next factor to consider is the statement the graduate student said to her roommate about going to the bar to get laid. Then walking with him to his place late at night after a verbal exchange that really bordered more on dysfunctional than flirtatious. This followed by her bathroom chant/mantra "Don't be a racist, don't be a racist, don't be a racist," after discovering the envelope of photos of nude women in sadomasochistic poses. As well, responding to his statement to take her shirt off (and ultimately all her clothes) and actually removing her bra practically immediately after she had just seen sadomasochistic pictures in his bathroom also makes the interpretation of the events more complicated.

Now, of course none of these actions erase the fact that she could still be raped. *No* means *no*, and men need to not only understand it, but act when they hear it, or even imagine they have heard it. As a matter of fact, if a man thinks there is a possibility a woman may say no to him, he should seriously consider not putting himself in the situation to have to respond to a no. And this anticipation of hearing no takes on more weight when the man is Black. Throughout American history Black men and Black communities have been decimated by false accusations of rape by White women (as was the case in Rosewood, Florida, and Tulsa, Oklahoma, and highlighted in the films *To Kill a Mockingbird* and *Freedomland*).

The word *nigger*, though, being stated during their sexual encounter wiped away for many of the White students any semblance of consensual sex. Since the graduate student initially wasn't willingly repeating what the professor desired to hear, somehow the sex became conflated with the statement and it became rape in their minds. His urging her on to repeat the word, urging her beyond her hesitation or socialization to hesitate, was probably seen as a form of violence by many of the students. I mean, why would a Black man want to be called a "nigger" by a White woman in a sexual situation?

Perhaps the desire to be called something most consider horrible as a sexual stimulant or form of verbal foreplay is beyond most people's comprehension. But that was also probably the case for most people who would shy away from admitting they appreciate a sensual spank but are walking around red-handed or red-reared. The head games that are played along racial lines don't stop on the playground or in the boardroom. They enter and exist in the bedroom too. If we deconstruct the context of their relationship and the events that led to their moment, it should be no surprise that something as provocative as challenging this young White woman's sense of social justice as well as self-worth could have occurred. Her representing the complexity of privilege (her Whiteness and seeming socioeconomic origin) contrasted with her minority status as a White woman dating a disabled man, wearing clothing that represented some dimension of her counterculture perspective (Malcolm X T-shirts representing a counterrevolutionary reality and Bo Jackson, an unconventional athletic icon), and then being overly patient and persistent in contributing to a possible tryst with her Black professor made her ripe for someone eventually to challenge her level of engagement. The Black professor's encouragement of her to use provocative language in the middle of a sexual moment could have been just one of those ways that people get turned on that others can't relate to. Or it could have been him pushing her to limits he was interested in seeing her respond to.

His motivation to challenge her to say such a thing could have been curiosity to see how far she would go to have a moment with him after he had basically given her very little positive energy. He may have realized that she could have seen the pictures while in his bathroom and decided from that moment onward that he was going to push the envelope to see where she would draw the line. Many women would have drawn the line when he requested of her that she remove her top, while he was still fully clothed. For them it may be about reciprocity or avoiding vulnerability. If she didn't stop complying with his request at that moment, then after his request that she remove all the rest of her clothes she probably would have stopped. If she did not stop him after those two things, then surely when he asked her to turn around while naked, with all his clothes still on, if she was hesitant to advance she could have ended the moment then too. She may have been intimidated by his presence and position but to call it rape is very complicated, perhaps naming and framing it appropriately, or perhaps overstating the case, especially within a context of the legacy of scenarios of false accusations of rape involving Black men and White women in America.

Most of the racially underrepresented students in the class saw it as consensual sex, while many of the White students saw the sexual encounter as rape. Why would they see the same event so differently? Well, aside from the political game that was soon to play out regarding the class itself, I believe it was the familiarity among Black people, both consciously and subconsciously, with the concept popularized by Angela Davis's (1981) "The Myth of the Black Rapist," and if not that myth, then "The Myth of Black Sexuality," as articulated in her book *Women, Race, & Class*. For Whites it would be the lack of knowledge or oral history of the problems with miscegenation. Most Whites would be unfamiliar with the White man's fear of reprisal from the Black man in response to the history of the Black woman's body being usurped during slavery. With little to no constraints that could seriously deter his lust, the White man either had access to the Black woman's body or, if he was ingenious enough, could orchestrate a scenario to gain access. When the tide so thought turned and Black people were so-called free, a paranoia arose among White men that the days of reckoning in most Black men's minds were near. Many White men feared retribution at the hands of their once enslaved chattel and couldn't give Black men the benefit of the doubt that they could resist the natural charms of the often portrayed symbol of beauty. Hence, the Black professor's desire to hear "nigger" emanate from her mouth during sexual intercourse could also be related to the Black man's desire to celebrate, if not overcompensate, his access to the White woman's body by also exercising control. Whether or not it is fair to women, or acceptable for certain types of men to act this way, is a debate that is unwinnable, just like whether or not an ass slap as part of a sensual moment is appropriate or demeaning.

Just as "some" Blacks overcompensate by playing the race card often as a last resort when all else fails them, and "some" gays play the homophobia card when it is their paranoia that is really the issue at hand, "some" women play the harassment card, and/or buy into the hype because of the scars they have incurred or are trying to avoid. The overcompensation by the Black man within the scripted film *Storytelling* is only one dimension of this story. The fact that after this film excerpt was shown in my Philosophies on Romance, Sex, Love, & Marriage course two high-profile and politically connected White students suggested that the mere showing of this film and resistance to acknowledging it could not be anything other than rape was evidence that their Black professor (yes, me, Dr. J. W. Wiley) condoned rape. They even went so far as to suggest my use of the clip was an attempt by me to sexually suggest similar possibilities with White female students. True story!!!

The fact that a female professional, who should be a colleague of mine in terms of promoting diversity and social justice through creative education, would instead immediately believe two disgruntled students, one male and one female, completely dismantled my sensibilities. I didn't receive one call from my so-called colleague inquiring into my reasons for showing the film excerpt. However, I did get feedback that the film excerpt that I used was then shown in one of her classes with discussion about me and my methods. Neither one of these students revealed to her that the male student (who at the time was a vice president in the student association) had raised his voice and interrupted another student's interpretation of the incident within the film not being a rape by calling that student an idiot for not agreeing with his previously articulated position that a rape had occurred. When I intervened and reprimanded the male student for his outburst, he and the other student with him, the young woman (who happened to be the president of the student association at that time), sat silently and I imagine then decided to take this incident elsewhere where they could obtain the justice they felt it deserved.

Both of these students and the female professional were academically linked to one another. So it is no surprise that their view of the world was similar on some levels. I am sure if we scratched deep enough, we'd find that I have similar views to them as well. However, casually suggesting and/or painting a Black professor as someone who would condone a rape just because he uses a controversial scene to provoke intriguing discourse on sex in a Philosophies on Romance, Sex, Love, & Marriage course is beyond the pale, over the top, and steeped in someone's yet to be healed scar tissue.

This scenario, like most, doesn't originate or exist in a vacuum. There was a moment in my early career where a female student of mine suggested that I had sexually harassed her after she received a B in one of my classes. Her first two grades in my classes in two consecutive semesters were A and A−. In her third semester of classes with me she obtained that B I mentioned as a teaching assistant and a B+ as a student in my most difficult course, The Philosophy of W.E.B. Du Bois. I imagine the deterioration of her grades was the reason she opted to initiate the harassment card to level what she perceived as an abuse of my power.

Her major was in the same discipline as that of the two students and female professional. When I was informed of this harassment charge brewing I challenged the person who brought forth the information to inform the student to please proceed. I knew that she was lashing out in the only way she knew how and that even her so-called allegations were so flimsy that they wouldn't go far. Apparently, though, knowing and choosing to believe this old unsubstantiated rumor about me sexually harassing a student reveals exactly how penetrating these gendered wounds can be. Once again we can see how $P = C = N$ is an efficient equation for this situation. I posed a problem for a group of people on campus who are/were intimidated by me and what I represented to them. The best way in American society to eliminate a problem is by framing the problem as criminal. The easiest way to make that frame believable is to somehow center the frame around someone who can easily be seen as a "problem," a "criminal," a "nigger." I have no doubt that Attorney General Eric Holder and President Barack Obama, in their quiet moments with their wives or very close Black friends, know this. Colin Powell knows this. Clarence Thomas discovered it and framed it when he referred to it as a "high-tech lynching." Enlightened non-Black people like Soledad O'Brien, Rachel Maddow, Anderson Cooper, Chris Matthews, George Clooney, Ann Curry, Matt Lauer, Mika Brzezinski, Chuck Todd, Willie Geist, Erin Burnett, Lawrence O'Donnell, Brad Pitt, Angelina Jolie, and Ed Schultz all know this too. Even Joe Scarborough kind of gets it. I mention them because I see them unrelentingly demonstrating an unending ability to fight the good fight for social justice. It is apparent that they understand this as well. They've been inside conversations with other Whites from all walks of life and have experienced what it feels like to be like Blacks seen as "the spook who sat by the door" through their experiences being "the ghosts who sit by the gate." But just as some people needed to see Obama's birth certificate to validate his citizenship, others would be apt to not struggle with seeing a Black professor in a mature sexual situation as anything other than a rapist when he provokes a young woman to say something provocative that might inspire him to a freakier performance. I personally know men who have told me that they have asked White women to say things not too dissimilar from what was said in *Storytelling*. Hey, whatever floats your boat, I've always thought. But we don't publicly and professionally try to ruin our neighbors for what we deem as sexually deviant behavior relative to our own, do we? Well, do we? This scenario got so ugly that my Philosophies on Romance, Sex, Love, & Marriage course was put under even more scrutiny when it came up for approval as a university course. Led by the professional female there was quite a bit of resistance to the class being approved. It eventually brought in some of the university's highest level administrators to lessen the hostility and keep all sides on their best behavior. In the end the class was approved and I still teach it, using the *Storytelling* clip to provoke conversation around race, gender, social class, and privilege every semester, but not without scars.

Women as Niggers?

The most significant lesson to be learned through all of this is that the nigger in all of us has us responding to things in a dysfunctional manner because we are trying to avoid being further oppressed. We have experienced the epitome of disrespect. We have had our voice taken away. As a well-educated, ever vigilant Black man I'm not stupid. If I am actually illegitimately *pimping* the system, leveraging my position and Blackness within my professional position for benefits others don't have and can't obtain, others may be more apt to try to solve their problem before it grows out of control. As their problem, I would be dealt with. In this scenario, my colleague was incapable of seeing how/why she had succumbed to seeing only the nigger in me. It may have been because she was struggling with the nigger in her.

> *Woman is the nigger of the world*
> *Yes, she is, think about it*
> *Woman is the nigger of the world*
> *Think about it, do something about it*
> *We make her paint her face and dance*
> *If she won't be a slave, we say that she don't love us*
> *If she's real, we say she's trying to be a man*
> *While puttin' her down, we pretend that she's above us*
>
> —John Lennon, "Woman Is the Nigger of the World"

John Lennon's provocative suggestion that women are treated like niggers shouldn't surprise anyone. It also begs the question, How do we engage Black women? If women in general are considered the "niggers" of the world, and Blacks are more often than not the racial group that receives the nigger designation, does a Black woman have to wear if not endure the nigger designation twice? This thought in itself has me wondering why Lennon didn't include a verse that addressed this oddity. At the very least it would have mitigated some of the backlash I "imagine" he may have received by using such a loaded term to make his point.

More so, consistent with my definition of *nigger* including $P = C = N$, we can see that any woman who steps outside of her routine threatens her status as "property" but nonetheless still carries the equation's P because she is now a problem. If her role has been designated as tightly defined with little to no life outside of her domestic responsibilities, anything contrary to that role could be/would be determined immoral if not unethical, possibly even bordering upon criminal, depending upon how rigid the relationship that she is in might actually be.

The oppression that women have endured at the hands of men has layers to it beyond those I've noticed as a man, son, brother, cousin, boyfriend, onetime husband, and lover of women. My professional colleague wasn't and perhaps still hasn't been able to put into perspective that all men aren't the enemy or a threat waiting to happen. But the scars that we carry from our interactions with people who have directly or inadvertently taken away our energy must be addressed, philosophically, metaphorically, as well as psychologically, or they will never heal.

In support of Planned Parenthood's efforts to communicate the problematic reality of rape, I was asked to create a conversation about rape to advance the public dialogue. As a father with two daughters, as a son who dearly loves his mother, as a man who has passionately loved women in his lifetime, and as a human being who believes everyone's humanity and physicality should be respected, I jumped at the opportunity. So, I decided to begin with a familiar point of departure for me. In the diversity class that I co-designed and co-teach at SUNY Plattsburgh with Deb Light—within our gender theme—we read an article from our invaluable text (Readings for Diversity and Social Justice) called "The Rape of Mr. Smith." In this very short but powerful (anonymous) essay, a parallel is drawn between the interrogation of a female rape victim and a male robbery victim. The essay demonstrates how the law is intolerant of female rape victims in a way that isn't on par with its tolerance for robbery victims. I will provide you an excerpt:

> *"Mr. Smith, you were held up at gunpoint on the corner of 16th & Locust."*
> "Yes."
> *"Did you struggle with the robber?"*
> "No."
> *"Why not?"*
> "He was armed."
> *"Then you made a conscious decision to comply with his demands rather than to resist?"*
> "Yes."
> *"Did you scream? Cry out?"*
> "No. I was afraid."
> *"I see. . . . What time did this holdup take place, Mr. Smith?"*
> "About 11 p.m."
> *"You were out on the streets at 11 p.m.? Doing what?"*
> "Just walking."
> *"Just walking? You know that it's dangerous being out on the street that late at night. Weren't you aware that you could have been held up?"*
> "I hadn't thought about it."
> *"What were you wearing at the time, Mr. Smith?"*
> "Let's see. A suit. Yes, a suit."
> *"An expensive suit?"*
> "Well—yes."
> *"In other words, Mr. Smith, you were walking around the streets late at night in a suit that practically advertised the fact that you might be a good target for some easy money, isn't that so? I mean, if we didn't know better, Mr. Smith, we might even think you were asking for this to happen, mightn't we?"*

I'm sure by now, you get the point. Aside from the fact that men can be raped as well, the reality of the situation is that it happens to men mostly in situations when they are incarcerated. Our women, however, the women whom we love, are under siege. The psychological scars carried by women who have been raped are much more than I can begin to fathom. The impact upon a woman who has avoided a rape is even difficult to imagine. I have never had a woman in my life (that I know of) who was raped or almost raped, but the thought of it terrifies me. As I said earlier, I have two daughters. One of the biggest fears I have is that one day some man will target one of them. Just as much, I harbor the fear that one of my daughters will be with a man who doesn't hear *no*, or doesn't understand what *no* actually means.

I recently had to admonish my son for not stopping when his sisters tell him to stop crowding them, or affectionately swatting them on the rear. I reinforced that teaching moment by telling him that historically men have had problems hearing *no* when they date women. I made sure he knew that the word *no* is especially not something for him as a young Black man to ignore because historically towns have been decimated over false accusations against Black men. I told him that in many places in this country, or in many people's mind, Angela Davis's articulated "The Myth of the Black Rapist" is still alive and well. I hadn't expected to have this conversation with my then-12-year-old son until much later, but it came up in the flow of conversation, and he was into girls enough that I figured, what the hell, might as well.

Coincidentally, I remember when my then-10-year-old daughter and I were channel surfing while grabbing a bite to eat in the kitchen and caught the very moment that Ike Turner rapes Tina Turner, his wife, in the movie *What's Love Got to Do With It.* Since it was on cable they didn't take it far, but ironically it went far enough for my daughter to ask me if Ike raped Tina. I wasn't pleased to know that somehow my daughter understood, on some level, what rape was. But I told her that he did and that once upon a time a man couldn't be convicted of raping his wife because she didn't have the right to say no to him. I told my daughter that while our society has changed quite a bit, it hasn't changed enough for her to not be ever vigilant about protecting herself against someone forcing himself upon her.

While no woman can fully protect herself against a rape, women can lessen the possibility of date rapes occurring by "really" talking with the young men who would like to spend time with them. I told her that it never hurts to make sure that the person you are involved with and you speak the same language when it comes to your interpretation of what *no* means. I also told her that I was doing my part by immersing men in conversations where rape was being discussed. After all, rape and suicide are probably the two most significant topics that require discussion that aren't being discussed.

I have always thought that when anyone is a victim of a hate crime, we are all victims of that hate crime. I have always felt that when anyone is physically abused, we are all physically abused. And yes, I have always believed that when anyone is sexually violated, we are all sexually violated. Why? Because yesterday the victim lived around the corner, today across the street, and tomorrow perhaps in your home. Now, if only we can get this point across to our youth so that they will join us in changing the game.

5

OF BEING COOL, CHRIS ROCK, AND CLASS CLUELESSNESS

> You got designer shades
> just to hide your face and
> you wear them around like
> you're cooler than me.
> And you never say hey,
> or remember my name and
> it's probably 'cause
> you think you're cooler than me.
>
> —Mike Posner, "Cooler Than Me"

Mike Posner's assertion that certain behaviors (certain social class markers like sunglasses or speaking to others) frame some more cool than others is problematic. But that is just my opinion, right? I mean, what exactly is cool? Who deems cool, cool? Is it cool to be the one who identifies things as cool? Is it cool "to be known" as the one who identifies things as cool. Is this even a cool topic to discuss?

Aaron Schwartz—currently my graduate intern and a SUNY Plattsburgh student who has taken every class I teach and been the teacher's assistant for most of them as well—and I recently taught a class on the identification of *cool* as a marker of a certain type of social class status. The class is called Examining Dimensions of Cool: A Study of Social Class. I got the idea for creating a course on social class using as a point of departure a cool book I purchased while at Dartmouth to speak for Martin Luther King

Jr.'s birthday. The book is titled *The Book of Cool*, and I kid you not, it is, yes, "cool." It is full of different perspectives on what is cool and what isn't, told through a popular-culture lens. After all, like the word *bad,*, which can mean "good," *cool* can mean "okay," as in "That was a cool movie." It can mean "compliant," as in "He has a cool disposition that fits in well with us," or "noncompliant," as in "It was cool the way he stood his ground," like Denzel Washington in *Man on Fire*. *Cool* can mean handsome, as in "George Clooney is so cool," when he is only standing there and we must be talking about more than the way he is acting. *Cool* can also mean not so attractive, as in "Humphrey Bogart wasn't as handsome as Errol Flynn, but he sure was cool." Though, like most takes on *cool*, it is quite relative.

Ironically, one of my students once applied the descriptor "cool" to the actions of Sean Penn's Sergeant Meserve versus the actions of Michael J. Fox's Private Erikson in the film *Casualties of War* (DePalma, 1989), which is based upon a true story. The gist of the film is that of a moral excursion into the inner strength and fortitude of one person against the power of many. Penn's Meserve, as the leader of a weak-minded, easily duped group of people, has them blindly following his lead toward actions that if they really, seriously considered should lead them to individually see him for the snake that he actually is and not comply. But Meserve is shrewd and knows the tools to use to get his followers to be faithful minions, so he plays them over and over again in various ways until the entire military unit is on board to sexually assault a Vietnamese woman except Fox's Erikson. Erikson, whose life was in jeopardy but ultimately saved by Meserve, stayed the course and attempted to take actions to live out his ethic responsibly.

Erikson was so adamant about not blindly following the crowd that he brings to mind Henry Fonda in *12 Angry Men*. In that film, when it wasn't cool to keep 11 other jurors overtime to deliberate on a murder case with severe consequences, Fonda did just that because he felt something wasn't quite "cool" about the case and he wasn't comfortable simply allowing the judicial system, with its many flaws and limitations, to resolve the matter. Of course, this made him uncool with most of the jurors, but so cool to those of us watching him stand up for what is right. It seems the courage to go against the grain occurs more in film than it does in real life. But in all those cases, we—as the outsiders looking in—see the lone wolf as cool, though those inside the moment see their leader as cool. Is it possible that within any given moment, as members of an organization, we are acting uncool if we could see outside of that moment? Have you stepped outside of a moment you were in lately and questioned your cool? If so, then this is for the cool in you!

Is it possible that both parties, Meserve and Erikson, can genuinely be cool? I say not if we are attempting to define cool in a socially just context. If we consider that Erikson's cool and Fonda's cool were both related to possible oppression, it is hard to take to task their actions, even more difficult to say they were uncool. However, if we look into their respective moments and consider the consequences that loomed large for the Vietnamese woman and the accused in *12 Angry Men* when someone arbitrarily decided to violate them by denying their human rights, it is quite difficult to anoint Meserve or the impatient jurors as cool.

Cool, while difficult to define, is something you can feel, like the real feel of temperature. It seems like people who try to "act" cool around really cool people become unraveled. I remember seeing *The Mike Douglas Show* on television years ago and watching Rick Springfield come out first. It was at the time he was a big heartthrob with his role as Noah Drake on *General Hospital* and his song "Jessie's Girl." He seemed like the man until John Travolta joined the conversation, and Rick Springfield just seemed to disappear before my very eyes. Travolta was classy and quite complimentary to Springfield, but it was like a man to a teenager in a conversation about life. The teenager, generally speaking, just doesn't have the life experience. How cool can you be at 14 when you still have to ask for money and the right to go places? Springfield was cool until Travolta emerged; then Springfield simply became chill. Chill is cool too, but just not as cool as cool. You feel me?

People who protest too much are hard to consider cool because cool listens. I don't know anyone who would define *cool* as someone who doesn't listen. Not listening is just uncool. Cool considers, but doesn't arbitrarily judge, especially based upon potential half-truths, or innuendos, as bell hooks (2004) suggests in this excerpt from her real cool book *We Real Cool*: "It is a fake stereotyped notion of cool that denies the history of the 'real cool,' which was not about disassociation, hardheartedness and violence, but rather about being intensely connected, aware and able to judge the right action to take in a given circumstance" (p. 152). As hooks suggests, cool is being engaged with a heightened sense of social justice. Cool is understanding the social implications of being called a *nerd* or a *geek* and not letting those terms or the speaker of those terms define you. What is cool is understanding that when you label someone a nerd or a geek what you are really saying is that they are not you, which often speaks to your own insecurity of not being well read or technologically talented. When we call someone a nerd or a geek it is because we think we are cool and they aren't. Before either word is out of our mouths we should realize that we just proved how uncool we actually are.

Cool is understanding that the very notion of cool is a social class marker for accepted behavior that everyone on some level wants but no one wants to be seen pursuing. Cool is understanding why some people feel the need to (or the lack of sophistication to not) designate certain areas as ghetto and people from differing communities as trailer trash. Depending upon your family's financial situation as you were growing up—understanding that things can be quite relative—someone could construe your neighborhood as ghettolike if not a ghetto. Depending upon your family's stability, the 3,000-square-foot home situated on two acres of land that you were reared on could easily become an 800-square-foot living space that you can barely afford. Conversely, the mansions on the other side of town come with their own misguided hype. The children of people who live in large, expensive homes didn't contribute anything to enjoy that unearned privilege. It also is the case that just because someone's parents own a large, expensive home doesn't mean their kids think they are better or "cooler" than you.

Cool doesn't backbite, backstab, character assassinate, or unduly influence, but instead gets inside of what's in question and coolly determines the appropriate action. I know this because I have been uncool like that before and fortunately realized exactly how uncool I was being.

Now, let's not get it twisted; it is possible to be duped by cool. Tiger Woods might come to mind for many as someone whom society once considered cool and now probably less so. Well, that is so wide open for interpretation it would be uncool for me to go there and may have been uncool for me to use Tiger as my example. However, I would go on record saying that if Tiger truly didn't think he and his wife could salvage their marriage, it was uncool for him to project himself as a repentant soul. It would have been much more cool of him to say he was forever going to make amends any way he could to Elin and his children, but wouldn't exacerbate the situation any further by acting like he should stay married. That would have been cool along the lines of a George Clooney type of cool because he has never gotten married and therefore never been forced to explain his control or lack thereof of his libido. It even would have been cool of Tiger to not succumb to the PGA culture by getting married if he knew he had an overactive libido.

I remember an *Ebony* magazine cover that had as its caption "Black Cool" above the head of Barack Obama stepping out of a limo, nattily attired. I thought he was so cool but know that everyone doesn't see him that way. As a parent, however, I see myself as cool when I sacrifice for my children. Is there any way that doing that is uncool? Yes, of course. Someone who can't do for his or her kids the way I may be capable of doing for mine might designate me as not only uncool, but pretentious. Pretentiousness is definitely not cool, unless you can be pretentious and not seem to be. And that still is not cool.

I'm cool as a friend when I answer the phone at a time I really don't want to but can see it may be a friend calling who is in need. I guess it is uncool when I don't answer it and a friend needed me. However, it is also uncool for me to answer the phone when I should be handling other things with more priority. Phones, though, as electronic gadgets a few keystrokes away from being computers, have become so cool, but nonetheless are so uncool at times.

I'm cool as a professor when I try to keep it real with my students. I'm even cooler when I always at least try to respect them as young women and men with minds and lives that are capable at times of teaching me as much as I may be capable of teaching them. Cool is being a part of a community that you genuinely care about and want to see even better than it is. Malcolm X was the epitome of cool. Cool is disagreeing with colleagues and still somehow having their back professionally while still finding and/or maintaining your groove. Cool is Oprah and the positive influence she has tried to have on American society if not the world. Cool is Sidney Poitier talking to a young brother (me) for 15 minutes at a film premier simply because he could/would. Cool is Skip Gates giving a young brother (me) an unsolicited autographed copy of his new book, *Thirteen Ways of Looking at a Black Man*. Cool is Cornel West inviting a brother (me) to join him for a Richard Rorty talk simply on the strength of two conversations. Cool is Martha Swan, her social activist organization John Brown Lives! and her Dreaming of Timbuctoo exhibit. "The Coolest" is Lupe Fiasco and his way of saying as a result of his way of seeing. Cool were the Kennedys, who, even though they had weaknesses, figured out some significant things along the way. Cool was Eleanor Roosevelt for what she did for the Tuskegee Airmen. Cool are the thoughts and effort put forth by the Reverend Dr. Martin Luther King Jr. Cool is anything by Michael Franks, but especially "When She Is Mine." Cool was Bogart and the original Rat Pack who stood up to the Red Scare. Cool is Kool Moe Dee, and LL Cool J. Cool is Jay-Z's "Feelin' It" and Earth, Wind & Fire's "Feelin' Blue." Cool is Beyonce's "If I Were a Boy." Cool was Ellen coming out of the closet on her nationally televised show. Cool were all the Republicans who voted for Obama because they weren't going to be regimented into voting for their political party's candidate just because they were members of that political party. Cool would be Democrats who also would vote for a Republican candidate. Cool are Independents who truly vote independently for the best candidate on criteria that are socially just. Cool is French-Acadian researcher Dr. Helene Fournier knowing more about American politics and Black American music than most Black people. Cool is Mos Def as well as his song "Umi Says." Cool is loving your faith and adhering to your religion without haughtiness toward others of different belief. Cool is James Dean in anything, Al Pacino as Michael Corleone, Jamie Foxx as Django as well as Ray Charles, and Ray Charles himself. Cool is Lil Wayne as a lyricist when he isn't dropping *bitch* bombs. Cool is hearing comedians Chris Rock and Louis C.K. and knowing that not everything they say is funny and some things are downright uncool. Cool are the movies *Frozen River* and *When the Levees Broke*, which both help to unmask the classism rampant within the capitalist system. So of course that would make the filmmakers, authors, and storytellers who push the proverbial envelope in their stories (Spike Lee, Steven Spielberg, John Singleton, Nora Ephron, Russell Banks, Courtney Hunt, W.E.B. Du Bois, bell hooks, Toni Morrison, Quentin Tarantino, Cornel West, Thomas Keith, Alice Walker) cooler than the other side of the pillow, as ESPN's Stuart Scott likes to say. One could make an argument, though, that cool doesn't exist any more significantly than beyond Queen Latifah's (1993) lyrics from her song "U.N.I.T.Y.":

> *Instinct leads me to another flow*
> *Every time I hear a brother call a girl a bitch or a ho*
> *Trying to make a sister feel low*
> *You know all of that gots to go*
> *Now everybody knows there's exceptions to this rule*
> *Now don't be getting mad, when we playing, it's cool*

Latifah's assertion that in some context *bitch* or *ho* can be cool is generous, though problematic as we already discussed thoroughly in chapter 4. If some boys/men are allowed to go there, to use such language with girls/women because they have it like that with those girls/women, it's an in-group dialogue thing and arguably people representing the out-group could/should look the other way. However, the repercussions are that the terms stay alive for appropriation by others who don't understand the required context for the use of these terms.

Cool is when we know we have made a mistake, owned it, and went about correcting it. I also think I am cool when I fight the good fight to correct whatever wrongs need to be corrected that others shy away from.

> "Any Black male who dares to care for his inner life, for his soul, is already refusing to be a victim."
>
> —hooks (2004, p. 149)

The previous quote is from bell hooks's book *We Real Cool.* Beyond defining *cool* in an array of creative and engaging ways, hooks challenges men to consider the far too often unthinking projection as well as protection of their overvalued masculinity. Her challenge, when accepted, has the potential to be empowering for men willing to step to it. For me, her challenge made me go deeper into my analysis of cool, which generated my interpretation of cool as follows:

COOL IS . . .

Acting more like a saint than a sinner
Recognizing in every so-called loser is a winner
Not prejudging her because you think she should be thinner
Cool is this and more . . .

Cool is . . .
Knowing you've got a little swag
Never calling someone fag
Sometimes being "it" in tag
Asking yourself how could he
Or why would she
Ever be a bully
Cool is this and more . . .

Cool is kissing her just right
Holding close but not too tight
No insecurity when she's out of sight
Taking a nibble instead of a bite
Picking your battles to lessen the fights

Speaking up for "the Other's" rights
Cool is this and more . . .

Cool is . . .
Using your vote
Making it more than just a hollow note
A whine not escaping our throat
Knowing when to share your coat . . .
Knowing we should never gloat . . .
Cool is this and more . . .

Cool is . . .
Knowing when to give a shit
Knowing when it's time to quit
Being authentic & legit
With courage to play the game
Treating everyone the same
Except with those that would doubt you're strong
Keep your cool and prove them wrong

Cool is . . .
What it is . . .
Not necessarily hot
Sometimes rather chill
Often engaging different thought
A provocative intellectual thrill
Similar to a lesson that can't be taught
Or a cure that's always sought,
Cool is . . . simply cool.

—J. W. Wiley

Benefit of the Doubt

People are cool when they are truly themselves, as long as their being them-selves doesn't oppress others. It is really, really cool when we give each other the *benefit of the doubt* as much as we possibly can.

I was tested on exactly to what extent I could give someone the benefit of the doubt when I first moved to Plattsburgh, New York. My son, Justin (at the time three years young), and I sat down to eat at a restaurant called

Lums, which is no longer in business. As we eased into our booth I noticed I was back-to-back with a guy talking to a woman. While I was sitting he never turned to see me, so either he truly didn't know I was behind him, or he had been signaled by the woman with him that a Black man and his little boy were seated behind him. Whatever the situation, he was talking to the woman, who sounded as if she was his sister. They were discussing another woman, who sounded as if she was their sister. They were discussing her Black boyfriend, to the utter disdain of the White man I was sitting back-to-back with. Left and right, he was relentlessly saying nigger this and nigger that, literally dropping *N*-bombs everywhere. Upon realizing I had just sat down in a precarious position I wanted to act. Imagining his teeth cracking against my fist wasn't an unattractive thought for me. However, I had already processed the fact that if I were to challenge this guy's language it could cause a scene. I had been living in the North Country for only about a week. I was single parenting and imagined that if this man and I argued or fought there would be a good chance he would be believed, not me. I also imagined that any altercation with him, or anyone else, might affect not just my livelihood, but Justin's freedom. I could easily see Justin taken away by Child Protective Services because I wasn't smart enough to maintain my cool. Fortunately, Justin was so immersed in the toys he was playing with that he didn't notice his dad's frustration and didn't appear to hear the man with the toilet tongue.

Cool was the walk my so-called Negroes and I were accustomed to doing on Venice Beach in Southern California in the late '80s. Ranging in number from 7 to 10 guys, in height from 5 feet 9 inches (me, always the shortest) to 6 feet 5 inches (usually my cousin Derek), we cut an impressive swath down the strand as we checked out people while hoping we were being checked out as well. One day while strolling along the strand there was a man, about 5 feet 4 inches, 120 pounds, vociferously voicing his opinion about Blacks. Upon seeing us, he ratcheted up the noise he was making even more, proliferating Venice Beach with *N*-bombs for all within earshot to hear. The brothers I was with immediately became agitated and were itching to put a foot up his ass. As one started toward him, a couple of us stopped him, challenging him to consider how odd it was for this unimposing White man to be aggressively agitating us. It was obvious that either he had a gun, or some of his friends were nearby anticipating trouble, awaiting his cries for assistance, or maybe he was mentally challenged. In any of the possible scenarios, it would have been stupid for us to act in response to his taunts. If we even thought he was packing heat, we would be lacking common sense to bring knives to a gunfight when we didn't even have knives. If there was a chance he was setting us up to be ambushed, we would be stupid to over-react. And lastly, if he was mentally impaired, then we were perilously close to engaging if not bullying a differently able person. Now that would have been totally uncool.

Suffice it to say, we put his ranting in perspective and context. Instead of any attempts to open up a can of whip ass on him we chose to marvel at him and his precociousness. On some level we pitied the fool, once we more thoroughly considered the source and opted to give him as well as ourselves the benefit of the doubt.

Bullying's Relationship to Cool

In the bullying film I made with Mountain Lake PBS titled *Dissed-Respect: The Impact of Bullying* (2007), we don't really go deep into a discussion about bullying and its relationship to "cool," but we should have. I've done enough work with middle school and high school students to know in no uncertain terms that one of the reasons people bully one another is an attempt to establish status. If a person can frame his or her reality as cool, then those not attached to that person's reality are not just uncool, but also the other. We attempted to frame this notion in a skit from the film titled "Egg Salad." It featured a conversation among four adolescent boys, three sitting together and one sitting alone eating an egg salad sandwich. The conversation went like this:

> **Boy #1:** Hey, Luke, what you eating?
> **Luke:** A sandwich!
> **Boy #1:** I know it's a sandwich. What kind?
> **Luke:** Egg salad!
> **Boy #1:** I'm surprised it's not fruit salad.
> **Boy #2:** I'm surprised you're not wearing a dress!
> **Boy #3:** Sissy! Maybe from now on we should call you Lucy!

Since we are talking about cool and not bullying I'll stay focused on the ramifications of cool instead of bullying, though I unabashedly make the argument that they have a symbiotic relationship. The boys' conversation with Luke wasn't really about the type of sandwich that he was eating, but their perspective on his difference. Luke, a mild-mannered, soft-spoken, full-of-love-for-life boy doesn't walk around trying to be seen as cool. Asking him to define cool and hearing his answer would probably be quite fascinating because he probably wouldn't naturally gravitate toward thoughts about it. However, the other boys are committed to, if not mired in, an attempt to establish themselves as cool. This is why the first boy attempts to display his wit in front of his peers by creatively challenging Luke as to why he is eating an egg salad sandwich instead of a "fruit" salad sandwich. What the boy is not so subtly suggesting is that Luke doesn't exude masculinity at the level that he surmises boys their age should. He also hints that Luke, at a very young age, displays some gay attributes since the word *fruit* has been negatively connoted with sexual orientation. More so, though, for the purposes of this chapter, what Boy #1 is also suggesting is that Luke is not cool. Perhaps it is Luke's demeanor, or the fact that Luke is sitting all alone, or the fact that Boy #1 is sitting with two other boys who somehow validate for Boy #1 the notion that he is cool. But because somehow this concept called cool is so important to our youth, many of our youth will pursue it at all costs, even to the point of harming others. Framing others as uncool is a way that want-to-be-cool kids ostracize, marginalize, and decenter others while indirectly proclaiming that they are worthy of attention, deserve to be in the center, and are undoubtedly cool.

Murray Milner (2006), in his book *Freaks, Geeks, and Cool Kids*, asks,

> Why are adolescents so concerned about who "goes out with" whom and who eats with whom? It is because they intuitively know that who you associate with intimately has a big effect on your status. In all societies food and sexuality are key symbols of intimacy. Where status is important, people try to avoid eating with or marrying inferiors—as executive dining rooms, upper-middle-class dinner parties, debutante balls, and the marriage and eating restrictions of the Indian caste system all indicate. In contrast, if the occasion is purely instrumental, status concerns are much less important: The beautiful cheerleader can work with a bright nerd on a class project, the Brahman can supervise Untouchables working in the field, the company president can spend all day in a meeting with subordinates and even share a "working lunch"—but, when work is done, they go their separate ways. (p. 5)

As Milner suggests, the concept of cool is really a conversation about status, which is a conversation about class, and in this case social class. The skit from *Dissed-Respect: The Impact of Bullying* features a typical day in the lives of four boys who through one of their daily meals have intimately defined their roles. Our children first learn their lessons on status and being cool in elementary, intermediate, and middle schools when they watch from afar the decisions made by older kids as to where they will sit, and with whom. Of course they wonder why, and probably associate the reason with an ill-informed perspective based on the trappings of consumer culture, attractiveness, popularity, and unfortunately identity politics.

In the same film, we have a skit involving five girls that reveals the way girls sometimes interact with one another in not so cool ways. It is titled "Fashion Statements" and features three girls sitting at a lunch table gossiping about another girl sitting alone within earshot of their comments:

Girl #1: I bet she got those jeans at the Salvation Army!
Girl #2: Those jeans were cool when dinosaurs walked the earth!
Girl #3: If my Mom got me those jeans I think I'd die of shame!

All three of the girls continue to whisper and gossip as they look at the girl sitting alone. Their scrutinizing her and prejudging her doesn't stop until another girl, much younger than them, interrupts the conversation after overhearing their conversation and witnessing their interest in the girl we can now call the victim. With all their attention fixated upon her, the younger, more demure girl speaks:

Girl #4: I'm only 5 and even I know that bullying isn't cool.

This conversation is taking place in middle school and high school classrooms all over the country. It's taking place because these girls have been taught that certain types of clothing are as important as the people wearing them. They also believe that they are seen as worth more, seen as more cool because they are wearing and can wear clothing that has been recognized as appropriate by the cool kids, instead of the freaks and geeks. What they haven't been taught is that what they are wearing is directly related to the fact that they may have been born on third base relative to the kids they are judging as less than them. These adolescent girls didn't go to work to earn the money to purchase their clothing.

> "Why are the latest fashions so important to teenagers? To gain status in any group you have to conform to their norms. But this means that insiders, and especially those with high status, have an interest in making conformity difficult for outsiders. Hence they frequently elaborated and complicated the norms."
>
> —Milner (2006, p. 5)

The ability to conform to norms is a privilege that everyone doesn't have. As such, some kids have as their destiny no options except to eventually be bullied since their families don't have the socioeconomic class status to drape themselves in the so-called proper garments and therefore will remain outsiders. Cool plays out in different ways, though. In the classic film *Rebel Without a Cause*, James Dean, often considered the epitome of cool both off screen and on, played the part of a young man who had recently just moved to town. Eventually, trying to connect with the cool kids he is denied access to them simply because he posed a threat to their status quo, or perhaps made those with beautiful girlfriends feel insecure. But as if inspired by the character's behavior in the film, Milner's assertion that norms are deliberately complicated to deny access to others is quite real, even more so when the other is "the Other." How much different would James Dean's experiences have been if he were comfortable being gay, or differently able?

Class Cluelessness

Who you associate with, fairly or unfairly, makes a statement about you. Is this more unfair than fair? Well, we know that when we associate with someone who has a very bad reputation we are apt to have our reputation tainted. Many of us go to an extreme to distance ourselves from people designated malcontents or of questionable character. But to what extent or extreme do we go to in our attempts to associate with people whose character is above reproach? More importantly, do we go so far that we start to question their identity, and end up playing identity politics? Are we hesitant to hang out with the new kid on the block because he is disabled and we anticipate others may be about to limit his access to the crew? Are we afraid to become friends with the new student at the university because she belongs to a different sorority and some of the more senior sisters have issues with that sorority? It was the singing group Earth, Wind & Fire that once framed the notion that life could be fair, but so uncool:

> *Glory seeker, fortune hound,*
> *don't you ever break it on down*
> *Ain't you been to school?*
> *Ain't you learned the rules?*
> *Ain't you paid them dues?*
> *The life you need is fair, fair but so uncool*
>
> —Earth, Wind & Fire, "Fair but So Uncool"

Being cool, while exhibiting class cluelessness, is a complex thing to observe. Earth, Wind & Fire's lyrics seem to suggest that chasing this thing called cool is actually quite uncool. The problems with our hypocrisy and the courage to overcome it and really be cool are complicated. Many of us want to believe we are cool, but when pushed to a limit we never anticipated having to face we are often left with more than we bargained for. The best example I can provide of this is from one of the experiences I had in the doctoral program I attended. I had a Black professor who was teaching his first doctoral cohort course. I had previously known him through the very small and yet intimate circle of Black folk in Vermont. As a result of that prior acquaintance, I was truly excited to have him as my professor.

I put serious effort into the first assignment he gave the class. I wanted to impress him and let him know, through my work, that I was taking his class seriously. I know as a college professor myself that often students who have familiarity with me think they will get some "love" from me if they slack off because, for some reason, they believe I'm cool like that. Well, I'm not! I'm cooler than that. I'm about getting all my students prepared for the next level of life they will encounter. If they receive a break here and there, a little "love" occasionally, that's cool too, but they should never, ever expect it. So, with my Black professor I was determined to overcompensate in prov-ing to him he wouldn't need to have concerns about my performance. Unfortunately, to my chagrin, he expressed appreciation of the work I had put into my project but said it wasn't what he expected. I pointed out to him that it was consistent with his instructions. He acknowledged that it was, admitted that he hadn't been quite clear in the instructions he had given us for the assignment, but still wanted me to redo the assignment. I was very irritated with him wanting me to redo the assignment because of his poor instructions. As a professor myself, if my students do inadequate work due to my subpar instructions I take the hit, not them. I felt as if he should have done this himself, but he didn't. As a result, I did redo the assignment but with nowhere near the effort of the first iteration. The result of all this was me receiving a C +, a worse grade than the previous score of B − given to me prior to being told I needed to do the rewrite. I was furious.

The next assignment was a book report. I wrote my report on the book *Trust and Betrayal in the Workplace.* In it I created/used a case study of a professor who had given poor instructions to "her" students and afterward was incapable of owning her inadequacy, so instead her students were rele-gated to busywork redoing their assignments if they didn't align with the professor's vision. Well, the gender part of the story aside, he recognized my case study was about him. He called me at home, admonishing me and insisting I redo the assignment. I did, and received a B.

The last assignment I had for the class was to create a consultant's proposal. As someone who had just recently had two consulting proposals funded and was currently working under contract for both of them, I just took one of these two funded proposals, reframed it a bit, and submitted it. This professor, whom I now had been battling throughout the semester, who had never done any type of consulting himself, trashed my proposal with comments like certain parts of it were "irrelevant." He ultimately gave me a C+ on it and a C+ in the class. I don't share this story as payback for a disconnect with a professor. I share this story to examine/unpack dysfunctional language, specifically the term *cool* in the context of social class. Although the grades were ultimately overturned, the C+ that this first-time professor gave me on my final project and as my course grade could have ended my doctoral aspirations. The cool that I had seen in him (and him in me, I imagine) had dissipated entirely and I was sad to discover that it was predicated solely on our being two of few Black men at the University of Vermont as well as residing in the northeast region of the United States. When push came to shove his social class had him situated to end my aspirations without a second thought about the similar path and requisite struggles we may have shared along our journey through higher education. Earth, Wind & Fire's notion of life being "fair but so uncool" couldn't have been more prescient. Babyface perhaps frames the experience even more profoundly:

> *Here we go round and round and round*
> *And back and forth you know*
> *Everybody goes through it sometime*
> *And that's just the way it flows*
> *So we go up and down and up*
> *And in and out the door*
> *Even though you know you've been through it before*
>
> *For every argument that we've experienced*
> *It's nice to know that you've remained composed*
> *And I wanna thank you for the chill in you*
> *Especially for you being so cool*
> *This is for the cool in you!*
>
> —Babyface, "For the Cool in You"

Babyface's lyrics were written for a romantic relationship but easily apply in this case to our dysfunctional interactions. The professor and I did a relentless circle dance that I imagine he must have done before, as I have with many of my students. While I somehow wrongly intuited that this Black professor would be cool with me because of our similar experiences, he wasn't. His ascendancy to a higher level of social class removed him from being able to remember from whence he had come. As Babyface further asserted, though, I am still able to thank him for the chill he exhibited, and still able to thank him for the cool he reflected. After all, uncool is still a dimension of cool.

Chris Rock, one of my favorite comedians, in one of his many moments of comic genius went into a routine whereby he claimed that he loved Black people, but hated niggers. He then drew a distinction between the two, with Black people being upstanding citizens and niggers being either criminals or too ignorant to understand and/or adhere to societal conventions. This piece from his *Bigger and Blacker* album is engaged by Randall Kennedy (2002) in his book *Nigger: The Strange Career of a Troublesome Word*. What intrigued me about Kennedy's take on Rock's piece is that Kennedy explores Rock's usage solely in the context of race. It isn't that Kennedy doesn't unpack "nigger" in terms of social class. He does, as evidenced in this passage where he is quoting Henry Louis Gates: "Black professionals soon learn that it is the socially disenfranchised—the lower class, the homeless—who are more likely to hail them as niggers" (p. 124). Kennedy's engagement with social class in this quote addresses who is more apt to refer to a Black person as a nigger. Essentially, Gates is stating that the disenfranchised and/or underclass have more of a propensity to use the term. The Rock comedy routine itself is used in my African American Culture class for the same reasons. One day, however, it occurred to me that whether intentional or not, Rock was really speaking to socioeconomic class more than race. There is no doubt it is a racial piece, because most people see the word *nigger* as a racial word. However, if *nigger* is to be considered by the definition I presented earlier ($P = C = N$, with P defined as *problem* in the Du Boisian sense of the word; C defined as *criminal*, albeit again in terms of Du Bois's inevitability of the occurrence; and N defined as *nigger*), it is difficult not to consider it as a term that addresses social class, privilege, and cool.

Norman Mailer, in an essay he wrote titled "The White Negro" (1957), defined the experience of being Black in White America in a way that is gripping in its earnestness, and refreshing in that he is a White man writing about White privilege before it was in the national discourse. More so, he was defining *hip*, which to a large extent is synonymous with *cool* as a phenomenon that comes out of Black people's response to oppression.

> Any Negro who wishes to live must live with danger from his first day, and no experience can ever be casual to him, no Negro can saunter down a street with any real certainty that violence will not visit him on his walk. The cameos of security for the average white: mother and the home, job and the family, are not even a mockery to millions of Negroes; they are impossible. The Negro has the simplest of alternatives: live a life of constant humility or ever-threatening danger. In such a pass where paranoia is as vital to survival as blood, the Negro had stayed alive and begun to grow by following the need of his body where he could. Knowing in the cells of his existence that life was war, nothing but war, the Negro (all exceptions admitted) could rarely afford the sophisticated inhibitions of civilization, and so he kept for his survival the art of the primitive, he lived in the enormous present. . . .
> So there was a new breed of adventurers, urban adventurers who drifted out at night looking for action with a black man's code to fit their facts. The hipster had absorbed the existentialist synapses of the Negro, and for practical purposes could be considered a white Negro.

Mailer's articulation of the Black experience is something to marvel at. Mailer's assertion that the Negro "lived in the enormous present" and "kept for his survival the art of the primitive" supports my assertion about how some Whites saw and still see Blacks. Possibly like some White people's preoccupation with tanning, which makes them darker—if not more Blacklike—though, heaven forbid it ever be framed that way, Mailer's suggestion that some Whites endeavored to be more hip/cool is quite an intriguing spin on cool and its social-class underpinnings.

The word *nigger* can be seen as a social class word when you consider how Rock uses it to draw a distinction between people of the same racial group. From the perspective of a racist against Blacks, an obvious outsider's perspective, there is no distinction. Rock's bifurcation of Blacks and niggers by determination of their behavior doesn't exist for this type of a racist so the class distinction is moot. However, from an internal perspective of the two segmented groups what Rock is asserting is that one group has a higher degree of social class than the other. Rock frames Blacks who aren't smart enough to know how to raise or take responsibility for their kids as niggers. He categorizes as niggers Blacks with criminal tendencies (shooting up theaters, breaking and entering); Blacks who lack education, a certain level of common sense, or sophistication; and in both cases Blacks who are problematic to the society in which they live. However, what isn't stated or implied in Rock's interpretation of niggers and what makes it so problematic for people listening to his routine is the fact that much of the ability to project sophistication about the world we live in comes from exposure and experiences. Someone who originates from a family unit that has had no family member ever obtain a college education would be categorized as a nigger, by Rock's description. Upon first hearing Rock say it as part of his comedy routine, with his timing and delivery, it is hilarious. However, upon second thought, and then a third consideration, it becomes a sad truth about the way we see one another. It is nothing if not a sad truth about the haves and have-nots. To racists who don't slice and dice Black people (as Rock once said about his perspective on Whites), Rock's Blacks and niggers are both situated the same, as niggers. What Rock ultimately, albeit inadvertently, suggests is that Black people are cool, and niggers ain't. Yet, rap music makes the argument that gangstas are the coolest motherfuckers around. It is this notion of cool that presents problems far beyond the reach of Blacks.

What is not cool by any stretch of the imagination is the appropriation and use of the word *nigger* as cool by people seldom, if ever, referred to as "nigger." Now, don't lose sight of the fact that while some of the concepts we are discussing in this chapter intersect with other concepts/chapters, I'm talking about socioeconomic class, not race or racism in this case, necessarily. So, my point here is that often the use of the word *nigger* isn't so much about "racism" as it is about "status." *Nigger* is often used for status. Back in the day, while definitely applicable in terms of exhibiting dysfunctional behavior around someone's race, even then it was also suggesting that the target of the word was a "nigger" and the speaker, when non-Black, was not. However, in today's often considered egalitarian society, when it is used by non-Whites toward non-Whites it is more often than not used for status.

Sometimes one of my teaching colleagues for my course Examining Diversity Through Film, Kevin Pearson, when encouraged enough, will tell the story of going to a party where there were only White people in attendance. At some point in the party there was a young White male yelling at the top of his lungs, "Nigger!" He wasn't yelling it at a Black person, because none were there. He was just yelling it. He wanted attention. He wanted status. Yelling *nigger* I imagine would paint him as a daredevil of sorts, though unbeknownst to him, it also framed him as a coward because he wasn't doing it in the presence of Blacks.

One of my nieces, a 12-year-old, shared a story with me recently of three of her White girlfriends visiting her home. Two of the girls were wrestling. One girl was dominating the other, who was quite a bit smaller than her. Appearing to get frustrated, the smaller girl said to the larger one, "Get off of me, nigger." My niece, the only Black person present, was infuriated by this and was seriously considering ending the friendship with her. I challenged her to not do so if she genuinely liked the girl and it was the first time something like this had ever happened. However, I told her that she needed to *really* talk with the girl to explore why she would have said such a thing. I told her if she was comfortable she may want to ask her friend the following questions:

1. Would you have said that to me if we were wrestling?
2. If not, why not?
3. Why then did you say it to someone who isn't Black, yet say it in a Black person's home?

Of all the stories I've heard around the word *nigger* none perplexes me more than this one. The irony of this event unfolding as I am writing a book called *The Nigger in You* is not just mind-blowing, but sensibility dismantling. The smaller girl, who was being easily handled by the much larger girl, was flummoxed by the situation and was digging deep to engage how it felt for her to be a problem. She was not only struggling with a larger person physically (albeit with playful intent) mugging her, but struggling with her inability to physically change their flow.

This isn't too dissimilar to what happened to me at a party I attended when married and living in Los Angeles. I had left my wife at that time, the lovely Adrienne Boyd, all by herself at this gathering where we were the only Blacks, as I mingled with other coworkers. After being away from her for a while, I turned to see where she was, what she was doing, who was talking to/with her. Eventually our eyes met and she looked as if she had just witnessed if not a murder something quite akin to that. I instantly broke away from my conversation and went to check in. Adrienne immediately told me that the woman she was talking with had told her that often her husband treated her "like a nigger." I now wanted to turn and ask the woman exactly what that meant, but Adrienne reeled me in. So, if you are the woman who said that to Adrienne that night and you are reading this, I'm still awaiting an answer to that question.

My son and daughter have often told me of non-Black kids a bit older than them who use the word *nigger* or *nigga* toward one another. My daughter, Autumn, ever the precocious one, eventually found the courage to inquire as to why it was being used. She was told by the clueless older girl that she wasn't saying "nigger," but "nigga."

My son shared with me that one of my favorite athletes on one of his sports teams whom I always thought was cool had just become cool in his eyes as well. Surprised, I asked him why just recently he felt that way. He then shared with me that the kid had stopped using the word *nigger* when upset. In disbelief I asked him if he was serious. He replied that many kids, when using expletives to show their frustrations, combine the word *nigger* with *fuck, shit,* and *damn.*

What makes matters worse is when non-Blacks and Blacks both justify it as not problematic because they have changed the ending. So, instead of nigger they are saying nigga, or niggah. Could this be any more ridiculous? What if you actually don't mean anything by it, have been taught not to say nigger, but instead to say nigga or niggah? In that quick moment of saying it and someone hearing it, is your diction going to be excellent enough to ensure there is no miscommunication occurring between your intent and that person's reception? Would the person be less apt to get his or her ass kicked by intolerant Blacks who are not trying—on any level—to hear non-Blacks even say the word *nice* because it starts with an *n*? It's like me saying to a differently able person, "What's happening, retar?" or to a woman, "What's up, bich?" While it is true that I am changing the spelling and my intention in the case of the change from *retard* to *retar* is to call the differently able person "cool," or in the case of the change from *bitch* to *bich* to refer to the woman as confident, the person hearing me say these uniquely spelled terms is not in my head as I speak them and doesn't have access to my meaning.

More so, unless the person is already a part of my crew I possibly if not probably won't receive the *benefit of the doubt,* nor should I. Besides that, there is also the all-important litmus test that allows us to really measure how just our actions are. Would non-Blacks use the term *nigga* if they were grossly in the minority, like a situation when they are outnumbered 25 to 1? I know I wouldn't use *bich* or *retar* or any other term that could get me into trouble if facing those types of numbers. However, I wouldn't use those types of terms if I was alone with my crew, my family, or even looking in a mirror because I would feel quite stupid. And if there is no other time for me to feel it, when I look in the mirror I'm trying to look cool, not stupid. But that's me.

However, there is that odd situation that arises that makes you have to slow your roll and consider certain actions in a larger context. I recall pulling into a gas station in Southern California and leaving my vehicle with the gas pumping as I headed toward the station to pay. As I walked away from my car I heard someone say loudly, "Yo, yo, yo, my nigga!" Of course this got my attention. So, I turned around with a bit of edge ready to engage whoever/whatever was awaiting me. To my chagrin, I realized that the greeting had come from a young Vietnamese male. He was speaking to his friend, who, unbeknownst to me, was just a few feet behind me. As I absorbed all of this, realizing at the same time that I could now round off some of my edginess, the other young man replied to his friend, "What, nigga?" At this point my analytical skills were kicking in. I couldn't avoid noticing that the body language, the tone and tenor of what I now surmised as late teens, was quite authentic to what I know of as the Black experience. If I had closed my eyes and not seen these two young men I would have sworn they were Black. It was like listening to now deceased singer Teena Marie and not knowing the infamous Vanilla Child was White until you saw her or someone told you. There was a bit of resistance to accepting it because it just didn't seem so. It was like Dr. Eddie Moore Jr.'s reaction to hearing one of my all-time, top-shelf youngbloods, Sean Matthews, a White male from Trinidad, when we presented "The Nigger-word" at SUNY Plattsburgh. Sean was talking in his heavy Caribbean accent, loaded with flava because Sean just has it like that, and Eddie walked over to me and said, "Man, it is blowing my mind to hear a White cat talk like that." So, suffice it to say, I caught my breath and smiled as the conversation culminated with their last two comments. The young man still at the gas pump said to his friend, "Nigga, don't forget my smokes." His friend then replied, "Nigga, I got you!"

> "One important result of my approach is that behavior of teenagers comes to be seen not as the result of immaturity or poor parenting and teaching, but rather quite reasonable behavior—given the social context they have been provided by adults."
>
> —Milner (2006, p. 9)

While I was no longer edgy, definitely not angry, and even appreciative on some level of the relationship they appeared to have with some dimension of the Black experience, I still left that gas station wondering how street savvy these two young men actually were. They didn't know me from Adam or Saddam and really could have been putting themselves at risk with their cavalier use of what Randall Kennedy refers to as a "troublesome word." I hope they realize the extent of their hypocrisy when they use *nigger, nigga,* or *niggah* to be cool when in the majority, but don't use it when they are not.

Recognizing the hypocrisy within our socioeconomic class status isn't always an easy thing to do. It takes a disruption in the benefits available to us from our socioeconomic class to heighten our awareness around this level of privilege some of us are fortunate enough to have earned or own. Because of the benefits I have through my job and my ability to make my copayments for the dental work I obtain, I am always complimented on my smile. This is an easy thing to not consider a privilege and an extension of my socioeconomic class. However, how different would my life actually be if I didn't have a mouth that distracted if not detracted from the salient points I attempt to make when speaking.

Class cluelessness is an odd thing. I know a woman in the North Country who, as a playful gesture to make others laugh, likes to wear a set of plastic false teeth as she flitters from one set of friends to another when she is drinking. Now, this woman is drop-dead beautiful with a set of molars that would have you wanting your tongue to be her toothbrush. She also is one of the nicest people you will ever meet—caring, gracious, loving in so many ways. Nonetheless, when I pointed out to her that the teeth she wears for laughs represent the actual reality of many people in the North Country (and of course many other places in this country and the world), she dismissed me as being too serious. She even scoffed at a more obvious point I made, that she might be in the face of people who have friends and/or coworkers with teeth similar to the plastic ones she was playfully wearing.

She would probably deny this, perhaps even argue with me about it, but she wore those plastic teeth because she thought it was "cool" to have others laughing with her. I questioned her on the possibility that everyone wasn't laughing with her, but instead some could be laughing at her. I thought it was uncool to have them laughing at a symbol of what others don't have. I thought it was uncool for a woman fortunate enough to have access to good dental care mocking others who don't. The last I heard she still wears the teeth.

I have had the pleasure of consulting to many organizations over the years, engaging in conversations with individuals ranging from CEOs and university presidents to cafeteria workers and custodians. In doing this type of work, often people aren't truly serious about wanting the change they hire you to facilitate but are more interested in the appearance of change being under way. For example, I consulted to a college in upstate New York that had a crisis occur within its community regarding some of its students inconsiderately donning KKK clothing as Halloween attire. One of the administrators there happened to be an ex–student body president at a university for which I had previously worked, who knew of my work, and who recommended me as the person to facilitate a community forum to address the situation. I was hired, and the conversation occurred with the 150 people anticipated being exceeded by 450 people. Yes, 600 people showed up to discuss the impact of the students wearing KKK attire on students who were grossly in the minority and students and faculty who understood the social justice implications of this type of action. Afterward, without little hesitation, I was hired to assist in changing the diversity and social justice ethos of the campus. I often think that people subconsciously hire me to work with them because they think not only will it possibly be beneficial to their organization but it also might be a cool experience working with me. However, as the commercial for Colt 45 Malt Liquor advertises, "Don't let the cool taste fool you." I know the advertisement actually says "smooth," not "cool." Cut me some slack here, will you. The bottom line is that I'm about effecting change and anyone who gets in my way of accomplishing that goal will be directly challenged in ways that the person can anticipate won't be cool, or smooth.

Immediately after being hired I should have realized something more problematic than I anticipated was amiss. I was approached by an administrator and told that one of the other administrators had a problem with the fact that social justice was being associated with my plan to implement diversity. Suffice it to say, over the next 18 months of my experience with this college it was quite unfruitful. Far too many of the administrators there were professionals committed to placating their peers instead of challenging them to do the right thing when it came to creating an egalitarian environment where everyone could feel safe as well as their voices valued. At the end of my rope working with the college's second in command, who appeared to be playing both sides against the middle, I finally went to the top and asked the college president to meet with me for breakfast. I was pleased that he made the time, and we spent a bit less than two hours chatting about the state of affairs at the college and my need for him to champion the diversity and social justice initiative. When he left the restaurant that morning I was amped and ready to marshal my energies to finally make things happen. Unfortunately, it wasn't long before I realized that the president's second in command hadn't gotten the memo about the president being poised to now champion the diversity initiative. My desire was to have as the centerpiece of the college a diversity course similar to the one we were teaching at SUNY Plattsburgh. This course would assist the college in developing an understanding of diversity and social justice while being an invaluable resource for those students, staff, and faculty who could benefit from seeing themselves in the curriculum of a highly touted course. It would also allow the college to develop leadership among its student population with return students serving as teaching assistants. Lastly, it would serve as a professional development opportunity for the staff and faculty, with them being able to participate as guest faculty in the class for a two-week rotation in any of the six themes offered (ability, race, gender, sexual orientation, socioeconomic class, and privilege). Unfortunately, feet were dragged, resources weren't made available, budgets were bemoaned, and ultimately nothing happened.

I then requested a meeting with the president's cabinet, which comprised his vice presidents, deans, and some directors. In this presentation I provided them a sneak preview of the class with a rationale for why it was important that they implement it. In the room I could see/feel the resistance of a few naysayers, including the second in command, who was adept at wearing the appropriate face for whatever moment he was involved in. I ultimately arrived at a precarious moment in the presentation when it was time to conclude and it occurred to me I could end the presentation with either a bang or a whimper. I chose the bang. My closing comments to the cabinet were "So, it's time we either shit, or get off the stool." Little did I know those would be my last comments to his cabinet.

Afterward I had quite a few of the administrators approach me and thank me for challenging them. Some of them even went so far as to express their excitement about the possibilities for their college. But the two phone calls that I made to check and see what our next moves would be were never returned. The e-mail I then wrote to the president to ascertain where we were presently with the diversity initiative never was answered. Yet, I continued to receive four of the last five quarterly installments I was owed per the contract. The president obviously had made the decision that he didn't want to work with me any longer, but would pay me anyway to avoid any potential bad publicity. I guess it didn't matter that I still could have earned those wages by doing some work with their students, or faculty, in some other capacities. I guess the president didn't know how to engage someone as edgy as me in a one-on-one dialogue to understand why I might have been frustrated enough to make the closing comments I made. He just decided to cut not their losses, but his losses. Perhaps you can discern the distinction?

I had hoped and expected that the college president would use his position to leverage a better experience for all of his students instead of just those situated adequately because of the social class they had on campus from their reality being reflected everywhere they looked. However, I gave the president the out he obviously needed. It is easy for me to say that because I stayed in communication with a few of the employees there and was apprised of the fact that nothing new had occurred to advance their diversity initiative.

As a result of my actions he did not have to do the real work of changing his campus from the top down or answer to those who might inquire. He no longer had to muster and exert real leadership in implementing one of the more difficult changes that can impact a college campus. However, he may have to forever engage how he chose to continue to allow the old-school mentality of the privileged few dictate the realities of the students he is tasked to educate. His underrepresented students are not the only ones who suffer from not being educated in an environment that reflects them. Their voices being silenced denies the rest of the students, faculty, and community the opportunity to hear them as well as learn from them. One other thing, though. The president, in his quiet moments, I am absolutely sure has reflected upon how it feels to be a problem since he represents the potential for change but is actually more of a representation of lip service. I am also sure at some point the president has had to own the fact that he paid someone off, not too dissimilar from bribery, which is a criminal offense, if I'm not mistaken. In other words, if you recall the equation $P = C = N$, yes, not only is he struggling with his cowardice, his inability to create a social class consciousness among his constituency that would better serve his academic community, but he is also grappling with the newly discovered nigger in him.

Class cluelessness can sometimes get downright petty and totally uncool. As a younger professor without my doctorate, I once worked in a department with five other faculty members, all having their doctorates, and tenure. The youngest one of them had just ascended to department chair of a group of faculty who were all highly respected on the campus and in the community. Now, perhaps it was an overriding desire to manage someone, but one day after playing phone tag throughout the course of the day, I received a return phone call just seven minutes prior to the start of one of my classes. After informing the department chairperson that I would call him back after my class, which I only had a few minutes to get to, I was told in no uncertain terms that I would talk with him now. To this demand I retorted, "You are essentially asking me to either disrespect my students or disrespect you, and that's not difficult for me to decide." I then hung up. This would go on for a few years, often with the provost having to get involved, until I eventually stopped working with this department. However, along the way we had another occurrence worth mentioning. At the bequest of the provost we were encouraged to lunch together to see if we could get on the same page. Across the first 30 minutes of conversation with the department chair, I sat quietly and listened to him wax philosophically about this and that, that and this. Not once was I invited into "our" conversation. Not once did he come up for air, slightly pausing so that I could interpret the pause as my cue to contribute. So, I deliberately drifted into another phase of my personality. I decided then and there that I was going to say something to him that would knock him from his perch of pompousness, something he would never forget. Leaning in, I said, "You know what, my man, it just occurred to me that if we had grown up in the same neighborhood I have no doubts that eventually I would have tried to kick your ass." He was so caught off guard that his jaw literally dropped. I then stood up and before I left the table added, "Look, you don't like me. I don't like you. So let's just try to work together as long as possible without any drama."

Why would I say this to him? Because in the halls of academia, with his doctorate and position, in this predominantly White community, he somehow thought he could disrespect me by taking away my voice. Perhaps it was his lesser status with the senior faculty within the department. Perhaps it was his discovery that without my degree, my lack of an equivalent social class to his, I still made $20,000 per year more than him (as a result of my administrative position). I'm not sure what it was, but I know that the only way you handle a bully is to look him or her in the eye. Whatever it was that made him think he could disrespect me prior to my comments had been replaced by the concern that I might snap and revert back to my street days.

> "As we climb the ladder of success what is our perspective
> on the rungs we leave behind?"
>
> —J. W. Wiley

My perspective on the rungs I left and am leaving behind is to use them delicately so that they will last, remaining in good stead for my return, literally or metaphorically. No matter how much success we achieve it stands on the shoulders of others. So, at the very least we should give back what we gave. After all, as Lupe Fiasco claims in his song "The Coolest," as we chase the "cool" we must still adhere to those "cool" rules of engagement.

If/when we do finally reconcile our attempts at being cool with our failures at recognizing our class cluelessness, often far too many of us aren't skilled enough to overcome the problem that we ourselves have become to our communities and/or organizations. As a result, if we aren't mindful and vigilant about how we morally represent ourselves, we can become amoral, immoral, and downright unethical, which if not leading to criminal activity can contribute to a counterproductivity that borders on criminality.

> *Imagine no possessions*
> *I wonder if you can*
> *No need for greed or hunger*
> *A brotherhood of man*
> *Imagine all the people*
> *Sharing all the world . . .*
>
> *You may say I'm a dreamer*
> *But I'm not the only one*
> *I hope someday you'll join us*
> *And the world will live as one*
>
> **—John Lennon, "Imagine"**

If we could only imagine Lennon's vision, and collectively move in that direction, we would not need material goods, everyone would be eating, and we would all be flowing harmoniously. If we could implement Lennon's vision, we could eradicate any need for class consciousness and end class cluelessness. That would be real cool!

6

OF RACES WHERE
NO ONE WINS

don't give the black man food,
give red man liquor
red man fool,
black man nigga
give yellow man tool, make him railroad builder
also give him pan, make him pull gold from river
give black man crack, glocks and things,
give red man craps, slot machines . . .

—Lupe Fiasco, "American Terrorist"

W hy in the year 2012 is it necessary for musical artist Lupe Fiasco
to have to assert that different racial groups have been systematically engaged in uniquely different ways that are more detrimental to them than beneficial? Perhaps because after the myriad ways we have
engaged race in this country no racial group is seen as the presumptive favorite to win. So why does it feel like a competition?

In the 18th century, Immanuel Kant and David Hume, two of the most
influential traditionalists in the history of philosophy, both publicly declared
their belief that the Black man was inferior. Cornel West revealed in his
book *Prophesy Deliverance*, published in 1982, an example of Hume's notori-
ous racism with this quote from Hume: "I am apt to suspect the negroes . . .
to be naturally inferior to the whites. There never was a civilized nation of
any other complexion than white" (p. 61). From his book *Observations on
the Feeling of the Beautiful and Sublime*, Kant added,

> Among the hundreds of thousands of blacks who are transported elsewhere
> from their countries, . . . not a single one was ever found who presented

anything great in art or science or any other praiseworthy quality. . . . So fundamental is the difference between the two races of man, and it appears to be as great in regard to mental capacities as in color. (p. 111)

Kant also added, "The Negroes of Africa have by nature no feeling that arises above the trifling" (p. 110). Even the third president of the United States, Thomas Jefferson, is cited by West as a contributor to the perception of inferiority surrounding the Black man still today. Jefferson said, "In memory they are equal to the whites; in reason much inferior . . . and that in imagination they are dull, tasteless and anomalous. . . . Never yet could I find that a black had uttered a thought above the level of plain narration" (West, p. 62). Now keep in mind Jefferson was one of the prime architects of our constitution. His influence on the American intellectual landscape is unquestioned. Is it far-fetched to believe that he wasn't influenced either directly by Kant or Hume or indirectly by one of their many students when in writing the Declaration of Independence he was heavily influenced by the British philosopher John Locke's *Two Treatises of Government?*

Kant also developed what has been recognized by many as the supreme principle of morality, the categorical imperative, which states that every person should "act only on that maxim through which you can at the same time will that it should become a universal law" (Pojman, 2004). Imbedded in that principle is an assumption of equality that necessarily implied that all humans are rational in contrast to beasts, which are nonrational. In both calling Blacks "men" and denying them rationality, Kant reveals a deep contradiction in his global belief set.

This is the type of racist thought that permeated the American society of yesteryear and still influences it today. It is the type of racist thought that insisted certain racial groups in America were not equal, thereby practically mandating that the racial groups lacking equality must compete at whatever levels necessary to obtain equality, while the hegemonic racial group must compete at a consistently high level to maintain its dominance. Only a thorough explication and understanding of this racist ideology and its effect will effect a change.

Many African Americans' perspective on race relations or, more specifically, on the nature of the European American is complicated. In certain pockets of the Black community the White man is considered the Black man's natural enemy, a blue-eyed devil who is never going to remove his foot from the throat of the underclass. Sweeping absolutist claims can be problematic. The use of terms like *all* or *every* invites the problem of induction to your very door. Therefore, a sweeping absolutist claim about all

White people is no more viable than Kant's or Hume's statements about "all Blacks." If the White man is our archenemy, committed to destroy or oppress us, then how did a once enslaved people acquire freedom in this country? Because enough Whites at that time knew that slavery was an injustice against mankind. Regardless of the reasons the Civil War was fought, we should never forget that many White lives were lost over the slavery issue.

There is also a misconception among some Blacks that Black people are the antithesis of Whites, that Blacks are good-natured compared to their White counterparts. This is unsubstantiated drivel. While problems with race relations in this country make it necessary to highlight the Black experience, there is no need to convolute the situation with a similar distortion of facts. An interesting thought experiment is a role reversal with Blacks as the masters of White slaves. Who can definitely claim that slavery would have been less horrific?

We should know to not be so wedded to an idea that we can't recognize when a better idea has surfaced. That is not to say that any opinion should be held loosely, as if it is only a matter of time before it changes, but that there are two sides to every coin, and from a philosophical point of view, don't forget the coin's edge—it counts for something.

Flirting With Miscegenation

I distinctly remember, as a child, approaching my mother after watching the Sidney Poitier movie *Guess Who's Coming to Dinner*, which is about an interracial romance, and asking her, "Mama, what would you do if I married a White girl?" Her response was, "What would you do if I married a White man?" The reverberations of her question totally dismantled my sensibilities. My response to her was, "Mama, you wouldn't do that, would you?" She replied, "Why not?" I then said, "What about my friends? I'd be embarrassed." She replied, "So if I loved a man who was White, I should walk away from that love because my son's friends would tease him and he would be embarrassed. Is that fair to me?" I remember leaving the room thinking to myself how complex that situation would be. My mother, displaying a philosophical acumen that I would see often in my future dialogues with her, appeared to be rather pleased with herself. Sometime later, I approached her once again and said to her, "Mama, if you fall in love with a White man, it's cool. You can marry him. But we will have to move."

Have I dated outside my race? Well, if I say yes believe me some Black women might say, "I knew he had dated a White woman," or "I knew he would date a White woman." Either proposition could be quite frustrating for Black women who sometimes process a Black man crossing the color line as if he is seeking a woman whom society might view more favorably. Don't dismiss this too quickly. Black men also have their anxieties about Black women dating outside the race. Spike Lee possibly captured the woman's take on this phenomenon best in the conversation he featured called the "war council" in his 1993 film *Jungle Fever*. Rumor has it that he just gave the women in that film's conversation a topic, interracial dating and the loss of Black men to White women, and then let the camera capture one of the most authentic conversations ever depicted in film. And for many if not most people who may not be the product of an interracial union, opinions on interracial dating are often fraught with stereotypical notions. Well, maybe I have dated outside my race, far outside of it, traveling in many directions and acquiring insight into different cultures and values along the way. Oh yes, and incurring the slings and arrows of opinionated people from both sides of the racial divide.

I remember the first time I crossed the color line to "examine diversity." I was 16 in Tulsa, Oklahoma, and my 15-year-old cousin was somewhat dating one of two sisters (really, hanging out is more appropriate to what was actually occurring) who were both eager to hang out with two Black males. I had never even imagined what a head rush it would be to be under a spotlight like the one that interracial dating puts you under. Regardless of your strong will and character, knowing people are looking at you out of the curiosity of witnessing two people whose skin color differs appearing to have some type of intimate relationship under way is quite intriguing. Knowing that people hate you for daring to do something that they have been taught is not right is incredible. Even admiring two people who enjoy one another can be quite invasive, and when they are attempting to enjoy one another amid society's stares and whispers, someone admiringly witnessing their relationship can still be problematic because of the couple's cultivated paranoia.

People of different race enter into relationships knowing what is in front of them, or do they? The layers of scrutiny associated with this type of dating run deep, and the scars associated with attempting to merge two very divergent races, cultures, and often religions, even at the least complicated level of simply dating, definitely make you wonder why anyone would do it. It gives another level of appreciation to the thought that many gays offer in the nature/nurture debate over sexual orientation: Why would anyone choose to be gay and deliberately put his or her life at risk in a dysfunctional American society?

Hanging out with the two White sisters and my cousin had its most intriguing moment when my great-grandmother discovered our relationship when these two young women drove from South Tulsa all the way over to the north side to "hang with us." My great-grandmother was gracious when we introduced her to them, but afterward when they left, something was alarmingly different about her disposition, mostly captured in the fact that she wasn't speaking to us. Of course, I pressed her for conversation and was blown away with her response. "Can you visit their homes?" she angrily asked. Wow! Her question was mind-blowing because both the sisters and my cousin and I knew we couldn't. Their father was adamant about the fact he didn't want them dating Blacks. When I answered her, "No, we can't," she responded, "Then I don't want them over here either."

To provide you some context, my cousin and I were living with our great-grandmother Mama Horn, a woman who was one of the pillars of the community because, for one thing, she carried the designation of being the first Black policewoman in the state of Oklahoma. My great-grandmother was also a survivor of the 1921 Tulsa Race Riot, a consequence of Tulsa's Black Wall Street (which you history buffs should Google if you want to see one of America's blackest eyes). Lastly, my great-grandmother was truly grand in every way, seldom if ever losing her temper. My response to her last statement was to just turn and walk away and attempt to process where her anger came from. It was over a period of years when I came to realize that her anger may have been wrapped up in her being biracial, and not as if her grandmother had a choice. Did someone say legalized, societal, systematic rape?

My great-grandmother was born in 1897, so her grandmother (my great-great-great-grandmother) was a slave, and many if not most women during slavery were not given the choice of whom they were going to create children with. Until recently our history books, television shows, and movies seldom depicted this reality, and if so, they whitewashed it (no pun intended, but appreciated, I hope). Even in the classic television miniseries *Roots*, rape was sugarcoated as "abuse." So, maybe her reaction was in response to a memory of that. Maybe her response was to the fact that her two great-grandsons were oblivious of the pain associated with dating outside the race. Just as American history has often been painted in a way to virtuously portray the victors, my relatives probably kept away many of the atrocities associated with our oral and actual history so that we wouldn't have to see our lesser-than reality, though it may have given us a better understanding of our current-day lesser-than reality. Maybe her pain was from the fact that we felt we had to import two White girls into our community, perhaps somehow suggesting a lesser-than status of the girls who lived in the nonetheless predominantly White neighborhood. Maybe her anger came from imagining the life we would have if we were stupid enough to think that we could date outside the race and not pay for it, in some form or fashion.

I often wonder how angry Mama Horn would have been if one of my two sisters had "hung out" with White males. Would the anger have been more or less? Since many scholars argue that White men are positioned in American society with more opportunities for success, would Mama Horn have somehow acquiesced to that interracial reality, and instead left it up to the young White males' energies to fight their lesser-than status from within their own community? How far have we come with this interracial dating? At local parks I see all these beautiful children running about, playing with one another, many without a thought about their differences. How many parents are comfortable with them playing but want friendship to be just that, friendship? The defense supporting the taboo of interracial dating is trite in that it implies the world's not ready for it. Yeah, right! People aren't ready for it because they are overtly concerned with what their friends might say. It makes me think of a line from a Dave Chappelle skit: "Oh, this racism is killing us!" I often wonder myself as a parent how I might respond if one day one of my children approaches me and introduces me to his or her interracial love interest. Hopefully, with less anger, I can later ask my child if he or she can visit his or her love interest's home. If not, then unlike my great-grandmother, I will observe a moment of silence on behalf of the limited vision of those parents, but I won't deny my child my support because of scars inflicted from a misguided, dysfunctional society.

All this discussion of interracial dating has made it necessary for me to ask some rhetorical questions:

- How many of you actually think that your choices, what you find attractive, or not attractive, aren't tied to some knee-high sermon or soliloquy you heard from your parents, uncles, aunts, friends, films, or books that forever framed for you a person who might have been your soul mate if the conversation ever had a chance to flow freely?
- How many of you instead settled for a person whom your family and friends approved of, as if they had to live with the person daily, and missed out on other worlds you could have visited?
- How many of you are now poised to pass that tradition on to your children under the guise of wanting the best for them, when it may

be more of wanting the best for yourself in terms of fewer questions to answer, and minimal anxiety about meeting and, dare I say it, getting to know the "Other's" family?

On some level considerations of dating outside your race are preposterous when really there is only one true race, the human race. Everything else is hype!!! Yet we buy into this hype with an aplomb that is as peculiar as it is particular. When we talk about race/racism in America it has a tendency to become a Black-White conversation. Assuming that we can agree upon a simplistic definition of *racism* as a form of prejudgment against someone's skin color, an illogical conclusion arrived at before all the facts are available, how could we limit it to a Black-White dynamic? It was Chris Rock who once said, "I don't slice and dice White people, I hate them all." Now, while we imagine Rock as obviously joking, there are nonetheless many people who hold the position that if your racial paint job differs from theirs, it's a problem.

Exoneration From Racism

Many of my colleagues, both White and Black, hold the position that you can't be racist if you are Black due to the lack of institutional power that Black people have. Joy DeGruy Leary (2005), in her phenomenal book *Post Traumatic Slave Syndrome,* is in this camp as well. She says:

> I then ask them to identify how black racism adversely impacts the lives of white people as a group and there is silence. There is silence, because while black people may have prejudices, and at times even feel hatred towards white people, perhaps even causing many fear, the reality is that black people lack the power to affect the lives of whites as a group. Black people's feelings towards white people do not preclude a white person's ability to get a loan, receive fair treatment by the justice system, acquire education, etc. (p. 23)

While I understand Leary's argument, and can appreciate it, I am not a proponent of this relatively popular notion. While I acknowledge Leary and I may be doing a semantics dance, sometimes people dance for the artistry of the movement and other times they dance for the exercise. I dance for both reasons, always.

Most people would agree that racism is largely predicated on unfamiliarity with the "Other." If Black people in pockets all over the country have a distinct feeling that they are not well received by Whites, will they love White folk anyway or perhaps be more apt to overcompensate and not be comfortable with Whites? If so, that discomfort could even develop into a lack of trust for Whites in general. It is easy to distrust someone you don't know. As these nontrusting Blacks ascend the ladder of success in this country to positions of prominence, doesn't their socialized distrust of Whites change, just because? No, there would have to be a reason. If there is no compelling reason for the races to trust one another, then everyone is tiptoeing around everyone mired in varying levels of distrust.

Whites can be paranoid around not just individual Black sentiment toward them, but the looming potential of Blacks in power who can affect the lives of White people as a group, and the other racial groups that have suffered from a racism that benefits Whites. What do people think is occurring with our politics? There was a time in America when Blacks didn't have power, beyond moral persuasion, to impact anything other than some Whites' consciousness. But over the years Black power has manifested itself in some intriguing ways. Blacks are situated in American society in ways that never could have been anticipated. The proof of this assertion resides in a white house located at 1600 Pennsylvania Avenue. The fact that property value is reported to have gone down since the latest tenants moved in is not the point. What is the point is that this biracial president is modeling access and leadership beyond a White paradigm.

Rumors are rampant that it isn't just a partisan power play to desire to recover the presidency as a result of the perhaps not so mythical fear of a Black precedence/president. The blind unflinching loyalty of underrepresented/underserved political pawns to a party that plays on their paranoia is more problematic proof of an oppressive hysteria stemming from "Black racism." That is, if the criterion for racism is the power to affect the lives of White people as a group Leary's book itself speaks extremely articulately about post traumatic slave syndrome. I would imagine there must be some type of syndrome that people go through, individually and as a group, when they know they've wronged others and the others are aware of it. I know that I would watch my back. As a matter of fact, any group that is dirty, doing dirt, and planning dirt should be paranoid.

However, the biggest problem I have with the argument that Blacks can't be racist is that it also doesn't allow for the power of one. I refuse to be told I don't have the power to be racist. That very thought leaves me feeling as if I might be suffering from internalized racism if I were to believe it. I'm not trying to be cute or coy as I assert this. I'm a college professor and administrator tasked with teaching classes, creating programs, and mentoring an array of very interested and passionate young minds. I could make an argument that the damage I could do to the perspective of some of the students who come through my programs and classes is as significant as the damage caused by the policies of White-run or racist-influenced institutions. I teach future teachers, future administrators, future parents, future political leaders, and yes, future criminals and terrorists, I would imagine, with the law of averages being what it is. Depending upon how I go about that has a direct influence on how many of my students fit into which of those categories. Since I'm about social justice, and I'm real serious and good at what I do, the last two categories, I would imagine, are infinitesimal compared to the first four. And I'm just me in the North Country of New York. Because of immediate influences like bell hooks, Cornel West, Peggy McIntosh, Beverly Daniel Tatum, Jane Elliott, Martin Luther King Jr., Tim Wise, Malcolm X, Dr. Thomas Keith, and Yvonne Wiley (you're damn right Mom's in that group), I and others like me are making social justice noise all across the country.

Institutions are made up of individuals. If the leader of an institution is Black and has scars from racial encounters with Whites, Latinos, Asians, and Indigenous peoples, must we find another term to frame their racism? Sorry, but I'll go against the grain on this one. While I go there I can't help but wonder if this isn't just another instance of Black people wanting to be above the fray, better than the oppressor. I mean, if it is semantics, why emphasize it? If it isn't, what difference does it make to assert that they are racist and we aren't? Does that give us more power as Black people to know that we don't have the power to systematically deny them opportunities as they can do to us? Listen, as the dearly departed attorney Johnnie Cochran once said, "If it don't fit, you must acquit." Or saying it another way, "That dog just don't hunt."

I'm in the camp—perhaps as a lone wolf, which is okay since it keeps me lean and focused when hunting—that anyone who is socialized in the United States is sexist, heterosexist, homophobic, ableist, and classist. So why wouldn't they also be racist? I can imagine some of you reading this wanting to take me to task about my position. Okay, well bring it! But recognize that while I have read many of the same foundational pieces many of you may have read in my journey toward my first doctorate, in philosophy and cultural studies (which I didn't complete), and my journey toward my second doctorate, in educational leadership (which I did complete), my assessment isn't just from reading others' theories (not to imply that yours is, so relax). My assessment stems from research both in and out of academia, personal experiences, logic, and the courage to buck the trend. I know similar arguments abound that women can't be sexist too, gays can't be homophobic or heterosexist, and probably people who are differently able can't be ableist. Well, if that works for you, cool. However, calling women who expect that I'm going to be the typical sexist man (picking up the check, getting the door, being into sports, focusing on my orgasms first) not sexist doesn't work for me. When a White colleague of mine told me that what I am is not racist, but biased, I respected his opinion. After all, he was just trumpeting the party line that many of my Black friends had already espoused to me. But a bias toward someone of a different race isn't racism if it comes from me? However, a racial bias toward me isn't racial bias but racism. Did Jamie Foxx's character, Willie Beamen, in the film *Any Given Sunday* actually coin the term for Black racism when he told Al Pacino's character, Coach Tony D'Amato, that perhaps it wasn't racism that D'Amato was practicing, but instead "placism"? With a different twist to it, perhaps that's it. I don't practice racism against other races because I lack the power. It's placism. I resent either the place they have in society or the fact that they would deny me my place if not dare to take it. Perhaps we can call it spaceism, because I want my own space, at least for me and mine. Somehow I missed the memo that explicated how we had to reserve terms for our differing problematic encounters around our diversity.

How do I lack institutional power when interacting with a Latino, an Asian, or a Native American? I can't be racist to Whites, but I can be racist to other groups that haven't necessarily arrived politically, economically, or perhaps even socially in America? Let's see, the attorney general is a Black man. The president of the United States is a Black man (okay, biracial, but the one-drop rule is in full effect). We've had Black generals, governors, senators, mayors, head coaches, baseball managers, even owners of major sport franchises. This situates Black people to better receive fair treatment by the justice system, acquire education, etc. Unless we are talking about racism in a constrained context what part of no institutional power don't Black people have?

Can Asians be racist to me or other Blacks? Can Asians be racist to Latinos? If I am a Black filmmaker and I consistently create negative images of Latinos and Asians that adversely influence policy-making Whites' perspectives toward these two groups, are they still labeled racist while I'm not? After all, they may be less apt to "get a loan, receive fair treatment by the justice system, acquire education, etc." (Leary, 2005, p. 23). If I was the progenitor of their racism, the root of their racism, how do I merit a pass? How do I escape the label?

When rap artists N.W.A dropped their controversial song "Fuck tha Police" and immediately had a sociopolitical voice that would grow with every million records they sold, were they still lacking power? Don't tell me the industry created around rap and racism isn't what contributed to getting Obama elected. While many others played a part, Oprah, Russell Simmons, and many, many other high-powered Blacks leveraged their power and relationships toward accomplishing a heightened consciousness.

Boycott the Mascot

Racism is an intriguing phenomenon in this country. Its relationship to so many dimensions of our existence can be seen or imagined if one is inclined to go there. For example, in the movie *Smoke Signals* (Eyre & Alexie, 1998), when Victor Joseph is releasing the ashes of his deceased father, Arnold, from a bridge to free his father's spirit, a poem is recited that symbolizes Victor's paternal plight:

SMOKE SIGNALS

How do we forgive our fathers? Maybe in a dream. Do we forgive our fathers for leaving us too often, or forever, when we were little? Maybe for scaring us with unexpected rage, or making us nervous because there never seemed to be any rage there at all. Do we forgive our fathers for marrying, or not marrying, our mothers? Or divorcing, or not divorcing, our mothers? And shall we forgive them for their excesses of warmth or coldness? Shall we forgive them for pushing, or leaning? For shutting doors or speaking through walls? For never speaking, or never being silent? Do we forgive our fathers in our age, or in theirs? Or in their deaths, saying it to them or not saying it? If we forgive our fathers, what is left?

This film is set in the turbulent '70s, more than a decade after the civil rights movement had helped ease some of the racism in American society but hadn't eradicated it; a reason why an indigenous father would leave his family in this period could be the loss of employment. He may have left his family for the opportunity of better financial support from the government with him absent, or simply because he did not understand the impact of the lack of a stable role model due to his father's absence when he was a child, and hence the cycle continues. All these reasons could have been exacerbated if not directly attributable to racist policies/practices. The unexpected rage, excess of coldness, inexplicable silence, and divorce could all be answered as consequences of racism.

Michael Eric Dyson (1996), in his book *Race Rules*, suggests that racism is frequently found in different forms with varying signifiers. He suggests that the concept of racism should be separated into three categories: race as context, race as subtext, and race as pretext. Race as context he defines as helping the nation to "understand the facts of race and racism in our society" (p. 35). Race as pretext assists in understanding the function of race and racism in America (p. 35). For the purposes relative to Arnold Joseph's dysfunctional parenting, it is Dyson's race as subtext that is pertinent. Dyson accentuates how various arguments have been utilized as a means of mystification or deliberate vagueness in regard to racism. Race as subtext describes the "different forms that racism takes, the disguises it wears, the tricky, subtle shapes it assumes." Dyson states that the understanding of race as subtext helps grasp the "hidden premises," "buried perceptions," and "cloaked meanings" of race as they show up throughout our culture (p. 34). It is the buried perceptions and cloaked meanings associated with our perspective of Arnold Joseph's decisions that I want to challenge you to consider. But first, I ask you to imagine.

> *Imagine a mother struggling*
> *Dealing with a system that don't give a fuck about who shot her son*
> *Imagine life you can't win*
> *When you get out of the ghetto and go right to the pen*
> *When you get out of the pen you go right to the jenz*
> *When you put back on the streets you get right back in*
>
> **—Snoop Dogg, featuring Dr. Dre, "Imagine"**

As accentuated by this excerpt from one of my favorite rap songs, "Imagine," it isn't very difficult for most racially underrepresented people in American culture to imagine social injustice. In many of their rap songs Snoop and Dr. Dre speak about social injustice; it just is imbedded in their edgy articulation of cultural happenings. In this excerpt they speak of the institutional injustices that far too often than not plague the racial underclass.

It must be doubly painful for Native Americans to just "imagine." Imagine living in a country that once exemplified the epitome of the notion of freedom for its indigenous people. Imagine having unlimited resources at your disposal. Imagine having pride in your heritage, culture, and identity while never having to consider it as something to not be proud of. Now imagine the trauma to any notion of self-esteem associated with your identity when in high schools and colleges, newspapers, restaurants, movies, and major sporting events televised for national and international viewing the historical image of your ancestors continues to be framed as savages. Kimberly Roppolo (2010), in her essay titled "Symbolic Racism, History, and Reality: The Real Problem with Indian Mascots," addresses the "race as subtext," as explicated by Dyson, that Native Americans must face, daily. From occurrences across the country that showcase symbols of Native Americans as mascots to the more extreme cases of cheerleaders yelling, "Kill the Indians," where does it end?

> Dr. Cornell Pewewardy of the University of Kansas calls this kind of racism "dysconscious racism," or in other words, racism that the people themselves who exhibit it are unaware of. The use of American Indian mascots falls under this category. The grossly exaggerated features of the Cleveland Indian, the cartooned vicious savages decorating high school spirit ribbons, the painted, dancing, fake-buckskin-clad white kids running down the sideline doing tomahawk chops, are all unintentionally stereotypical and aren't even perceived by most Americans as negative. . . . The average American engages in this behavior without ever being aware of it, much less realizing that it is racism. (Roppolo, 2010, p. 75)

Roppolo also addresses the level of inconsideration that continues to be perpetuated throughout our society by those like Ted Nugent who would don the Plains chief's headdress to attract attention, Disney's stereotypical caricatures within *Pocahontas* and *El Dorado,* and terms like *Indian giver.* Even those of us who have experienced racial oppression contributed to the denigration of the Native American by unwittingly joining in the dysfunctional celebrations. I can still see a Black man wearing a Native American war chief headdress running along the sidelines at Washington Redskins games, televised for millions to see. The irony of that image haunts me. Especially since that very same Black man wearing Native American attire would scream "racism" at the top of his lungs if a White person were wearing blackface in a field picking cotton for the fictional football team the Carolina Cotton Pickers.

I attended a high school that had as its school sports name "Braves" with an Indian image as its mascot plastered on all of its sports gear. Growing up watching cowboy and Indian movies, I never once considered the plight of the indigenous people, and none of the adults in my world ever took the time to challenge me to do so because apparently they weren't considering it either.

Professor and Native American scholar Ward Churchill (2003) also unpacked the societal subterfuge that he claims is designed to placate the oppressive consciousness of the typical White American, when he states:

> The fact that any society could subject another to such ongoing misery by indulging in a subterfuge designed solely to enable its own constituents to nonetheless "feel good about themselves" reaffirms our earlier conclusion that a genocidal mentality is at work among North American settlers, although this time with respect to contemporary rather than merely historical circumstances. (p. 78)

If historical anecdotes are continually told in ways that detract from the humanity of the victimized by rationalizing the reasons of the victimizer, how dysfunctional will the worldviews and various levels of privilege and oppression be for all involved. I can't provide any better evidence of this than the fact that as a little boy I was obsessed with the Jessie and Frank James fable. In any given situation where I might be playing bank robbers or cowboys and Indians with my friends, I would insist that I played the part of Jessie James, whom I saw as so cool. Little did I know that Jessie James was one of Quantrill's Raiders, a Confederate guerilla group that refused to accept the fact that the Civil War had ended and, as a result, took it upon themselves to continue to terrorize pro-Union sympathizers and abolitionists, people who would have supported the freedom of my ancestors. But Hollywood's framing of the Jessie James story was packaged in such a way that it had me as a youth wanting to be a man who might have executed me (had I lived at that time) as he ransacked and pillaged a town that would have sympathized with my plight as a Negro. For that matter, he might have murdered some of my ancestors. This is what the reality of America's indigenous people was and tragically still is.

> "Racism against American Indians is so intrinsically part of America's political mythology . . . that without it this country would have to do something it has never done: face colonial guilt." (p. 75)

Roppolo's assertion that America without the intricacy of racism imbedded within its national psyche would have to assuage its "colonial guilt" is taken further by Churchill (2003). He ultimately and unequivocally calls for the decolonization of America or at least America owning its hypocrisy (p. 82). Enlightened and motivated by Roppolo and Churchill, I embarked upon a conversation with a valued colleague of mine, the superintendent of Peru Central Schools in upstate New York, A. Paul Scott, about changing the name of the school mascots from, ironically, Indians to something that isn't offensive to any specific group. I pleasantly discovered that, as a progressive, forward-thinking administrator, as early as one year prior he had already laid groundwork for the change and really only needed an ally. So, in alliance, we were prepared to use Roppolo's compelling arguments augmented by her authenticity and passion as a Native American as well as Scott's profound and well-intentioned research. Rappolo (2010) asserted:

> If we had sports teams named the New York Niggers or the Jersey Jigaboos, Americans would know this was wrong. The average American, who would clearly perceive the Louisville Lynched Porch Monkeys as a problematic name for a team doesn't even realize the Washington Redskins emerges from a history of the literal bloody skins of American Indian men, women, and children being worth British Crown bounty money—no one's skin is red. American Indian skin is brown, at least when it is on our bodies and not stripped from us in the name of profit and expansionism. African Americans, thank God, have raised the consciousness of Americans enough through the Civil Rights movement to keep the more obvious forms of racism usually hidden, though it took publicly armed Black Panthers, the burning of Chicago, and even the riots of Los Angeles to get this point across. American Indians are frankly so used to being literally shot down if we stick our heads up, we aren't nearly as likely to do so. (p. 75)

This excerpt from Scott's (2010) comprehensive research further supports Rappolo's assertion and reveals Scott's commitment to social justice and insights into some of the challenges we had before us:

> It is evident that because one group of people believes it is their entitled right to use American Indian people as their mascots or symbols, the relationship is one of superiority vs. subordination. As anyone who has been involved in working to retire institutionalized "Indian" sports tokens can attest, those who favor retention of "Indian" mascots often exhibit an almost pathological sense of proprietary ownership of the symbols, mascots, and nicknames. The use of "Indian" sports team tokens is therefore not unlike a symbolic slavery that allows those who use the symbols, nicknames, and mascots to control, manipulate, and exploit such things and their meanings in any manner that best suits their purposes.

That the use of "Indian" mascots, nicknames, and symbols frequently continues even after many American Indian people and advocacy groups have repeatedly requested a cessation of such uses further illustrates the fundamentally "racist" element embedded in the issue.

It should be noted, however, that "racism," or ethnocentrism, takes several different forms. Sometimes it is overt and willful while at other times it is the result of an innocent lack of awareness and sensitivity often borne from many years of socially and culturally ingrained beliefs and practices. While both types of "racism" can be seen in conjunction with this issue it is frequently the second type in which most people, at least initially, unwittingly participate.

Ultimately, we didn't go forward with the initiative. The combination of Scott's school district's budget cuts, his impending retirement, and my kids having to live and attend school within a community where many would not appreciate what Superintendent Scott and I would have attempted to do made it too daunting a task. People say they are socially just, try to do the right thing, and love their neighbor, but somehow they will fight you tooth and nail when you challenge their perspectives and/or comfortable lifestyles. Yet, ironically, if a billionaire bought the school district guaranteeing better resources and educational opportunities for all involved only if the name was changed to the "Peru Privileged" or the "Peru Predominantly Whites," screams of bloody murder would be discernible across Lake Champlain. What those resistant to such a change don't realize is that all across America school districts and the people who populate them are now making statements contrary to their *once upon a time* lack of consideration for others, their blatant hypocrisy once they've been informed of the social injustice taking place, and their hesitance to relinquish their unearned privileges by retaining these antiquated racist demarcations of time long past.

This is why the poem from *Smoke Signals*—perhaps more so than any other I've ever read—frames the reality of many racially underrepresented fathers trying to parent in a racist country designed to emasculate, eviscerate, and deny them opportunities while promoting privilege.

The poem also tells the story of my father so vividly that I have never been able to hear it or read it—since my introduction to it while watching the film—without crying. More problematic, though, were the years it took me to forgive my father for both his physical and spiritual absence. Like Victor's father, Arnold Joseph, who died a sudden death, my father, Joe, was murdered after perhaps willingly not seeing his children the last six years of his life. At 15 I wasn't prepared to forgive him in his age. My level of sophistication with race and racism wasn't evolved enough for me to understand and/or comprehend some of the mitigating factors that contributed to his actions. I just missed the love. I didn't forgive my father in his death either, choosing to not go to his funeral, not to cry for years. However, I did forgive my father once I came to realize what it may have been like for him at that time. The poem asks, "If we forgive our fathers, what is left?" Well, I chose to do everything in my power to create a reality whereby my son would never have to forgive me for sins similar to Arnold Joseph's. The only way I could enhance the possibilities of never situating my son where I commit sins similar to those of Arnold Joseph is to engage race and racism, gender and sexism, sexual orientation, homophobia and heterosexism, temporary able-bodiedness and ableism, and socioeconomic class and classism until their adverse effects on our society have lessened and, dare I say, possibly, hopefully, even vanished.

The Subtext of Racism

"Consequently, most of the early information we receive about 'others'—people racially, religiously, or socioeconomically different from ourselves—does not come as the result of firsthand experience. The secondhand information we do receive has often been distorted, shaped by cultural stereotypes, and left incomplete."

—Tatum (CWT, p. 79)

I recall, in terms of the secondhand information that Tatum suggests, stories about Asians that I imagined were stereotypes but that I wouldn't put to the test. Asians as martial artists was probably the most significant one in terms of its impact upon me. Probably a consequence of the Bruce Lee phenomenon in America at that time, I nonetheless had a level of paranoia about any type of transgression with an Asian male. I was committed in my youth to stay away, as much as possible, from drama that might lead to an ass whipping. As someone who could take care of himself I wasn't apt to run from a situation. However, if the possible combatant was Asian I was going to try to find every way possible to amicably come to an agreement.

So, how did this stereotype of Asians affect my perspective and that of others like me? Well, first and foremost, Asian is such a vague category for such a large and diverse group of people that it is racist to think you could actually reflect all their different ideologies under one limited rubric. The notion of Japanese and/or Chinese Americans as the model minority might contradict the realities of recent Asian immigrants like the Vietnamese or Hmong. Many of these groups recently arriving have the pressure of trying to make ends meet, but they nonetheless must find ways to transcend expectations that they will be the smartest in the class, good in math, and, of course, good fighters.

These stereotypes apply only to the men. I don't recall any stereotypes associated with Asian women except that they are more passive than White women, who are stereotypically depicted as even less aggressive than Black women. So, if we know that these stereotypes of Asian men and women don't benefit them in their daily lives, how are the stereotypes still alive?

They stay alive because we don't stop to consider "the Other" in a context that will enable us to move beyond Dyson's notion of "race as subtext." Dyson's (1996) assertion that an understanding of race as subtext will assist us in navigating our way through dysfunctional depictions of other cultures applies here (p. 34). The culture of the United States comprises many cultures, hence why the United States is considered a multicultural society. Within the United States many of these subcultures are inadvertently (or perhaps inconsiderately) pitted against one another when situated in lower socioeconomic living situations while vying for their piece of the American pie. The struggles of two subcultures (Blacks and Mexicans) to respect one another culturally while trying to consider actions to combat social injustices that threaten to cause more tension between them is exemplified in this excerpt from the motion picture *Bobby* (Estevez, 2006).

> **Scene 5:** *A group of cooks are seated around the table in the back kitchen of a restaurant, ready to eat the food the chief chef has prepared.*

Miguel: Chef's special, Edward?
Edward: Miguel, you know if I could, I would.
Miguel: Bullshit, man. I see you servin' the brothers the good stuff. White folks, too. You don't see them eatin' this dog food.
Edward: Lord, today. Do we have to do this every day, Miguel?
Miguel: Every day you keep puttin' the brown man down, Edward. (*Edward chuckles.*)

Keepin' the brown man down.

Edward: (*Chuckles*) I'm puttin' the brown man down. That's right, let's keep the brown man down. Let's send the brown man back across the border to his sweet senoritas and refried beans.

The men around the table laugh and make, "Oooh!" sounds.

Miguel: First of all, we didn't cross the border, the border crossed us; and our senoritas are better than your fried-chicken eatin' mama with the big backyard.

Men "oooh!" again.

Edward: Hey, you smell that? Look at that, my very own special berry cobbler, fresh out of the oven! But, since you had to put my mama in it, excuse me, (*Hands the cobbler to Jose, who is seated next to Miguel*) here you go, Jose. Enjoy.

Jose: (*Accepts the cobbler and chuckles*) Oh, thank you.

Miguel: Come on, man.

Edward: (*mockingly*) "Come on, man." (*The men around the table laugh.*) You Mexican boys can't play the dozens. I don't know why you keep on, Miguel.

Jose: Yeah, man.

Miguel: (*To Jose*) Man, what do you know about the dozens?

Jose: I know that I got some cobbler and you don't.

Laughter around the table.

Miguel: Sellout, man.

Jose: You know.

Edward: Hey, it's good ain't it, Jose?

Jose: Mmm-hmm.

Edward: That recipe was handed down by my great-grandmother.

Miguel: Let me have some of that. Come on, brother.

Edward: We ain't brothers, amigo.

Laughter around the table

Miguel: And we ain't amigos, "bruh-thuh."

Laughter around the table

Edward: Go ahead.

Jose: (*To Edward*) You um . . . workin' a double shift like the rest of us?

Edward: I most certainly am not.

Miguel: You must be the only one.
Edward: And you know why.
Jose: Why?
Edward: Too good-looking for that mess.

Laughter.

Miguel: You ain't workin' a double 'cause whitey's afraid of your black ass, man. They're afraid you're gonna go all Huey Newton on 'em, all violent. See, they ain't afraid of us yet Jose. Not yet, man, but one day, they will be, man. We're gonna get the respect that we deserve. We're gonna take back California, take back our land, man.
Edward: (*rises a bit so he is in Miguel's face and hand is on Miguel's shoulder*) I want you to take that anger and park it in my kitchen, young man.
Miguel: I want you to get your hand off my shoulder, Negro.

(Men "oooh")

Edward: (*sits back down*) All right, keep it up. See, the first few times I tried to make this dessert, I couldn't get it right. Too much sugar one time, not enough sugar the next time; couldn't find the balance. I realized I was forcing it. Trying to make it taste like my mama's or her mama's. Mine didn't have any poetry, didn't have any light. And then I realized, I was trying to force it to taste like my mother's, taste like her mother's. See it had to be Edward's creation. Mmm-hmm. It had to come from me. Now you, Miguel, you've got . . . shit to offer. You've got no poetry. You've got no light. You've got no one looking at you and saying, "Damn, look at that Miguel. I want some of what he's got." All you got is your anger.
Miguel: I ain't angry.
Edward: I'm sorry, I didn't hear you. Come on, speak up . . .
Miguel: (*shouts*) I said I'm not angry!

Men around the room mutter

Edward: All right. I used to be just like you. I had anger. And then after Dr. King was killed . . . well, anger like you can't even imagine. White folks ain't trying to keep you down, Miguel. White folks just don't like to be pushed into a corner. They'll come around. You just gotta make it look like it was their idea, like they're the ones that thought of it. They need to feel like they're the great emancipators,

like it was theirs to give in the first place. Let 'em have it. I mean, if
that's all it takes, let 'em have it. Can you dig it? Well, I know my
man, Jose, can dig it. Can't you?

Jose: Yeah.

Edward: Hmmm.

Daryl enters.

Daryl: Edward? Is that your famous cobbler I'm smelling down in my
office?

Edward: (*stands up*) Yes sir, Mr. Timmons. I just pulled a fresh batch
out of the oven, I'll make sure some gets to your office directly, sir.
(*sits down*)

Miguel: (*mockingly*) "I'll get some sent to your office directly, sir."

(*Laughter around the table*)

Step-and-fetch it motherfucker.

(*Edward takes Miguel's plate which prompts Miguel to exclaim*) Hey!

Edward: I'm not workin' a double shift today, though, am I . . . amigo?
(*Men "oooh."*)

Scene ends

The characters' cross-cultural banter began light, witty, and harmless.
Miguel's passionate desire to take action against oppressive forces flirts with
overriding his reason. He acknowledges—as an accomplishment of Black
organizations like the Black Panthers and Black Muslims—respect from the
hegemonic culture acquired as a result of Blacks actually inciting fear by
their actions or their strategic posturing of potential action. He also implies
Brown people (Mexicans) were inspired to adapt the same strategy validated
by Black people's successful social progress movements. This implication by
Miguel reveals a one-dimensional knowledge of Black struggle: that it was/
is essentially violent and its success doesn't result from respect for Black
intellectuality, but instead is predicated on a fear of Black physicality.

Edward's statement about Miguel's lack of poetry is a statement about
Miguel's inability to eloquently articulate his political positions. Miguel's
inability to demonstrate his "light" is symbolic of his inability to situate
himself creatively in a light benefiting him sociopolitically. Miguel's lack of
poetry and light prevents him from becoming an effective leader.

When Edward tells Miguel he has got "no one looking at [him] and saying, 'Damn, look at that Miguel. I want some of what he's got,' " he is really saying that Miguel has avoided modeling leadership. He points out to Miguel that his anger's only positive purpose is a release of tension.

However, it is Edward's statement about White folk not being pushed into a corner that is perhaps his most significant leadership moment. Edward suggests to anyone listening a certain expectation by Whites of a type of behavior from Mexicans, Blacks, and any racially underrepresented group. With Whites having had dominion over someone simply because of their Whiteness, making an adjustment to an equitable distribution of power that is possibly not in their favor can be challenging for them, and probably anyone. Edward's assertion is not far-fetched when you consider that Whiteness reflects the hegemonic racial subculture and that many Whites are accustomed to things being done the White way as opposed to perhaps a so-called right way. Edward is correct in that White folks can accept the idea of them becoming enlightened if it is articulated by Whites, instead of underrepresented voices. Peggy McIntosh, Robert Jensen, Tim Wise, and other White social justice authors get a great deal more mileage out of challenging resistant Whites about their White privilege. When I attempt to do it as a Black man I am often seen as whining. When Whites frame White privilege they are seen as articulating, on some level, their enlightenment.

When Edward asserted that Whites need to feel their power validated he could not have been more provocative in his realistic depiction of how power can be leveraged in strategic doses, even by those coerced into relinquishing it in small doses.

Humans are creatures of habit. A challenge extended to them to consider some of the habits they internalize that may be counterproductive or dysfunctional is something that may actually get their attention, especially if they are made to feel ridiculous for succumbing to the way they have been socialized or are still being socialized. This socialization process never truly ends. For example, when I present my Diversity Enlightenment session and we get to my dysfunctional language section, I usually get a reaction from having the word *Hispanic* displayed as a dysfunctional term. Many of the Latino participants don't understand how it could be dysfunctional. Then I inform them that my being reared in California among Mexicans and Chicanos in my adolescent and young adult life introduced me to the abhorrence these two Spanish-speaking groups had with the term *Hispanic*. Like Black folk with the term *Negro*, Mexicans/Chicanos saw the term *Hispanic* as a one-size-fits-all label affixed to them by the U.S. government. Chicanos especially, like Blacks (who didn't appreciate being labeled Negroes), rebuked the term and embraced their current-day labels as a statement of power, a statement of their ability to name themselves.

The socialization that accompanies the way we see race reveals itself in some intriguingly problematic, unanticipated ways. In early May 2004, a moment now referred to as the "'heritage, not hate' incident" occurred at a local high school. Those are the words that a parent used to justify some students wearing shirts that bore the Confederate flag to school. This prompted me to seek out the definition of *heritage*, which is "practices that are handed down from the past by tradition." While the definition makes sense in an open-ended context, in the context of students using the term *heritage* to defend their wearing of attire that represents something horrific to others, the term is being used to manipulate, to deflect the pain of certain "traditional practices" that were far from civil. People who celebrate the Nazi swastika cannot avoid the moral responsibility of its other meanings simply because to them Nazism may be counterculture or cool. Morally responsible citizens do not wear T-shirts that celebrate the bombing of Hiroshima and Tulsa's Black Wall Street. Morally responsible citizens do not emblazon their sweatshirts with the images of those infamous members of Columbine's Trench Coat Mafia, Dylan Klebold and Eric Harris, even though they may be said to represent an aspect of our American heritage. And don't try to justify these insensitive outrages with rationale or rhetoric. We each must ask ourselves if we would have a problem with the glorification of someone who did evil to us. I would imagine most of us would agree that freedom of speech is not divorced from moral responsibility. In the grand scheme of things, though, because of our fixation with race, we continue to find ourselves in a contest where no one wins.

7

OF PRIVILEGE, POLITICAL POSTURING, AND LEADERSHIP MOMENTS

When the world needs someone to do the really big stuff, you need an American.

—Mitt Romney, RNC acceptance speech, 2012

I wish I was White!

—Autumn Blake Wiley (at age 4)

These two quotes, which may appear to be not only different but totally unrelated, are actually more connected than it would seem. Mitt Romney, the ex-governor of Massachusetts and the GOP nominee for president in 2012, was making his statement in the context of astronaut Neil Armstrong. While he didn't in any explicit way refer to President Obama, it is not too far-fetched to read into his statement a veiled reference to America's first Black president's racial heritage. Why else would he have phrased it just that way? Yes, Romney could be a jingoist and sometimes poses as a jingoist, and he often has admonished Obama for supposedly apologizing for America, questioned his patriotism, and weakly denied the "birthers" movement. But more so, the veiled reference that Obama has something different about him that precludes his ever having passion for the American way is what makes this "Americans do the really big stuff" comment troubling. Romney unequivocally sees himself as an American, which gives him added privilege depending upon whom his conversation is with at any given moment. He also denies President Obama the privilege of being American because in America, in our current-day political milieu, he can.

It links to my daughter Autumn's comment because as a Black girl if she does not feel included within the definition of American, or can't easily see herself as an American, then she may begin every day of her life—after having bought into such a notion—feeling inadequate and vulnerable to so-called Americans whom she may encounter. Wishing she was White at the age of 4 is essentially wishing she was a full-fledged nonhyphenated American instead of "just" an African American. It is recognition of lacking a privilege that others not only have, but often don't even recognize they have. Essentially, one dimension of privilege is the ability to not have to consider certain things about your identity. Autumn is always situated to consider her lack of privilege. On some level Autumn is really declaring, "I wish I had their privileges." This point is accentuated better by this quote from Tim Wise's book *White Like Me* (2011):

> Inequality and privilege were the only real components of whiteness. Without racial privilege there is no whiteness, and without whiteness, there is no racial privilege. Being white means to be advantaged relative to people of color, and pretty much only that. (p. 179)

Of course, my lovely daughter at 4 years of age wanted this thing called privilege that she couldn't begin to comprehend or even fully understand. Most people don't have an inkling of their unearned privilege. As a matter of fact, most people also think their often considered "earned privilege" is actually earned. They don't see the friends they made in sports connected to their *ability* as a healthy person, or the friends they have on the debate team connected to their not being impaired mentally. Most people don't see their "earned privilege" connected to their *socioeconomic class*. They don't see the relationship between the clothes they wear, the car they drive, and the neighborhood they live in as relative to, if not influencing their choices in whom they desire as friends and whether those desired friendships are reciprocated. Far too often we naively attribute our relationships to our personalities alone.

> "Social class is probably the single most important variable in society. From womb to tomb it correlates with almost all other social characteristics of people that we can measure."
>
> —Loewen (1995, p. 203)

> "Ultimately, social class determines how people think about social class."
>
> —Loewen (1995, p. 205)

> "As a result of the class you are born into and raised in, class is your understanding of the world and where you fit in; it's composed of ideas, behavior, attitudes, values, and language; class is how you think, feel, act, look, dress, talk, move, walk; class is what stores you shop at, restaurants you eat in; class is the schools you attend, the education you attain; class is the very jobs you will work at throughout your adult life."
>
> —Langston (2004, p. 398)

In the Examining Diversity Through Film (EDTF) class I co-teach with colleagues at SUNY Plattsburgh, we had a very intriguing moment arise as we exited our much less anxiety-ridden "ability" theme and cautiously entered our "race" theme. A young woman, who often is very much *in the game* in terms of the energy and insight she brings to a conversation, admitted that she struggled with the notion that because she is White she is privileged. She argued that she has never felt that way and that when she accomplishes something of merit she doesn't want it undercut by assertions that her race might have been a factor in her achievement. As the discussion ensued, it was pointed out to her, and of course the rest of the class, that the reason White people often don't/can't see their racial privilege is that it is a dominant attribute and as Beverly Daniel Tatum (2004b) asserts we are less apt to focus on those qualities that give us unearned privileges (p. 11). To frame this point further, I asked the students whether they thought men had an advantage (privilege) over women in our society. They concurred. I then asked whether they thought it was more advantageous to live a heterosexual lifestyle, or to not have a so-called disability. Upon her agreeing with the fact that some cultural groups in our society do have privilege (advantages), I then asked why would the dominant race in our society be any different? It is an intriguing thing witnessing students grapple with realizing and then owning the fact that they have privilege. However, it is even more intriguing when a struggle with privilege occurs among professionals who are themselves either surprised by the discovery or oblivious to it.

An example of this occurred with my son, Justin, when at age 14 while sitting in his class another Black boy entered the classroom. Upon seeing him, my son greeted him with the words, "What's up, my Negro?" That's right! His salutation to the other Black boy was a slight twist on the popular culture greeting that has permeated Black vernacular for years: "What's up, my Nigger?" So, though all he said was hello to his friend in a very informal, comfortable manner, the response from their White teacher was to send my son to the principal's office. What was the grievous offense perpetrated by my son greeting the other Black boy upon his entering the class? Was it his fault that the teacher was unfamiliar with the myriad of ways two young Black boys, teenagers in the age of hip-hop, might greet one another? I mean, with the creativity of language that permeates rap music, do you think that two generally perceived as cool and popular teenagers are always going to just say "hello"? Was he wrong in extending the greeting to the other teenager? From what I understand he didn't yell it out, but definitely said it with no shame. Is there a problem with expressions of culture like this that are not profane? If an Italian had said to another Italian, "What's up, my Italian?" would the student have been sent to the principal's office? Come on, be real. Of course not. So, why did "What's up, my Negro?" cause such a stir? Had the word *Negro* become profane overnight? The implications of unearned privilege being given in this scenario abound. A White student could have said hello to another student using an array of descriptors like "What's up, my Swede," or "What's up, my Irishman." But something about "What's up, my Negro" was problematic. Are there limitations to the way underrepresented people can express themselves if they make the overrepresented uncomfortable? Another way of framing this is if underrepresented people embrace or celebrate their oft-called minority status in a way that makes members of the hegemonic culture have to consider their dominance, it is not only deemed unacceptable, but highly problematic? This is the reason Justin ended up in the principal's office. So, there is a level of unearned privilege, racial privilege that is available to not just the White students in class in terms of what they can/can't say, but also to the White teacher in terms of her social class privilege. Though in a position of authority to teach a class, is she absolved from acquiring a modicum of sophistication about her students to know, at the very least, that the word *Negro* is not an offensive term among Blacks, especially when said from one Black to another? More so, the word *Negro* is not synonymous with the word *nigger* though they both start with an *n* and are often identified with people with chocolate skin.

Wait a moment now, before you start to act as if I'm being racist (because I know some people enjoy putting that jacket on the diversity guy), catch your breath and realize that still, to this day, when I am in a restaurant in the North Country of New York, I am almost always the only Black man in that restaurant the entire time. However, just days before this incident, I was in a local sushi bar sitting next to the director of a local fitness center who was White, whom I just happened to encounter there. Then two other Black men entered the restaurant within a five-minute period of one another and flanked the two of us. I knew all of these men, although they were unfamiliar with one another. The other two men were president of an auto dealership and a vice president of human resources for a significant local business. Yes, this White man was surrounded by three professional Black men, all craving sushi, but discovering a rarity, that the stars don't necessarily have to align for three Black men from different places and locally different spaces to share social graces while they serendipitously meet and touch bases. We fell into a rhythm whereby eventually, perhaps due to the sake, martinis, and beers being imbibed, our socially constructed differences became irrelevant, as long as our discourse didn't awaken us from our sushi-induced slumber of sorts. The one White man amid three Black men had acquired honorary (albeit temporary) "brother" status while everybody was getting their eat, or should I say "sushi," on. We discussed this, that, and the other thing (you don't really think I would tell you), and for me I must admit it was one of the best impromptu moments I've had in Plattsburgh.

Being very direct, I must say it is a rarity to ever see three professional Black men sitting and dining in a restaurant in the North Country. For that matter, seeing even two? More so, seeing three Black women who aren't related out and about is like seeing two pink unicorns having tea. This would be no different if there were Asian women or Latinas dining out in predominantly White enclaves. Well, how many times have you considered the fact that the person(s) you are dining with understands some dimension of your struggle? Perhaps you've never had the thought because in terms of race you may never have had to struggle or felt under siege, or been paranoid because once again you couldn't shake the feeling of being "the Other." The White fitness center director didn't seem extraordinarily ill at ease at the beginning of his experience of being the racial other, but he definitely wasn't as relaxed as he would become an hour later. Was it just the alcohol and sushi, or perhaps his discovery that given time with people who are different from us, along with an open mind, the commonalities between us and those we perceive as different could be more hype than anything else? Have you ever considered it as significant or cause for celebration for racially underrepresented people to have access to one another? Have you ever considered the reasons why some people wouldn't see it as significant? Well, if you haven't figured it out yet, this relates to the two Black boys encountering one another in the classroom. Two White boys don't see their racial privilege when they are situated as part of the racial majority. In the racial majority they are not threatened. However, let them walk out of a class of 20 students, whereby 17 have racial paint jobs like theirs, and immerse them in a class where they are the only ones with their unique coloring. They then may be greeting one another with the salutation, "What's up, my Caucasian?"

Perspectives on Privilege

The subtleties of having privilege are easily missed. When I do my Diversity Enlightenment workshops I often simply walk across the stage or front of the room and ask people what they noticed. Seldom does anyone say what, on some level, should be quite obvious. When you watch me walk your mind doesn't go anywhere toward a thought about me being disabled. You might notice I'm male, probably might think about the fact that I'm Black, will check out my clothes, might think about my height, might hate on my sweet-ass boots, but won't think at all about the privilege I have of being able bodied. The boys/men will notice that I'm male but won't think about how lucky I am to not be female. The girls/women will think about how I am male but probably won't immediately designate me as an oppressor because of my gender.

Most of us aren't adept at engaging our privilege. As a result, when we hear someone discussing it, it really gets our attention. When the person discussing it is a comedian and can lace the profound points he or she is making with his or her sociopolitical commentary, it can and more often does really get our attention. On the topic of White privilege, Louis C.K. is the Tim Wise of comedy. Check him out for yourself:

> Sorry I'm being so negative.
> I'm a bummer, I don't know, I shouldn't be. I'm a very lucky guy.
> I'm healthy, I'm relatively young, I'm White, which thank god for that shit, boy.
> That is a huge up, like are you kidding me?
> Ugh god, I love being White, I really do.
>
> Seriously, if you're not White you're missing out, because this shit is thoroughly good.
> But let me be clear, I'm not saying that White people are better; I'm saying that being White is clearly better.
> Who could even argue? If it was an option then I would re-up every year.
> Oh yeah, I'll take White again, absolutely.
> I'm enjoying that; I'll stick with White, thank you.

Here's how great it is to be White.
I could get in a time machine and go to any time and it'd be fucking
    awesome when I get there.
That is exclusively a White privilege.
Black people can't fuck with time machines.
A Black guy in a time machine is like,
"Hey anything before 1980, thank you, but I don't want to go."
But I could go to any time.
The year 2, I don't even know what was happening then.
But I know when I get there
"Welcome, we have a table right here for you, sir."
"Oh, thank you, it's lovely here in the year 2."
I could go to any time, in the past.
I don't want to go to the future and find out what happens to White
    people because we're going to pay hard for this shit, you guys got to
    know that . . .
but for now, WEEEE!

If you're White and you don't admit that it's great you're an asshole!
I'm White, and I'm a man.
How many advantages could one person have?
I'm a White man; you can't even hurt my feelings.
What can you really call a white man that really digs deep?
"Hey Cracker"
"Ugh, ruined my day. I'm White, shouldn't have called me a Cracker,
    bringing me back to owning land and people, what a drag."

C.K. is funny in both the ironic type of way and the slap your knee type of way if you are into knee slapping. He's funny in the way that you can actually get tired of laughing. But his ironic funny makes you think deeply. I've been told that his comedy routine on White privilege makes White people notice their privilege in ways that an academic lecture doesn't. Perhaps it is the release of endorphins that occurs as you are hearing something from a person who normally makes you laugh but this time is saying something that isn't silly, but instead quite profound.

    C.K.'s rationale on White privilege, being something that is easily missed by most Whites, ideally accentuates how the notion of privilege transcends race. His references to a time in history where Blacks wouldn't want to return also speaks immediately to male privilege, sexual orientation privilege, and ability privilege, if not more. All the people oppressed in the context of any of these underprivileged groups have moments in history they'd prefer not to visit.

Observations on privilege aren't easy to articulate and can just as easily place people on the defensive. However, if you promote an approach of "keeping it real," then no one is above criticism as long as privilege is articulated in as diplomatic a way as possible. Consistent with diplomatically keeping it real in the second teaching of the EDTF course at SUNY Plattsburgh, an intriguing moment arose that I have never and will never forget. This class was co-developed by Deb Light and me. We had been colleagues at the Center for Diversity, Pluralism, and Inclusion for five years and knew that we could better serve our university in a teaching capacity if we were part of the teaching mechanism. As a result, we designed EDTF to create conversations around difficult themes of diversity and social justice, leadership, and development of allies. Well, after one class, when our students were milling about discussing their upcoming projects with Deb or one of the 8–10 teacher's assistants available, a young man who was in the very first EDTF class we taught sauntered up to me, leaned against me, and whispered in my ear a thought that was as profound as it is true. He said in response to seeing Professor Light in consultation with one of our female students,

"Look at them, swimming in privilege, yet drowning in oppression!" (Angel Acosta, INT303 EDTF Teacher's Assistant, Fall 2005)

It was so on point that I stopped cold in my tracks and asked him if that statement was an Angel Acosta original. He said yes, it was. I then informed him that I not only would never forget his statement, but was positive I would use it often. He smiled, turned, and walked away with an Angel Acosta swag that up to that time I hadn't noticed. As he walked away, I thought what may have prompted him to say that was the opportunity to have a witty moment with one of his favorite professors. However, why it resonated with me so profoundly was the way it poetically framed our multiple identities. At any given moment we are just one heartbeat away from morphing from oppressed into oppressor.

Another example of this type of privilege can be seen in the never-ending debate over same-sex marriage. I was saddened when I heard President Obama state that arriving at his perspective on same-sex marriage was challenging for him. I applaud his honesty in admitting the fact that as a leader he is not always clear on the issues he must engage. Far too often our leaders act as if uncertainty on an issue is something to be ashamed of. James Loewen (1995), in his chapter titled "The Land of Opportunity" from his renowned book *Lies My Teacher Told Me*, once said that historians have felt it necessary to whitewash the truth so as to hide any doubts that our leaders may have had. This he gives as a reason why in our high school history textbooks we had not been told of Abraham Lincoln's indecisiveness on the slavery issue (p. 179).

In the economic/political climate where countries are going bankrupt and nations are clamoring for democracy, many of the positions President Obama takes are greatly influenced by keeping America situated in a safe, resourceful space. However, as a Black man (or, at the very least, a biracial man) you would think that his understanding of the struggles of Blacks to obtain an egalitarian status within American society would make him not just more sympathetic to others' struggles to achieve the same within the United States, but more committed to being an ally in assisting others to overcome their struggles. Is his hesitation in supporting the eradication of homophobic practices *political posturing*, or earnest angst? As odd as it sounds, I hope it is political posturing. I expect Obama did the necessary posturing required to increase his chances of being reelected so he could then make the difference he couldn't make cleaning up an inherited mess.

Nonetheless, an Obama "swimming-drowning" moment is evident in his maleness contrasted to his race. He experiences another swimming-drowning moment as a member of the upper class contrasted with his humble beginnings as the son of a single mother. It is, however, his heterosexual lifestyle/marriage contrasted with the sociopolitical voice he allowed to be muffled in the same-sex marriage debate that had me reflecting on the lyrics from soulful song stylist Marvin Gaye's "Inner City Blues": "Makes me want to holla, throw up both my hands."

It makes you wonder why more people don't consider stepping into a leadership moment. It is without question easier to mindlessly follow a leader, no matter how unethical he is in a given moment, when the majority of people in the room have already succumbed to his dysfunctional leadership. It takes serious intestinal fortitude to transcend the mob mentality. It takes serious self-confidence to walk in a direction opposite what scholar Beverly Tatum (2000a) frames as "the moving walkway":

> I sometimes visualize the ongoing cycle of racism as a moving walkway at the airport. Active racist behavior is equivalent to walking fast on the conveyor belt. The person engaged in active racist behavior has identified with

the ideology of White supremacy and is moving with it. Passive racist behavior is equivalent to standing still on the walkway. No overt effort is being made, but the conveyor belt moves the bystanders along to the same destination as those who are actively walking. Some of the bystanders may feel the motion of the conveyor belt, see the active racists ahead of them, and choose to turn around, unwilling to go to the same destination as the White supremacists. But unless they are walking actively in the opposite direction at a speed faster than the conveyor belt—unless they are actively antiracist—they will find themselves carried along with the others. (p. 81)

If leadership were easy everyone would be a leader. Since it isn't, we often find leaders making comments that give the appearance they are comfortable with sprinting on the moving walkway. Republican presidential candidates Mitt Romney and Rick Santorum attempting to appease their constituents both made statements during the Republican primaries of 2011–12 about America that were problematic to decipher as anything but privileged, if not pejorative.

Romney's statement about living in the "real streets of America" is troubling. Romney, an extremely wealthy man, stating that he lives in the "real streets of America" makes about as much sense as me saying that I should be starting in the NBA All Star game instead of Michael Jordan because of the fact that I hit three jump shots in a row over my 16-year-old son. No doubt Romney's experiences are real for him, and he lives as much as anyone in America's real streets, but the notion of real for Romney versus real for me, or you, can be so very different. Romney's assertion that the streets he has lived on are real, or perhaps more to his point, more real than others, suggests that others' experiences on American streets dissimilar from those Romney has lived on are not valid.

Santorum's statement was, "There are no classes in America. We are a country that doesn't allow for titles, we don't put people in classes." Santorum's assertion that there are no classes in America is as awkward and difficult to process as Romney's "real streets of America" comment. His assertion that there are no classes in America saddens me in that it reveals how pathetically inadequate we are at educating future leaders. Unless Santorum was *politically posturing*, saying it to just placate his audience within that moment, how could it be possible that a person as well traveled as this previous senator could not have a clue about socioeconomic class distinctions? I'm not trying to label the senator as an opportunist, or am I? Well, I'm not trying to bail him out for possibly saying what he feels his constituency wants to hear, instead of what those individuals need to hear.

Santorum is a male who doesn't allow for abortion, even in cases of rape. In the instance I've outlined he has a level of access to things that others don't who aren't Rick Santorum. In the scenario of rape with no choice to abort, his maleness gives him the privilege to not even conceive the harshness of a reality wherein a woman must carry the scars of being violated simply because others have legislated it so. It begs the question, Would his position be the same if it were his 13-year-old daughter who was raped and faced with such an ordeal?

Interestingly enough, my point about specific types of education that must occur early in our development as leaders could not be better framed than by the experiences I have with college students both on my campus and off. Around the country when I am engaging students about diversity and social justice in general and socioeconomic class specifically, I am actually made privy to their personal epiphanies surrounding the different dimensions of social justice. It is no exaggeration to say that nothing is more exhilarating than to have one of your students reveal the benefits of her education in a personal way, as done by Shanah Van Deventer in her socioeconomic paper for my EDTF course:

> To assert that, "we in the United States are reluctant to recognize class differences," is cleverly understating the great efforts that Americans have and continually demonstrate when dealing with class. I am ashamed to admit that I was extremely reluctant to even read through these articles. I had to ask myself, why? After reading about class structure it was just another smack in the face as to how privileged I am because of my race and class combined. Does this bother me? Yes. But how can benefiting so greatly from something bother an individual? For me it's thinking about how casually my mother puts 100 dollars into my bank account each week when there are so many individuals who are grateful to find change on the sidewalk that day.

Shanah's reluctance to "even read through these articles" is related to her having to engage how problematic some dimensions of her worldview had been up to the point of her personal epiphany. More so, it is also a statement about how lacking in sophistication some aspects of her upbringing were in terms of diversity and social justice. None of this is something that Shanah, or any of us, for that matter, should be ashamed of. We learn what we learn as children without the opportunity to tell our parents, uncles, aunts, clergy, neighbors, and friends that we only want to learn what will make us ideal citizens as adults. We couldn't order that level of consciousness if we some-how had that level of insight.

The fact that Shanah—a very intelligent person who represents herself extremely well in all regards I am familiar with—would assess how she has processed the world around her (after being challenged about her possible privileged perspective) is why diversity and social justice educators are inde-fatigable about engaging and challenging previously unchallenged perspec-tives. Shanah's consciousness, once awakened, can never again rest peacefully in the face of social injustices.

So what would Shanah do with Romney's and/or Santorum's state-ments? Probably something quite similar to what I would do except perhaps with more edge. Why? Because Shanah would recognize the leverage she has to challenge others who have succumbed to their White privilege. She would not only challenge the statements, but lean into the challenge, knowing that if she didn't fully engage the dysfunctional moment, it might fester and grow.

Problematic Purveyors of Privilege

Perhaps no one has contributed more to the creation of White allies against racism over the first decade of the millennium than Dr. Eddie Moore Jr. Eddie, a very close friend and colleague of mine whom you might notice I continue to mention in this book, is the architect, founder, and president of one of the fastest growing academic conferences in the United States, the White Privilege Conference (WPC). Having both attended and presented at Eddie's conference, I nonetheless, as a confidant of Eddie's, someone whom he is comfortable being challenged by, once challenged him about the name of the conference. I was positive that he would get more mileage, especially in terms of diversity and social justice, if he named his conference "The Privilege Conference." My thinking was that naming it WPC might be polarizing and limit participation by people seeking more than an extended conversation on racism. I thought naming it The Privilege Conference would invite more people to feel included to articulate their struggles with other forms of privilege. Eddie's judgment turned out to be accurate, because a decade later the WPC is still growing, while his conference engages many forms of privilege.

My plea for assistance in battling other forms of privilege was heeded, because as the conference grew, so did its conversations along many dimen-sions of privilege. However, in the North Country of New York it was racial privilege and socioeconomic privilege that I would find myself battling more than anything else. An example of this is best illustrated by an unexpected response I received from an In My Opinion (IMO) article I submitted to the largest newspaper in northeastern New York, the *Press-Republican*. With a Barack Obama presidency looming potentially large on the horizon in August 2008, I penned a satirical piece that posed questions about how America might perceive a Black family in the White House. Here is the IMO:

> All of the changes in policy aside, is America ready for the varying differences that will also be visited upon the White House by its possible Black residents? If Barack Obama ascends to the presidency and the accompanying benefit of residency in the presidential mansion, the White House, what will be the impact on one of America's most sacred symbols?
>
> How many more ridiculous stereotypes will a so-called Black president have to endure/avoid than other previous presidents? The White House has not been known to have little Black children running down its hallways, or never had a preponderance of Black folk deep within its inner sanctum! How will the nation respond to the sounds of Coltrane, Hyman, Vandross and Sade possibly resonating throughout the halls of its most hallowed domicile?
>
> What will be the reaction if residents and overnight guests are often witnessed fluffing out their Afros in the hallways or having their hair braided on the White House lawn? Am I exaggerating when I say that America's way of seeing its president and the presidency itself will greatly change if Obama ascends to the position as it would have if Hillary had taken office? McCain in the White House might be different in how he handles his business, but in terms of the social dimensions of this White House under McCain's administration, the house would be no less White! Is that a problem? Why or why not?
>
> Am I making a mountain out of a mole hill, "Soul Train" out of "American Band Stand," "The Cosbys" out of "Father Knows Best" when I say the White House is headed for darker days? Does that have to be a bad thing? Seriously, how devastating will it be for the presidential photo gallery to have some racial diversity? Won't it benefit America to have a leader who looks more like the majority of people in the world at least every now and then? Questions about his ability are moot! Even a fool knows that America would not elect a Black presidential candidate if he were incompetent, though as comedian Chris

Rock once said, America not long ago did elect a C student. But this disconnect between what America wouldn't do with a Black presidential candidate and what it recently did with our currently sitting president isn't really symbolic of more profound, if not troubling statements about American hypocrisy, is it? Well, is it?

If the Obamas celebrate Juneteenth, will that finally elevate this Black celebration to at least a symbolic holiday status? No other president that I know of truly celebrated this holiday. Will it at least provide an additional symbol of the different America underrepresented people often live in, even to the point of significant holidays that some groups share that many others don't have a clue about (Juneteenth being the celebration of the date that slaves in the deep, Deep South [Galveston, Texas] finally received word [over two years late] that they had been emancipated).

Will Air Force One pick up the nickname Soul Plane? If the Obamas hire an all-white staff, will this surreal inversion be any more replete with irony? After all, since presidents have a tendency to appoint political colleagues to pivotal positions, will people recognize the unwarranted scrutiny and hypocrisy leveled against the so-called Black president if the majority of Obama's appointments are as Black as other presidents' appointments were White? In the grand scheme of things, should any of that even matter? Not really! Unfortunately, for many, it will!

That is why we need this political Jackie Robinson to not only enter the majors, but be as successful at that level as Jackie was! Only then will the floodgates be thrown wide open for the other underrepresented individuals who will have to endure the insensitive stereotypes before them until this new reality becomes the rule instead of the exception. Since many Black men somehow inspire a certain level of comfort in unfamiliar people, allowing them to assume familiarity with another (did someone say privilege), will it be just a matter of time before Obama isn't seen as Mr. President, but instead as Brother Barack? Maybe that will instill an additional change in the way the presidency is viewed as well as the ensuing actions emanating from within the Oval office. Maybe this president/brother will be our keeper, or a keeper himself!

Now, seriously, I don't enjoy admitting that I was so naive I didn't expect any response to my satirical piece. However, if I had expected a response what I received was beyond my wildest imaginings. Here is an excerpt of that response:

> The recently published In My Opinion by J.W. Wiley was offensive, if not for its blatant hypocrisy, then for its thinly disguised contempt of local voters who happen NOT to be African American.
>
> Only Wiley could emerge unscathed after writing, ". . . the White House is headed for darker days," a juvenile reference to the possibility that Barack O'Bama [*sic*] and his family might one day occupy the White House. Whether it was intended as humor or not, imagine the reaction if a white author had penned similar words. That poor soul would be labeled as "insensitive" and a "closet racist." The Press-Republican would be forced to apologize for having published such drivel, and Wiley himself would describe the entire affair as "troublesome."
>
> But Wiley doesn't stop there. The author, whose job is to direct the effort at PSU for "Diversity, Pluralism, and Inclusion," presses on with a prediction of stereotypical blacks who loiter on the White House lawn beading their hair into cornrows, while friends of Obama are "fluffing out their afros" in the hallways of the Executive Mansion. This racist contrivance is presumed to frighten the reader and so Wiley scolds us for not wanting a president who "looks more like the majority of people in the world."
>
> And then, in a breathtaking display of specious reasoning, Wiley declares that any "questions about his (Obama's) ability are moot"—as if the only litmus test for presidential candidates is the color of their skin—and further asserts that Obama is the "Jackie Robinson" of American politics.
>
> Obama's supporters should be insulted by Wiley's sophistry, and fans of Jackie Robinson should be equally incensed . . . Barack Obama is no Jackie Robinson.
>
> And no one, especially J.W. Wiley, should argue that the color of a man's skin is more important than his ability.

Now, the author of this rebuttal is not just founder and president of his own corporation, an adjunct professor at a local college, and one of the most politically powerful men in the North Country of New York, but also one of the leaders of an ultraconservative Republican Tea Party that arguably if not oddly enough grew out of the Obama presidency. As a result, it isn't surprising that prior to the election that gave the United States its first Black president (and resounding Black precedent) any hint of such a thing would thrust people subconsciously—if not consciously paranoid about such an occurrence—into a frenzy. However, framing my lighthearted satirical assertion that the country might be headed toward "darker days" as a "juvenile reference" was a bit hard hitting. Of course, we must not look beyond the fact that in-group dialogue allows me to say things as a Black man that another non-Black person shouldn't dare say. Whether it seems right or wrong, certain dysfunctional language among members of a group is often deemed acceptable whereas outsiders using the same language are easily cast as perpetrators of blatant disrespect toward the very same group. But the obviousness of my satire, especially in the larger context of my IMO, could only be interpreted as problematic by someone choosing not to appreciate my attempt at satire with the possible looming scenario. More evidence of a predisposition toward wanting to take me to task for my Obama satire can be ascertained when considering his personal attack on me and other comments from his response to me. For example, how does "having their hair braided" become "beading their hair into cornrows"? The reality of braiding and beading isn't necessarily that different, though beading their hair into cornrows definitely requires beads, and I made no mention of cornrows. More so, why is it seen as me trying to "frighten the reader" just because I mention different scenarios available to spectators? I am accused of "scolding" the reader and "specious reasoning." I am chastised for "scolding" North Country Whites for not desiring a racially underrepresented person. My reasoning is deemed specious for being emphatic about the fact that Obama's qualifications more than adequately frame him as a very different type of leader whom others, many who resemble him, will joyfully celebrate.

Of course I responded. How could I not? As one of the primary architects for social justice in my community I couldn't all of a sudden lose my voice, especially after a public affront by someone apparently looking to use me as a point of departure to further advance his political agenda. Hence, my response:

> TO THE EDITOR: How does it feel to return to your community after using an ad hominem argument? Sorry you weren't receptive to my hypothetical scenario of a new dynamic in the White House. Aren't you concerned that not only didn't you get it, but didn't get it to such an extent that you embarrassed yourself publicly by going after me more than the points in the In My Opinion (IMO) piece I wrote?
>
> Even worse, in the process of attempting to ride to the rescue of local voters, you insulted them. Your inability to recognize the attempt

at satire in my IMO may have been exacerbated by an inadequate representation on my part, but matters worsened when you declared I had "disguised contempt of local voters" and then didn't substantiate the claim. How was I exhibiting contempt of local voters?

You take me to task for a series of "what ifs" surrounding Barack Obama's possible ascension to the White House. What is it really that perturbs you? You called my reasoning specious, but seldom if ever addressed anything that would provide ostensible evidence of your understanding. Don't just read, but think about what you are reading.

I am intrigued by your take on me attempting to frighten the reader. How is my articulating the possibility of Black folk fluffing out their afros or braiding their hair frightening? Just because the possibility of that occurring may be frightening to you, doesn't mean it is to others. It is always so fascinating to unpack the subtleties of what people say!

I know my presence represents change and when change takes place, often certain privileges are lost. It takes a courageous person to be receptive to change, even when its benefits aren't guaranteed.

J. W. Wiley

Ironically, after this high-visibility exchange garnered publicity and further framed him and me as rivals, we were approached about furthering our discussion in a debate format before a Rotary audience, which we ultimately did. The day it occurred I walked into the dining area as one of only two Black people in the entire room of more than 100 people. The other was a college sophomore who had an Afro fully fluffed out in a fashion popularized by scholar-activist Angela Davis. This young woman also happened to be my daughter Vanessa. Her brown-skinned loyalty amid a sea of Whiteness was something that I can't quite articulate in terms of its significance to me. Vanessa and I were also accompanied by a near and dear friend of ours, a beautiful, brainy blonde whose very presence with me may have ruffled more feathers. Suffice it to say, while it was refreshing to not be the only Black person, little did I know that the debate would breed confrontational moments with other Tea Partiers. As if this altercation with a community leader wasn't enough, when I also challenged a state senator about her hypocrisy—relative to same-sex marriage—the Tea Party leader's college-age son then attempted to take me to task in a fashion similar to that of his father who wrote the earlier In My Opinion critique of my satirical piece on the Obamas in the White House. Just as I had written the satirical offering that speculated about an Obama White House, I wrote the following piece challenging the very well-respected politician. I hope you notice how much I went out of my way to project respect toward the senator while nonetheless challenging her political stance.

Could the *Press-Republican*, a well respected newspaper, have been reporting accurately on the comments of State Sen. Betty Little in their article headlined, "Little spurns gay-marriage alternative" (Friday, April 24)? Is it possible that Sen. Little, a well received, seemingly sophisticated politician could have actually made the comments that reporter Joe LoTemplio stated she made in his article? Say it ain't so, Joe!

The article quoted the esteemed Senator as saying, "Life still evolves, and there are ways to give equal rights, and I think we can do that through civil unions and other ways."

Until I read the part where she reportedly said "civil unions," I thought she was talking about race relations and the phase in American history where "ways to give equal rights" to disenfranchised so-called Negroes were through legislation that was called "separate but equal." Yes, if I believed that Sen. Little had actually said the above statement attributed to her, I would possibly think that she believes in a separate-but-equal approach. Could civil unions—which essentially separate gay unions from marriage while pretending to make them equal to marriage—be the solution to upholding the so-called sanctity of marriage?

Allegedly, Sen. Little also added, "They are thrusting their beliefs on people, to some extent." That statement sounds like something people might have said about the abolitionists who were "thrusting their beliefs on people." Thankfully, they thrust their beliefs forcefully enough, or I'd be called in from the cotton fields to be whipped for even mentioning a white woman, let alone questioning a Senator's comments. Oh, no, that's not the case, because the women's movement benefitted directly/indirectly from the abolitionists' efforts regarding slavery. In other words, if I were still a slave in this country, so might Sen. Little have just been somebody's Betty, a second-class citizen herself with little more rights than the beast of burden I would still have been.

The reason this is so difficult for me to comprehend, in terms of Sen. Little actually saying something so short sighted, is that her statement "Life still evolves, and there are ways to give equal rights, and I think we can do that through civil unions and other ways" is probably what some man once said about women's rights. I am certain that Sen. Little must recognize how dire the plight once was for women in their struggle for equal rights. I am certain Sen. Little understands that, all too often, underprivileged groups, upon attaining privilege, forget the intricacies of their struggle and become so complacent, perhaps from the efforts to achieve their egalitarian status, that they lose their sense of justice and slip into self-centered seats of comfort.

On some level nowadays, accepting Black people, or at least acting as if we accept Blacks and other races, has become hip, and/or cool, or the politically correct thing to do. So most people at least try to wear that sheep skin to hide the wolves they really are, at least in terms of cloaking their xenophobia. Somehow, though, in this millennial moment, people believe that it is okay to have an open season on gays, lesbians, transgendered and bisexuals, saying whatever they want to say, when they want to say it. Come on, haven't they figured out, like the commercial of days long past suggested, that we don't ride in our parents' Oldsmobile any longer?

I have been reading Joe LoTemplio's writing for quite some time. I know as a professor I have biases that come through in my teaching and I often tell my students to use their heads and analyze thoroughly what I teach them, as well as other lessons they learn or have learned. If it doesn't fit, don't embrace it. Mr. LoTemplio also isn't above succumbing to his biases, either. Maybe, just maybe, he got Sen. Little wrong. Maybe this is the poorest reporting Mr. LoTemplio has ever done in his career.

Maybe I was dreaming and imagined the article, and like Pam in that infamous Dallas episode, it never happened, though it felt so real. Or, maybe my take on the fair-minded Senator from Queensbury was incorrect.

Maybe I'm wrong about her, and she is only as fair minded as she is open minded! Oh, say it ain't so, Joe!

Obviously, my philosophical training and appreciation of Socrates's reputation as the gadfly of Athens had gotten me into trouble again. I imagine to those who were dedicated to maintaining the status quo I was becoming the pest of Plattsburgh. As a result, in various circles it may have been determined that someone had to take me down, or attempt to do so. The fact that it came from the son of the man I had debated earlier, who also happened to be an ex-student of mine, made it even more intriguing. I remember wondering when he took my EDTF course after I had debated his father that he might be affected by the enlightening dialogue that the class was becoming famous for having. Apparently I was wrong, as evidenced by his response in the form of the following excerpted IMO:

> In a *Press-Republican* In My Opinion Mr. J.W. Wiley claimed that Sen. Betty Little's position against gay marriage is similar to those who opposed women's suffrage or racial equality. Not only is this insulting to our state senator, it is hypocritical of Mr. Wiley, the self proclaimed leader of tolerance for our community and for SUNY Plattsburgh.
>
> It should not be necessary to remind a man of Mr. Wiley's intellect of the history of women in America, let alone black history. Throughout the better half of the 20th Century, African-Americans were lynched, tarred and feathered, unjustly prosecuted, fire hosed, and even prohibited from enjoying a nice dinner out into town. Until 1920, women in America did not have any say as to who would represent them in Congress or in the White House. For the longest time in our history, women were not even allowed to own property.
>
> With this brief history lesson in mind, I ask you, Mr. Wiley, when was the last gay couple fire hosed? How many gay couples were turned away at the voting booth in the recent 2008 election? Which real-estate company prohibited a gay couple from purchasing a house? Which bank denied a mortgage loan to a gay couple? Have you recently seen a drinking fountain for homosexuals and another for heterosexuals? The barriers, torments, and the humiliation that women and blacks had to face as well as overcome throughout American history, are a far cry from the social or legal discriminations that homosexuals rarely face, if at all, in today's society.
>
> Sen. Little's position against gay marriage is a moral and religious point of view. As an A student in one of your previous classes, I was told by you that, as sophisticated human beings, we should be open to and accepting of other viewpoints, regardless of that person's background, religion, race or gender. Anything less than that would be "intolerant."
>
> You also instructed your students to believe that insulting a person with a different viewpoint is a sign of intolerance and should not be accepted. I would like to assure you, Mr. Wiley, that your comparison of a New York state senator to a segregationist or a male chauvinist is extremely insulting and a sign of your own intolerance.
>
> Let me calm your fears, Mr. Wiley: You will not see our state senator fire hosing homosexuals in the streets of Plattsburgh.

Unlike you, Sen. Little managed to express her opinion in the *Press-Republican* without insulting those of a different viewpoint. Sen. Little is a woman of integrity, honor and courage, and for that she deserves the utmost respect. It is a sad day in the North Country when the "spokesman" for tolerance feels compelled to insult a woman simply because she has a viewpoint that differs from his.

It is a shame that you feel compelled to refer to our state senator as "Betty," the second-class citizen. The rest of the North Country, including myself, refer to her as the 45th's finest—Sen. Elizabeth O'T. Little. God Bless America.

It is quite intriguing how someone sets the table for his or her criticism of others. However, beyond the fact that this young man was president of a politically conservative organization on campus, I came to discover that he may also be the senator's godson. Nonetheless, in the son of the Tea Party president's response I am presented as a self-proclaimed leader of tolerance, which couldn't be further from the truth. I have never promoted tolerance, though I can appreciate it as a rung on the diversity and social justice ladder. And I have never anointed myself as anything but a concerned citizen with no hesitation to voice his opinion. I didn't appoint myself to direct the Center for Diversity at SUNY Plattsburgh, though I work diligently and passionately to always deserve the appointment. As such, I once again deemed it necessary for me to publicly respond to this attempt at publicly chastising me for my challenge to a state senator.

TO THE EDITOR: Though you were an "A" student it seems it's time to teach you again.

It is possible to get an "A" in a class and not learn much. Anyone who has taken a class from me knows I don't teach tolerance. Tolerance is an antiquated notion of what diversity is about. Someone else taught you that diversity is synonymous with tolerance and somehow, with that in your head, you went through my class, which addresses something contrary and you never heard it. Oh, and people tolerate babies crying on airplanes, headaches, and students that don't thoroughly read the articles that they are attempting to take someone to task over.

Reread the In My Opinion I wrote and notice I didn't identify Sen. Betty Little as "Betty." I said if men had held the same position against women that Sen. Little held on same sex marriages she would have never become Sen. Betty Little. Instead she may have only been "somebody's

Betty." There is a difference between becoming somebody's Betty and being Sen. Betty Little.

Your points about gays not being whipped/beaten or disenfranchised reveals how immature your world view is, as well as your inadequate attention span. While you earned the "A," that you mentioned as leverage to attack me, we watched "Boys Don't Cry." Teena Brandon's experiences in that film contradict your point. Were you in class that day?

It isn't intolerance to challenge a politician's opinion; it's a civic duty. I respect any person who contributes their time/energy towards making this world better. However, if she hasn't considered the implications of certain statements she makes she must be challenged. If what I did to Sen. Little was intolerance, then everyone would be intolerant or no one would ever challenge anything.

J. W. Wiley

He did not respond, though, surprisingly, someone else from the community did:

TO THE EDITOR: Reading the In My Opinion regarding J.W. Wiley's article [on Betty Little], I wondered if [the author] and I read the same piece by Wiley. So I reread Wiley's comments about State Sen. Betty Little's gay-marriage stance. It appears [the author] cherry-picked one reference to the senator in which she was referred to as "somebody's Betty," solely in the context of the second-class citizenship she "might" endure today if not for the women's rights equality struggle. There are at least eight other references by Mr. Wiley where he writes respectfully, "Sen. Little . . ."

[The author] calls Mr. Wiley the "self-proclaimed leader of tolerance for our community and for SUNY Plattsburgh." Mr. Wiley's title of director of the Center for Diversity, Pluralism and Inclusion at PSUNY hardly seems "self-proclaimed" and more than qualifies him to speak on issues related to unequal treatment of any U.S. citizen. [The author] has the right to sing the praises of Sen. Little, and "self-proclaim" his excellent grade (A) in Mr. Wiley's class. However, it is not clear to this reader that he "gets" the true meaning of diversity, pluralism and inclusion. His statement that "homosexuals rarely face, if at all, social or legal discrimination in today's society," mystified me.

> A college education is not just about career preparation or fluffing one's political resume. Its broader purpose is to engage in critical inquiry and stretch our awareness and understanding of society and the human condition beyond our own parochial interests or personal bias. [The] Young [author] delivers his version of a history lesson about the discrimination of blacks and women, while blithely minimizing and ignoring the countless, historical occurrences and harmful impact of social and legal discrimination against homosexuals (i.e., [Matthew] Shepard). A simple Google search would have sufficed.

The response of support from a community member whom I didn't even know is evidence of how important it is to have the courage to put your voice out there. My doing that inspired her to join me in challenging the illogical rhetoric of two prominent voices that were confident in setting the tone for the political discourse in the area. I am not sure if my/our not being intimidated, combined with an adequate amount of eloquence, is what staved off any more attempts at using me to gain momentum for launching and/or maintaining the modicum of privilege that this father-and-son duo steadfastly desired to keep. It also could have been the emergence of an ally who prevented the two Tea Partiers from any further public attempts at spitting in my coffee. But whatever the case, I have not heard a word from either one since. While I saw their efforts at trying to gain momentum for their political agenda, I also can appreciate the sentiment of Warren Blumenfeld (2000), when he stated, "Individuals maintain oppressive behaviors to gain certain rewards or to avoid punishment, to protect their self esteem against psychological doubts or conflicts, to enhance their value systems, or to categorize others in an attempt to comprehend a complex world" (p. 271). Blumenfeld's analysis on the motivation of some individuals to oppress others may assist us in unpacking some of the most problematic purveyors of privilege. I have no doubt that both father and son were looking to justify their untenable positions so as to "protect their self esteem against psychological doubts," to "enhance their value systems," and to "categorize others in an attempt to comprehend a complex world." It is difficult for me to imagine how anyone could justify playing a role in supporting a political party that committed to undercutting a newly elected president who hadn't even taken office yet. So, in an effort to insulate themselves from psychological doubts it became somewhat necessary that they devalue President Obama and any of his support systems. By devaluing Obama, a Democrat, they might think they enhanced their own systems. Along the way if they could categorize me as dysfunctional and a walking contradiction in terms, then their blatant hypocrisy as played out in how they were responding to this American president would not necessarily be seen as nonsensical.

Mirrorless Masters of Menace

> *And I'll never let my son have an ego*
> *He'll be nice to everyone, wherever we go*
> *I mean, I might even make 'em be Republican*
> *So everybody know he love white people*

> —Kanye West and Jay-Z, "New Day"

While Kanye and Jay-Z's lyrics, if interpreted literally, could be construed as overcompensation, if not paranoia, can we really dismiss the sentiment as not indicative of the type of action that many people who are disenfranchised might consider taking to advance their child's situation? After all, how many Americans believe at the very least that Americans are all about fair play? What American parent would then look the other way after a staged scenario involving their daughter's denial of the opportunity to be the first female class president because precocious boys prearranged a method to discount votes from the girls' classmates, which might have won her the election? Is this the American way? If so, who modeled this "fair" behavior for them?

Anyone ascending to any presidency in this fashion is pathetic, and definitely not the type of leader I would follow. Any presidency obtained in such a manner would forever be tainted by her or him winning—perhaps not illegally—but definitely immorally.

What is occurring around the country in response to possible voting fraud, voting rights, and what ultimately amounts to voting suppression is reprehensible. No one wants election fraud, and taking precautions to address such things makes sense if it is a legitimate concern. However, if there is little to no history of voting fraud in a region, and yet a plan that could make it more difficult for some to vote than others is devised to protect that community against possible fraud, something is amiss.

It is unimaginable that people would attempt to win at the cost of obstructing an American birthright, one that people died for. Are the individuals orchestrating the suppression of voters fearful of something? Perhaps it is paranoia about the ascension to political prominence of possibly divergent voices? Is it far-fetched to imagine there may have been overt concern about the possible immediate success by a precocious president who *audaciously believed he could succeed?*

How do we explain the attendance of Paul Ryan, a vice presidential candidate in 2012, at a certain meeting the night of the January 2009 inaugural ball? Per Robert Draper's book *Do Not Ask What Good We Do: Inside the U.S. House of Representatives* (2012), it has been revealed that a plan was devised to undermine a yet-to-be-inaugurated president. All the participants were allegedly committed to the task of essentially (character/politically) assassinating the president. You couldn't make this stuff up.

I challenge students who stand by and watch bullying occur. I tell them that they themselves are also bullies if they could have played a role in eradicating bullying and conveniently chose to look the other way. If voting suppression occurs—whereby it potentially further disenfranchises those already somewhat disenfranchised—are those conscious of the transgression anything more than bystanders? How millions of adults can stand by, turn the other cheek, and benefit from their party's affiliates' not so subtle subterfuge is one of the most intriguing happenings I've witnessed in all of my years of watching American hypocrisy cloaked as American democracy.

What do we tell our children if / when they get wind of the way some Americans manipulate others for their own advantage? I tell mine that bullies exist everywhere, not just students in schools, but adults in business, politics, and national governments. I tell them that actions that enhance xenophobia, and bolster bullying, promote privilege.

I tell them that bullies demonstrate their insensitivity, cowardliness, and ignorance when they attempt to elevate themselves at someone else's expense. We must imagine bullies as "mirrorless masters of menace," because if they had mirrors how could they stomach to see—within their own reflection—a vacant soul devoid of the humanity to consider others' hearts? I try to teach them that often bullies seek and survive in the shadows. Ultimately, they know that both bullies and societies on the whole will benefit greatly when we shine the light on these "captains of coercion" early and often and force them to either crawl back under their rocks, or change their ugly ways.

It is incomprehensible to think that these "mirrorless masters of menace" would "elevate themselves" at the expense of the American public. By doing so, they reveal themselves as "insensitive," "cowardly," and "ignorant" if they think that they alone know what is best for "all" Americans, can manipulate others to accomplish their goals, and are fooling anyone.

Even after all this consideration of politicians' privilege imprisoning them it is difficult to understand how people not only protect their privilege, but also articulate certain positions that further and illogically promote such problematic protection of privilege. For example, Rush Limbaugh's comments about President Obama's position on same-sex marriage reek of his White-heterosexist privilege: "We've arrived at a point where the President of the United States is going to lead a war on traditional marriage" (Limbaugh, 2012). Limbaugh's assertion about President Obama's endorsement of gay marriage is racist because he knows that his audience, since November 2008, if not earlier, are not fans of President Obama. Hence, any reference to Obama's differences further endears Limbaugh to those who revere him and his Obama bashing. Limbaugh's assertion that Obama (or anyone else, for that matter) is leading an assault on traditional marriage implies that traditional marriage is an ideal that should not be challenged. Since the traditional notion of marriage involves a heterosexual couple, and Limbaugh projects himself as heterosexual, it can easily be construed that he wants to protect his privilege of being heterosexual in a society that rewards him for being such.

Limbaugh's attack on traditional marriage is nonsensical when logically considered. Two men or two women marrying doesn't necessarily affect the way so-called traditional marriage is viewed. After all, what is traditional marriage? At one time it was only validated if within the same race, socioeconomic class, or religion. At one time a woman with thoughts of having a voice in a marriage was doomed to be a spinster, or perpetually be sent to the proverbial woodshed. Eventually that changed. President Obama's existence itself is proof of how untenable Limbaugh's position is, considering Obama is the product of a nontraditional marriage. As well, Limbaugh himself has been married "traditionally" four times. It seems Limbaugh himself was engaged in his own war on marriage if we consider its intended sanctity.

Limbaugh makes problematic statements that then provide a larger buzz for him to find ways to even further exacerbate, like this racist statement he made about the NFL: "Look, let me put it to you this way: the NFL all too often looks like a game between the Bloods and the Crips without any weapons. There, I said it" (Limbaugh, 2007). So, then, by Limbaugh's assertion hockey must resemble the Republican Party. It would be difficult to refute the parallel. Its players, coaches, and owners are predominantly White, as are the local, regional, and national politicians. But Limbaugh doesn't make statements like this because it wouldn't get him any mileage. Referring to the NFL as an interaction between the Bloods and Crips contributes to America's seeing these mostly well-educated, high-priced athletes as thugs if not criminals more than role models. It is statements like this and Limbaugh's lengthy record of being socially inconsiderate that situates him as one of the many culprits that I deem the Paranoid Prisoners of Privilege.

Engaging Stereotypes/Exclusion With Leadership Moments

Most people, though, don't have the ability on their own to witness the dysfunctional path they are heading down until invaluable energy that they can't retrieve is lost. We sit in these conversations where people are ridiculing others, labeling people from one interaction, painting everyone in a group with the same brush, and don't truly unpack our actions.

The opportunity to step into a leadership moment and change the game is always available to someone who can transcend the routine of going along to get along. Most of us are in a habit of maintaining our privileged flow and are appreciative of no interruptions. We don't think about the long-term problems that arise from allowing one moment of social injustice to play out in our presence. Challenging a 10-year-old Barack Obama to think about his casual usage of the phrase "you guys," to consider how it keeps men in the center of conversations adversely, or a 10-year-old Rush Limbaugh who had a predisposition to call women girls, which infantilizes women, may have been significant enough to serve as a catalyst for a change in their consciousness around this type of discourse. If all of our leaders in their precocious youth were introduced to some of the subtleties of the language we use to engage one another, the games we all play, consciously, subconsciously, or dysconsciously, would be quite different today, if not lessened or gone. Instead, though, we continue on with our inconsideration largely because it has become habit forming. We have been accepting as well as using the easiest, most convenient ways of verbal exchange. Once it is brought to our attention, though, we are better armed to avoid succumbing to cowardly behavior.

> "Condemning people out of habit is easy.
> Overcoming deep-seated prejudice requires courage."
>
> —Corvino (1997, p. 144)

It requires courage to take ownership of our leadership moment. Ideally, a leadership moment should have occurred somewhere earlier in the political process. Such a moment might have circumvented the problematic pursuit of privilege by those who would deny privilege as the cause of their anxiety.

As stated earlier, leadership moments are when opportunities for leadership within a context of diversity and social justice have occurred, or could have occurred. A leadership moment is that moment when an individual could make a difference, educating others by the action she takes, or perhaps modeling behaviors that inspire others to take similar actions. Unfortunately, a leadership moment is also a missed opportunity when someone was situated to make a difference and did not.

I frame leadership moments as an instantaneous opportunity to accentuate leadership choices within a context of diversity and social justice. As an example of the bold and provocative embracing of a leadership moment, consider Steven Spielberg and Woody Allen, two highly successful filmmakers. Spielberg's *The Lost World: Jurassic Park* and Allen's entire corpus both present intriguing dimensions of leadership moments. A person with a predilection toward changing the world in a globally just manner could find it strategic to use Spielberg's *Jurassic Park* and/or Allen's first 16 films as educational tools. A person with a disposition toward social justice—coupled with a moderate sense of fair play and an understanding of the power and subtlety of media messages—who is familiar with both Spielberg's and Allen's work might find it difficult not to engage their films for their imbedded messages after considering my articulation of them. I unpack some aspects of both of their works within this chapter because they are two world-renowned filmmakers who can ignite intellectual curiosity and/or perhaps assist in cultivating critical lenses.

The *Jurassic Park* excerpt provides a philosophical, sociological, methodological, political, and educational perspective. All of those perspectives are important tools allowing us to try to open our minds to the possibility of receiving layered or textured messages that we otherwise could somehow have missed. I mean, after all, when you really think about it, do we actually get the full message of any film? Of course not, because there are both intentional and unintentional messages all throughout any film.

After teaching essentially film classes, or classes where I utilize a lot of film excerpts, I am convinced that my students' way of "seeing" films becomes quite different from the way the average person "sees" them. My students learn to see, "really see," considerate/inconsiderate behavior. My students learn that intellectual curiosity is second only to intellectual discourse. My students understand how significant a leadership moment can be. They know that a leadership moment that is acted upon now is not just doing the right thing today, at this time, in this moment, but also possibly diminishing the possibility of requiring such a moment later. The students know this because of how much they have learned from participating in well-formulated conversations that feature an array of perspectives on film, many of which they really thought they had fully accessed.

Within Allen's early work, the first 16 films from his corpus, he was not consistent with the general public's perspective of New York City. Since Allen has always positioned himself as an enlightened liberal, one could argue he is living proof of Anaïs Nin's famous quote: "We don't see things as they are, we see them as we are." Woody is about as enlightened toward racism as I was about sexual orientation when I left South Central Los Angeles, where I was reared from age 2 to adulthood. Growing up, I was clueless about any aspects of a gay person's humanity because the only reference I had to gay people was profanely dysfunctional because I had never been in a discussion about sexual orientation. Sexual orientation, what is that? But my dysfunction was played out from no platform at all, at least none outside of my neighborhood in Los Angeles. I had little to no influence that was worth mentioning back in those days. Allen's dysfunction, however, played out on the international stage for all to see, though many of his viewers may not actually have known they were processing it. In his defense, I believe he did not know the impact he might have been having, or is even still having when people watch his earlier films about New York City living. Woody was guilty of perpetuating what I frame as *stereotypical inclusion* and *systematic exclusion*, two dysfunctional concepts that are ripe for leadership moments when they occur.

Stereotypical inclusion occurs when underrepresented people are portrayed in a (not necessarily deliberate) unflattering fashion. An example of this would be the Asian American friend who is always portrayed as loyal and dateless. That representation, which at first glimpse isn't seen as awkward, features the person in limited ways that further exacerbate his or her various realities as somewhat dysfunctional. *Systematic exclusion* is revealed through story lines in film that would have obvious multidimensional social dynamics playing out but unbeknownst to the viewer the writer/director may have made a decision to not include certain types of persons. An example of this is a story about urban New York that totally obliterates any notion of a Black presence, or gay presence, or socioeconomic strife, etc. More often, though, inadvertent racism (and other isms that arise authentically) reflects and/or reveals either stereotypical inclusion or systematic exclusion.

For example, while we easily see gender, socioeconomic class, race, and/or privilege at play in a film like *The Godfather*, upon its initial release it was not necessarily being assessed for its sexism, classism, or heterosexism. Nor was it scrutinized for its stereotypical inclusion and systematic exclusion, because they were both there, just not necessarily where the viewer would consciously note it. Knowing that these challenging concepts were hampering a socially just consciousness would be a good thing, except it often requires someone pointing it out. At the time *The Godfather* was being made, there was little discussion of social justice, which meant that little thought was given to one's propensity for succumbing to stereotypical inclusion or systematic exclusion or their implications. So, as part of an evaluation of films for use in leadership development in a context of diversity and social justice, I analyzed Allen's racism in film, with considerations to how he succumbs to systematic exclusion as well as stereotypical inclusion.

In Allen's defense, we really could have focused on almost any filmmakers, picked one of their societal blind spots, and taken them to task as well. Nonetheless, I use Allen films to accentuate his inability to step into a leadership moment, to challenge and/or transcend America's way of further perpetuating "isms." His films reveal him succumbing to many dysfunctional messages around differences, and then subjecting others to his representation of them as well. On so many important levels Allen's films frame the concept of leadership moment so well in the context of an ill-advised message that doesn't necessarily need to exist, but that isn't easy to contest.

It serves my purpose well to assess specific filmmakers as active agents in leadership moments for the constant deluge of dysfunctional messages that they inadvertently subject their fans to simply because they are not consciously aware of their blind spots.

> "Leadership and learning are indispensable from one another!" (from undelivered Dallas speech of November 1963)
>
> —J. F. Kennedy

> "We may not have polluted the air, but we need to take responsibility, along with others, for cleaning it up. Each of us needs to look at our own behavior. Am I perpetuating and reinforcing the negative messages so pervasive in our culture, or am I seeking to challenge them?"
>
> —Beverly Tatum (2004a, p. 80)

I am a strong proponent of the fact that leaders who understand how important it is to be savvy and sophisticated about the needs of the constituencies they may lead must continually pursue knowledge, as indicated by the John F. Kennedy quote. As well, as suggested by the Beverly Tatum quote, a leader looks inward and is realistic. It does not matter if this situation that requires leadership from someone was not caused by us. If we have the skills to alter an adverse course of events, then we need to make that happen. In the process of leading, we should also be ever vigilant in not only guarding against any negative messages that we could inadvertently put out there, but also challenging the ones that we recognize are occurring.

Examining leadership moments within a context of diversity and social justice makes sense since life inevitably represents a wide array of scenarios that ultimately reflect the wide-ranging reality of any given constituency at any given time. Effective leaders care about their constituencies and not coincidentally their constituencies are *always* quite diverse, whether they realize it or not. A common misconception about diversity is that when racial diversity is lacking there is no diversity present. This thought dismisses the other dimensions of diversity as inconsequential.

More so, understanding the influence stereotypical inclusion and systematic exclusion have, in general, requires either that we fully embrace the leadership moments necessary for us to return to an unfettered space that may arise from these influences, or that we remain oblivious to them. Articles and books that address leadership development far too often omit the topics of diversity and social justice, unless those topics were stereotypically included or systematically excluded. I am an unwavering proponent of the fact that any articulation of a concept of leadership that is bereft of diversity and social justice is inadequate.

Allen's early films, centered in New York City, often provide prime examples of stereotypical inclusion and systematic exclusion. It just does not seem plausible that Allen could articulate the New York City perspective (in 16 of his early films) without a significant characterization of a racially underrepresented person in one of them.

> "By excluding entire groups of people, those in positions of power obtain economic, political, ideological, and other privileges."
>
> —Blumenfeld (2000, p. 271)

Is it justifiable to take an artist to task for having limited vision in his or her art? Some jazz musicians do not feel the need to record country music, and rock artists do not have to perform rap. Neither is it the case that a director like Steven Spielberg has to direct a movie and perhaps pursue a socially just leadership role by undertaking a theme outside of his national character or national origin. The fact that he may choose to do so would often be predicated on economic considerations of return on investment and a belief that he might influence others more than anything else. However, omissions that do not make sense or appear to transgress the borders of reason must be evaluated for their content. Jerry Seinfeld and Larry David, writers of the hit television show *Seinfeld,* articulated Judaism in many of their episodes, but occasionally included some of the other cultural characters who reside in New York City. Because of this constructive inclusion, *Seinfeld* parodied "the Other" without being unduly censured or chastised.

Steven Spielberg in *Jurassic Park* cast in the role of Jeff Goldblum's character's daughter a young Black girl. In the movie, Jeff Goldblum's character is a White man. There was no portrayal of Goldblum's character's ex-wife, his daughter's mother, in the film. Because of this omission, there was no reason to portray the daughter as anything other than White as well. Spielberg's casting of a Black in the role of the daughter of a White man in a major motion picture was bold and provocative and perhaps the act of a visionary leader. I interpret this act by Spielberg as not just a moment of visionary leadership, but also calculated and extremely political. It was calculated because Spielberg knew that portraying a White man with a Black daughter would not be inconspicuous. It was a political action because Spielberg knew he was making a statement about race and society that could be interpreted across multiple aspects of the movie production process, including motion pictures in general, film casting, and interracial relationships. It was visionary because he may have been telling a tale that he chose to situate in his notion of an ideal world.

The statement Spielberg made about motion pictures is that there is not and does not have to be a one-dimensional approach to filmmaking. Just because the traditional postmillennium method of romantic seduction in a movie is "boy meets girl, boy kisses girl, boy desires girl" does not mean that the escalation to ecstasy cannot be like the more two-dimensional approach depicted in the film *The Truth About Cats & Dogs,* where the seduction went more like "woman meets man, man and woman have phone sex, woman kisses man." Spielberg cast off conventions with his lineage of Black girl from White father with no necessary relationship having been established in the story line prior to the revelation of the relationship between daughter and father. What is more, Spielberg never went back into his narrative to explicate the tension that this unique aspect of the story may have caused his racially cognizant viewers. As a Black man, when I saw *Jurassic Park* and the Black daughter was introduced, I waited the entire movie for her parental lineage to be resolved. It never was.

Spielberg's casting of a Black person in a role traditionally and logically reserved for a White actress reveals Spielberg's incorporation in his work of a *calculated ambiguity*. His inclusion of Blackness in his film has the language of nation creating a language of race, except from a conflicted position. Spielberg, a Jewish liberal, is inverting Paul Gilroy's (1991) conception of calculated ambiguity by giving an authentic voice to an underrepresented constituency. Spielberg's wealth and Hollywood influence allow him to position himself politically, where the language of nation he presents is conveniently available for articulation as the language of race. Spielberg overrides White privilege in this one particular film when he introduces a Black girl into a film where it would have been much easier if she were White.

An undeniable statement that Spielberg made regarding interracial relationships is that he approved of them. If he had not approved of them, then he would not have presented the audience with a scenario that may have only come from such a union. Spielberg made an overt statement about his politics on the issue of interracial romance when he gave Jeff Goldblum's character a Black daughter. Spielberg's impact, though, is manifested best through his ability to express his "vision" in a nonthreatening, nonpreachy manner. Unlike Allen, Spielberg's inclusion of an "Other" was not stereotypical in the least. Instead it was included in the best tradition of leadership moments. On some level Spielberg, in his telling of *The Lost World: Jurassic Park*, may have modeled his ideal world. At the same time he challenged his viewers to consider another dimension of privilege, the unearned privilege of having two parents, or two parents of a racial reality consistent with the prevailing hegemony. It should not take much convincing that having two parents who are not disabled, or both of the middle class, or both heterosexual is an unearned privilege. Society's stressors will be far less onerous to families that reflect standard hegemonies. That this would include race is without question.

> "There is nothing more delusional than when privilege is wrongly perceived as prowess."
>
> —Maurice McGlothern

What labor relations professional Maurice McGlothern is really speaking about in this quote is unearned privilege and fits well with trying to consider privilege that isn't so obvious, like having two parents with very few identity hurdles to clear.

Hardworking people who situate themselves for some of the benefits they will obtain in life have earned certain privileges, right? Or can their privilege also be contested? When we adapt a holier than thou posture to those who "have not" or "have less," we often haven't effectively scratched the surface of our own realities, unpacked or fully engaged whose shoulders we have stood upon to obtain what we think is our earned privilege. This is why it is perhaps always better to operate from a position of appreciation of what we've got, and consideration of what others may not have.

Perhaps no one did this better than John Brown. Brown, a White man, an abolitionist, was perhaps one crop away from poverty when he died. He also died defending, often by attempting to inflame opinion, the cause of social justice. He was essentially hung for attempting to exacerbate the further injustices thrust upon unjustly enslaved so-called Negroes. The fact that he was a staunch proponent of the right to an egalitarian status for once enslaved dark-skinned people is difficult to question. Even before his apprehension at Harper's Ferry he had participated in a plan financed by wealthy abolitionist Gerrit Smith to assist a voteless people in obtaining the franchise. By moving to the Adirondack Mountains and teaching so-called Negroes how to cultivate virtually barren land, as landowners, they had an opportunity to obtain the right to vote. Considering this, it should be very difficult for anyone to interpret mixed messages from Brown's actions. Instead, as a result of his commitment to the cause, Brown was often painted more as crazy than crusader. But to many others, Brown was/is considered as sly as a fox and an unparalleled ally, especially to many in dire need of one. He was not a person who would wallow in his unearned privilege, or be apt to politically posture. On the contrary, Brown's life was exemplary of what it means to unceasingly live within leadership moments.

8

OF BULLYING, HYPOCRISY, RESPECT, AND CONSIDERATION

A bully doesn't fully understand the pain he causes
To himself and others when he breaks emotional laws.
There's a flaw, in the way that his parents stand in awe
When the teacher says their child has a problem, like a scar
They only see the effect but refuse to see the cause
So they pause, askin' themselves, "Whose fault? Is it ours?"
Not all together, 'cause the bully has a choice
To let his voice be positive and speak words that rejoice
And won't tear down a person of the opposite race or class
'Cause when the faces clash, it's a disgrace that lasts.
Why don't we recognize that disrespect leads to disconnect
Let's think from the perspective
Of who the bully is and what he thinks when he's bullyin'.
Maybe then, we can help him change his ways and pull him in.
'Cause in order to cause pain, you must have hurt before.
So let's get his story prior to closin' the door.

—Vanessa White, "Dissed-Respect: The Impact of Bullying" (2007)

I was a junior attending Central High School in Tulsa, Oklahoma. We were on our way to our off-site track practice aboard the school bus. Suddenly, without notice, Alonzo Powell, the new transfer student from McClain High School, pulled out his penknife and began jabbing people in the leg. Now, he was a bigger kid than most, definitely bigger than me. But what was menacing about Alonzo was his edge. He had a reputation for having no qualms about fighting and you could easily imagine he probably enjoyed it, and rumor had it he fought often. He also just looked as if he would be a nasty fighter, someone who would do whatever it took to win.

At first, watching people jump from the knife pinching their skin was funny, but only for a moment. Then I realized that there was a degree of terror in some of the other athletes' faces as they watched our different teammates either getting knifed or cringing in anticipation of what might be coming their way. I also felt a twinge of anxiety when Alonzo had his knife out. Would he come after me? He never did. However, there was one primary victim of Alonzo's who seemed to get more than his unfair share of penknife treatment, a boy we called Little Watson. It was really rather odd how he ended up being victimized by Alonzo more than the others. He wasn't the most likely suspect, primarily because he was actually a cool little kid. He was a sophomore, very thin, who had barely made the team. Everybody liked him and he never gave anybody grief. So, this one particular day on the bus ride back from practice he had the unfortunate fate of sitting directly across from Alonzo. Little Watson must have been jabbed a half dozen times because eventually he started to cry. Tears among athletes back then were rare, but especially among football players. It caught everyone by surprise, yet didn't stop Alonzo. I sat there really tired of seeing Little Watson being bullied. I sat there really wanting to say something to Antonio, anything that might get him to stop abusing this cool little guy. I sat there. What's worse, Alonzo liked me. He undoubtedly thought I was cool because he would always go out of his way to acknowledge me and kick it with me. So, in those moments when he was acting like a bully I may have had enough clout with him to suggest he chill out. Me speaking out just might have made a difference. No one had ever questioned his antics, and it was well overdue.

Instead, though, I sat in silence, happy I wasn't being jabbed in the leg, happy I wasn't being bullied.

I sat in silence trying to own the fact that I was a coward.

I often tell this story when I'm presenting to middle schools, high schools, even colleges when I facilitate discussions on bullying. What I have articulated here is also a scene within the bullying film *Dissed-Respect: The Impact of Bullying* (2007). I also tell this story in Dr. Thomas Keith's hit film *The Bro Code*. Every time I tell this story or even see myself telling it on film, every time, I have to work feverishly to avoid tears. It takes me back to one of my most disappointing moments. The shame that envelops me, that frames my cowardice, is often inconsolable. I know how much it has meant to me when people have come to my aid, and for me not to have done the same haunts me, and will forever haunt me. This is the message I try to teach students regarding bullying: If you don't want to have profound regrets when you get older, you have no options except to take a stand now.

The bullying that occurred back then hasn't changed, necessarily. But kids are more in the game today than we were back then, largely because we challenge today's kids to consider their actions as well as become allies much more than we did when we were populating the educational pipeline.

I recently asked the "which came first, the chicken or the egg?" question of a group of people endeavoring to facilitate diversity for a very large county in Southern California. After they considered their response, I then challenged them to answer this: "Which occurs first, bullying because of our ignorance on how to respond to differences, or inconsideration of differences that contribute to bullying?" I was a bit surprised when they admitted they had never envisioned diversity and social justice education as an invaluable resource for eradicating bullying. However, I shouldn't be. People have been more concerned with telling people that it is wrong to do and that they shouldn't, than figuring out why it occurs, outside of the psychology of the bully, and the predisposition of victim types. Bullying is about the socialized differences that exist and our society's inability to educate our populace sufficiently enough, early enough, to make the difference.

Some time ago my assistant at the Center for Diversity, Kristie Gonyea, and I facilitated three presentations at Peru Central School. As a result of a series of different bullying incidents (which often are connected to inadequate preparation of students/parents on diversity and social justice) that had occurred around the North Country, the Peru administration decided to accept some assistance and provided us access to the middle school students to create a conversation about diversity, social justice, and bullying.

In these types of interactive educational sessions I spend quite a bit of time establishing a rhythm with the students. As is always my way, I endeavor to primarily bat cleanup in a conversation that I create with the students and really only want to facilitate their voices, with necessary provocation. On this day the eighth-grade students were amazing! Quiet when they needed to respect a voice, vocal when a question was put to them, we were pleasantly surprised by the energy, focus, and consideration they gave the subject matter. Afterward I told my son, one of the eighth graders, that I was going to write a blog on my blog site, "Wiley Wandering" (hosted on the *Press-Republican* newspaper's website), about the rewarding experience I had that day with his classmates. I told him I would link it to my Facebook account so that his friends could see it. I then also decided to double dip and see if I could get both middle school students and adults to contribute to the conversation. These are the questions I wrote on my blog:

If any middle school students actually read this blog, my questions to you are:
1. What was the most personal thing that you got from the diversity/bullying session today?
2. If you were to describe to your parents what you experienced today, how would you describe it?
3. Why was it important for you to have a session on bullying/diversity?
4. Do you think the bullying/diversity session will make a difference with your classmates, and why/why not?
5. Do you think all students would benefit from more diversity sessions like the one you had today? Why/why not?
6. Do you think your parents would benefit from participating in a session on bullying/diversity?

I was pleasantly surprised when the middle school kids, led by my son, Justin, actually decided to weigh in. I didn't expect them to answer all the questions—though some did—but was pleasantly surprised with the depth of their answers. I chose not to clean up their grammar and spelling, thinking it adds to their authenticity. Here are some of their comments, with some of their comments bolded for emphasis, followed by my responses set off by asterisks:

Dad,
I enjoyed you coming to my school and enlightening all of my friends and piers. The most important thing you talked about today in my eyes and ears were the discussion of why we use the following words to hurt people: "Gay," "Fagot," "Queer" and "retard." **I felt you made the students realize what image they were putting out to people and, what they are really saying when they say "gay" etc.** I truly think you have gotten inside my piers heads. I thought it was important for 8th grade students actually teenagers at all to learn about bullying and what these hurtful words mean and, **I also strongly think that the session truly got in students head making them think of what they're saying and doing.** I think that all students would benefit from this enlightenment session it makes a lot of young students think and it's getting inside their heads.

*** Son, it may take you having a child of your own to realize this, but one of the most difficult conversations to create is one that includes your children and their friends. I was sincere when I said it was eerie how respectful the 8th graders at Peru were to us. That said, I agree with you that it is about getting certain thoughts in student's heads and keeping them there. I planted a few seeds, but now it is up to you and your crew to make sure they grow.

You also will never know how proud I am of the fact that you have posted to my blog for the first time. How cool is that . . .*****—J.W.**

Posted by: Justin Wiley | October 29, 2010 4:15 PM

The presentation today really made me think in a different way. It made me sad when Mr. Wiley had to explain to us how his son was being bullyed and his son was being called names. Then lots of people started crying thinking of how sad it was. I feel like this really helped are school and everyone should put some effort into changing, and trying not to be mean, and hurtful towards people.

*** I appreciate the empathy from you and your classmates. If you recall, my going into the story about my son's experience 7 years ago was in response to the one girl asking me to explain the word "nigger." I chose to tell a story that would reveal the pain associated with dysfunctional language instead of just giving all of you some stodgy academic definition of the term.

The bigger lesson I hope you all got from it was that we must be responsible for the things we say and do. As teenagers it is no longer acceptable for any of you to not think about your actions. So, as Justin mentioned earlier, language that ranges from what appears to be relatively harmless like "nerd" and "loser" to language that we frame as mean-spirited like "retard" and "queer" all have the ability to cut like a knife at different times.

Thanks for joining the conversation on the blog. *****—J.W.**

Posted by: Anonymous | October 29, 2010 11:19 PM

Mr. Wiley,

Your speach inspired me so much today. It made me think back of all the times that I bullied someone or made fun of someone. Two periods of you talking can really change someones life, like it did to mine. When you told me the story about Justin when he was a little kid, it was so hard for me to hold back my tears. **Before I walked into the assembly, I didn't think that the speech would be so touching and a good life leason.** You are so cool and amzazing!

*** Isabella, most likely when you previously bullied you just weren't thinking of the impact it was having on the victims. All I did was challenge you to consider your actions towards others. It is you that is cool and amazing because your mind

is open enough to accept a challenge to change some of your ways. Now, don't just halfway do it, but take it all the way. Remember, we talked about how great the 8th grade class could actually be. Well, go out and become that great individual that has been quietly residing within you. ***—**J.W.**
Posted by: Isabella Schaefer | October 29, 2010 11:31 PM

Mr. Wiley,
Your presentation was amazing! I agree 100% with you. **I hear and see people being bullied all the time and I hear all the name calling that was discussed. It bothers me so bad, and I'm glad that somebody finally took action!** What bothers me the most, is the use of the word "gay". I think you really got through to us, and I don't think we have ever been so quiet at an assembly. Thank You!
*** I appreciate your posting to the blog Michaela, but remember, the people that "really" need to take action are the ones that often are far too comfortable as bystanders. Don't be a bystander! Make sure you and your "now aware" crew of like minded students find ways to include those students that often are left out. That is when you really start to build a community. ***—**J.W.**
Posted by: Michaela | October 30, 2010 11:08 AM

Dr. Wiley,
Thank you so much for coming to our school! **I think bullying is the whole reason people are committing suicide these days.** Those pictures of kids with autism and the comments made everyone very sad. Also when you said Justin got called the 'n' word, people around me were crying, and I kept my tears in though. I think thats horrible that this 5th grader was talking to him like that. I think there will be alot less bullying in the halls and the classrooms. Coming to our school made our school a lot better than what it has become. **I think you should go all over the U.S talking about bullying,** and seeing how much schools you have changed. Thanks again for coming to our school!
*** Karly, you are correct in recognizing that bullying contributes to people's lack of self worth, which contributes to many people taking their own lives.
The 5th grader who called Justin "nigger" seven years ago when he was a 1st grader was a product of his environment. Hopefully, as an adult now he has grown and changed. Like I said when I talked to your class, that 5th grader wasn't born with that type of language. He unfortunately was taught hateful language. Now its time for us (you, me, your classmates) to find ways to re-teach those who are likely to bully, right? As well, it is also time for us to make sure that we aren't somehow bullying ourselves. Karly, thank you for being the leader that I know you

to be. Keep working hard on bringing out the greatness you have within you. *****—J.W.**

Posted by: Karly Dynko | October 30, 2010 1:10 PM

I really enjoyed your speech the other day, i feel as if people will change now after you gave us that speech about not to bully and how it affects other peoples lives if you bully. **I really connected to you when we were talking about the word "bitch" because it seems as if i get called that a lot, even by people i dont even talk to.** I don't get why though because i've never done anything to them. I also tend to get called "fake" and a "whore" constantly. **It affects me in life because i feel as if i'm not good enough to be here.** I hate seeing people get bullied to, i want to do something about it. and i want to put a stop to it. i know i've bullyed people to, and i do regret it. i may say something but i don't realize it offends people. i do regret the things i've done in the past to people. and i hope in the near future, people will change. Your speech really affected a lot of people that were there because i feel that most of them connected to you and realized that it's not right to do. **Everybody's different, no ones the same. so why dont we bully everybody?** everybody's different in every little way. lets change . . . lets not bully those who are different then us, because were all different. We just have those people that we fit in with, but that doesnt mean that they aren't different then you. because they are. everybodys different. whether it's the way you dress, look, your body feautures it doesn't matter, everybody's beautiful. treat people they way you'd want to be treated.

*** Lindsay, thanks for looking at yourself and owning the fact that you have bullied. You are smart enough to know that you are young enough and caring enough to change. So, do what you need to do to be the person you want to be, instead of not giving any thought to the person that you are.

You are correct that everybody's different. If we all really focused on the fact that we all want our differences to be appreciated and if possible, celebrated, then most of us would be far less judgmental. Make a commitment to yourself Lindsay to stop judging others, even those that prejudge (which is what prejudice actually is). Most people that exhibit prejudiced behavior have never stopped to realize what they are doing. After the talk at your school you and many of your classmates now realize it so you no longer have an excuse. Time to take your game (respecting others) to another level, right? Thanks for contributing your voice to the conversation. *****—J.W.**

Posted by: Lindsay A. | October 30, 2010 1:12 PM

Dr.Wiley, after **seeing the presentation the first time at SUNY Plattsburgh my life changed** about using the words that are hurtful to others and put them down.

I haven't changed completely but **everyday I think about being a leader and trying my hardest to be a better person. Yesterday my life changed again. Now i feel that someone needs to make a change and stand up to be a leader. I am going to take the opportunity and try 100%** to be an outstanding factor in the Peru school district. I believe you really made change in the way 7th and 8th graders from Peru will act in the future. You nailed the presentation, Congratulations Dr.J.W.Wiley.

*** Cameron, Thanks for introducing me yesterday. You are a leader, that is obvious, but with the power leaders have if/when it isn't used properly it can be very dangerous and detrimental to others. So, measure your actions young man, with care and consideration of others. I look forward to seeing the role you will play over the years in making Peru Central School District one of the best schools in the country. Are you up for that? *****—J.W.**

Posted by: Cameron Rock | October 30, 2010 2:03 PM

Dr.Wiley,

Thank you soo much for comeing to our school yesturday and telling us about diversity. It was really sad to hear about the story with justin and hat 5th grader calling him the "n" word. **It really affected me and now I a going to think about the words that i say and when other people are calling girls or boys names I will stop it now** since i have watched those videos that you showed us. **I am starting to become a better leader**, and now since you showed us that presentation I will be thinking harder about what I say and do and iI will deffinately become a stronger and better leader! Thanks Dr.Wiley.

*** Bryn, you are very welcome. You can really demonstrate your appreciation by being an ally for the people who are often alone and preyed upon by bullies. Be the leader that you want to be and help us change the game at Peru to one that all can play, fairly! Thanks Bryn for contributing to this conversation. *****—J.W.**

Posted by: Bryn Mousseau | October 30, 2010 2:51 PM

Now, my son and his friends are among the more popular kids in the school. I know most of these kids, and they are, generally speaking, kind and considerate. They are probably considered the cooler kids. As a consequence, they would be less apt to experience bullying. This is an important point because their perspectives are not so much from the perspectives of victims as they are from the perspectives of bystanders if not bullies themselves. This is why hearing them speak about suicide should garner immediate attention. As well, hearing them validate the need for these conversations resonates profoundly. Kids entering their teens are primed to embrace the leadership moments awaiting them, but their voices and vision require cultivation.

Usually when we think of bullies, we think of their targets, the recipients of their attention, their victims. Sometime thereafter thoughts of bystanders enter our minds too. These kids own all three of the roles in their comments. Like most of us, they are experienced with the role of bully, victim, and bystander. Unfortunately, like most of us, they are inexperienced with the notion that when we see a bully what we are far too often seeing is an entertainer. Bullies act out for attention, or out of frustration.

When we see a bully joined by two bystanders and the victim, most of us see three very distinct categories of people exhibiting unique behavior relative to their categories. After creating conversations about bullying with very different groups of people I have come to see those four people as one. They are all victims. They will remain victims until we find ways to educate all of them about the reasons why they are bullying. My experiences teaching college-age women and men reaffirm my insight that since no one exits the womb as a bully it is a learned lesson, a socialized secret, an indoctrinated idiosyncrasy.

A valued colleague of mine, then–Plattsburgh City School Superintendent Dr. Michelle Kavanaugh, years ago cemented the thought in my head that considerations/conversations and strategies that include diversity are invaluable to engaging bullying and inseparable from one day successfully eradicating it. She had hired me to consult on the development and production of the film *Dissed-Respect: The Impact of Bullying*, with Mountain Lake PBS, which situated me to work closely with media lab director Richard Allen. It was our mutual decision that he would match my intensity in making the film. So, when I began to exceed my contractually required 30 hours (I actually ended up working 300 hours), and he eagerly took the ride, I began to engage and better understand bullying.

Throughout my career, the Center for Diversity, Pluralism, and Inclusion at SUNY Plattsburgh has been immersed in enlightening people about the dimensions of diversity. Bullying, a form of hatemongering, is one of the many things we engage. Revealing bullies as overrated assailants and/or disrespectful duelists, we teach that these privileged pugilists would change their approach greatly if they were not stronger, larger, or members of the majority. As a matter of fact, bullies don't bully from an inferior position; they couldn't. Bullies begin their treacherous journeys from a seat of power, a privileged position.

Friedrich Nietzsche, a philosopher, once claimed that this Christian-like defense of the underprivileged, this "the meek shall inherit the earth" sensibility, is nothing but a slave morality opposed to other popular claims like "survival of the fittest" and "might makes right." However, it is hard to imagine that everyone doesn't experience that moment when they are not "mighty," or most "fit." When it occurs, how many of us invite others to trample upon us?

The national discourse has placed bullying in schools front and center. Our Diversity Enlightenment (DE) sessions are consistently solicited as a response to bullying. Because I unflinchingly believe that bullying occurs because of the differences that exist among us, the articulation of people stepping into their "leadership moment," the elimination of xenophobia (a fear of strangers), an emphasis on responsibility and respect, and the cultivation of community are some of the lessons taught in the DE sessions. Participants come to recognize that bullies succumb to their xenophobia, hide behind their privilege, and undermine if not eventually destroy their community. Xenophobia appears when a person wearing glasses is called four eyed, weird because the person dresses differently, or a nerd because the person doesn't meet some mythical level of social acceptance.

Bullies usually become privileged because of the security in numbers that is available to them when they disrespect or attack someone. In the case of the racial epithet once hurled at my son when a first grader, we need only to flip the script for an interesting analysis. Would that fifth grader have said the "*N*-word" if he attended an all-Black primary school where he was the only White kid? Be real! Would that fifth grader have been so daring as to project the same pejorative term to a seventh or eighth grader who was quite a bit larger than him? Yeah, right! As well, would anyone at a local high school that had students wearing T-shirts emblazoned with Confederate flags have worn what they claimed was heritage clothing if he or she attended Locke High School in South Central Los Angeles, a predominantly Black high school? No! This is where you can truly begin to see how privilege rears its ugly head. Because they have the *privilege of being in the majority*, bullies don't have to consider any other perspective or opinion and can somehow rationalize away the discomfort or pain they cause.

Bullies exist everywhere, not just in schools, but in academia, businesses, city politics, and national governments. Everywhere would include within each one of us when we aren't vigilant about not going there. For example, I was speaking to a colleague as I was writing this book and he surprised me

by thinking one of the layers to the title of this book was a nuanced suggestion that a victim of the word *nigger* isn't the stereotypical Black person who
is called the term, but the person who uses the word *nigger*. I was astonished
that my colleague could actually believe that would be my thought/method.
No way! That would be an instance of me hating the hater. No one should
be called *nigger*, or *retard*, or *fag*, or *bitch*, or *trailer trash*, or anything else
other than the person's name. It isn't about turning around and calling
someone who calls me a nigger the same term because I somehow am convinced that I'm so witty that I've found a way to justify that creativity. It's
also not about turning the other cheek. I'm also not down with that. I don't
want to be slapped twice, though on the right day if it happens I may endure
it. But I'm not interested in promoting accepting humiliation, or a verbal or
physical ass whipping. It's about finding a creative way to educate the perpetrator so that he or she is ashamed, through having been enlightened, which
sometimes requires a bit of philosophical edginess. Any other action on my
part could inadvertently promote more bullying.

I'm from the new school of thought that actions that enhance xenophobia promote privilege and also trumpet traditional transgressions. That these
actions must cease is a no-brainer!

Bullies reveal their callousness, cravenness, and ignorance when they
promote themselves to someone else's detriment. As a result we have no
choice but to see bullies as "mirrorless masters of menace." I often refer to
bullies that way because if they had mirrors, they would be incapable of
seeing anything within their own reflection beyond a soul devoid of the
humanity to consider others' hearts. Perhaps our biggest error is in attempting to avoid bullies. In avoiding bullies we eliminate the opportunities to
challenge them, and therefore eliminate opportunities to defeat them since
bullies survive in the shadows while they assess their potential victims. The
world will benefit greatly when we reveal bullies as "captains of coercion,"
forcing them to be more considerate of others or ironically possibly become
an other because of their self-absorbed dysfunctional behavior.

So, how do we successfully challenge bullies? First, by getting them into
a dialogue where they can see that they are undeniably bullies. Often, people
don't recognize this fact and it really is a situation where people/bullies are
inconsiderate with no consciousness of being that way.

As co-producer, co-writer, and co-director with then–Media Lab Director Rich Allen of the film *Dissed-Respect: The Impact of Bullying*, I myself
discovered I had been bullying my son. In an interaction with him at home
one day, to further make a point to him, I used my physical presence to

further influence his behavior. Upon recognizing that I was in essence bullying him, I stepped back so that I could step off. I haven't stepped to him in
such a manner since. Now I use my words to get my messages across, which
is what we teach our kids, right?

Conversely, Justin was one of the stars of a bullying movie, yet still
succumbs to the tactics, though usually he is found implementing them to
the chagrin of his sister, who, unfortunately for him, happens to be my
daughter. He knows that when he bullies his sister he is disrespecting my
daughter and in essence disrespecting me. But the more significant point
here is that at kids' impressionable ages if kids aren't constantly reinforced
about our propensity to bully they will probably fall prey to it again and
again. It is part of our culture.

Horrendous events near Tucson, Arizona, got everyone's attention in
January of 2011. The wanton murder of 6 people and wounding of 13 more
at the hands of a deranged assailant was hard to ignore, especially when they
were gathering to discuss democracy. Undoubtedly, because Congress-
woman Gabrielle Giffords and Judge John Roll were two of the shooting
victims, it ensured that the visibility of this heinous crime would be more
than that given to some drug-related drive-by shooting in an impoverished
neighborhood. However, the tragedy became even greater when one of the
victims was a child, a 9-year-old, who was in attendance only because of her
love for politics and desire to acquire insight into how our democracy works.
What would she think of our democracy if she were home watching the
aftermath of the shooting instead of becoming one of its victims? After all,
no matter how we slice it, the shooting occurred at a political gathering,
which makes it some sort of statement about our politics. Whether the
shooting occurred because of a crosshairs map highlighted by a reckless politician who was an election away from being our vice president, or because
of heated political rhetoric that disturbingly reflects violence, like "If they
bring a knife to the fight, we bring a gun," or something as inconsiderate
as a politician publicly stating "Don't retreat, reload," when/where does it
stop?

When President Obama, in his closing remarks at Tucson's event
memorializing the victims, stated, "We should do everything we can to make
sure that this country lives up to our children's expectations" (January 13,
2011), the film *Crash* came to mind for me. There are only a handful of films
that every time I watch them, they invoke in me emotion. The ending scene
of *It's a Wonderful Life* saturates my sight, especially when George Bailey

realizes that his life had much deeper meaning through his journey of witnessing how the world would have been without his loving, unselfish presence. Then there is the scene in *Cast Away* when Helen Hunt is responding to the ultimate dilemma, being restrained by her new husband from her first true love, whom she has just recently discovered is actually alive after being thought dead for years. And the most powerful one for me, the scene from *Crash* where the little Mexican girl is shot trying to save her father because he isn't wearing the invisible cloak he had recently transferred to her to protect her from the random violence that far too often occurs in their neighborhood. Unfortunately, I must watch the *Crash* scene every semester during the race theme in our Examining Diversity Through Film course. We show it because it symbolizes how pathetically inconsiderate we are of our children when we constantly put them in harm's way as a result of our actions. Prior to that scene, the little girl's father, who is a locksmith, and a Persian store owner have a disagreement that actually is over more than whether the lock on the Persian man's business can be fixed. What they are actually arguing over is the stereotype in the Persian man's mind associated with the Mexican man's trustworthiness, exacerbated by the frustration of the Persian man being stereotyped himself earlier by a gun store owner. It is stereotypes like these and the frustration accompanying them that contributed to the attempted murder of the Mexican father in *Crash*, resulting in his daughter using her body to shield her dad.

How do we avoid/avert the type of hurt inflicted on little Lara in *Crash*, or ironically, the innocently politically curious Christina-Taylor Green in Tucson? Are their shootings more about the randomness of the universe, or inconsiderate references and disrespect within our language? Is there a cause-and-effect relationship between our inability to systematically eliminate our propensity toward negativity when we frame those different from us as "the Other" and our then somehow justified or rationalized actions?

In schools all across the country educators are feverishly trying to eliminate bullying and the language that exemplifies it. *Trailer trash, retard,* the F-word, the B-word, the G-word, and the N-word have all been carefully considered while thoroughly engaged and targeted as problematic in their further perpetuation of dysfunctional attitudes and behavior. We have finally focused on the bullying that takes place in our society, obviously as a result of school shootings. At what point will we stop to ponder the fact that it may be virtually impossible to end bullying at the adolescent level if we are clueless about our modeling of it at the so-called "adult" level? This can't be any more evidenced than by the acts of Fred Phelps, a bully who calls himself a minister, who in 2006 chose to disrespect the gay Republican mayor of Plattsburgh, New York, as framed by me in this In My Opinion piece:

COVERT WOLVES WITH OVERT HOOVES: THE SO-CALLED MINISTER AND HIS SO-CALLED MINISTRY:

At Mayor's Cup this year (2006) we may have an episode of bullying unfolding involving our mayor and a bully posing as a representative of God. Our mayor has more than proven his worth to our community, exceeding his duties many times over from what I've witnessed. However, he is being taken to task as a morally corrupt individual because he doesn't live the lifestyle others think that he should. People that take Mayor Stewart to task for his job performance are entitled to their opinions. I constantly teach and challenge people to respect the opinions that diverge from their own. However, that doesn't mean everyone has to agree with those opinions. The most critical aspect of interacting with different people is really making the attempt to hear and understand them.

In good conscience I would feel like an idiot addressing anyone with the title of reverend, priest, pastor, chaplain, or minister when the messages they forward are steeped in hate. So, you won't read any reference to the "so-called minister" by his name or title. If anything it takes an exorbitant amount of energy not to refer to people in God representing professions who seem to have very personal agendas as "culprits of the pulpits." The sheer hypocrisy of an organization, spear-headed by a so-called minister of God, who interprets God's word in a language of hate, is manipulative, mean-spirited, and malicious. This minister once celebrated the brutal murder of a young man because of his sexual identity? If you have ever been oppressed or disrespected for some arbitrary reason, how can you be dispassionate about the so-called minister's mission?

The so-called minister is a vagabond who thrives on victimizing the vulnerable. He is no better than a hoodlum hauling and hurling hate that harms. The so-called minister is an instigator who endeavors to initiate ignominy by enticing the illiterate and uninformed into idiotic ideology.

Many of the so-called minister's assertions are so extreme that they threaten to dismantle your sensibilities. This definitely is the case with the so-called minister's perspective on people's sexual identities. Unfor-tunately, the so-called minister could be demonstrating his insensitivity, cowardliness, and ignorance by attempting to promote himself at someone else's expense. I see the so-called minister as a bully, "a mirror-less master of menace," because fixating upon himself in a mirror might cause him to discover his inability to consider other's hearts. Bullies are vanquished when they are challenged, because "bullies seek and survive in the shadows." We make a huge mistake when we attempt to avoid bullies. Shining the light on these cowardly captains of coercion early and often forces them to crawl back under their rocks or change their ugly ways.

How is it that this misguided miscreant in minister's clothing has actually developed a following? Unfortunately we live in a world whereby people are followers by nature. It takes more energy to challenge tradition than it does to simply adhere to it. The adage "we didn't create the pollution that plagues our world, though we must take responsibility to clean it up" is appropriate here! Why would we allow anything to pollute the world we inhabit? Arguments that attempt to frame same sex partners as pollutants are the first cousins of arguments that were made against miscegenation, Winter-Spring relationships, and marrying outside of your social economic reality. Within certain contexts all of these arguments have been problematic because of their myopia.

If God hates anyone it would be people who appropriate God's name for their own purpose. God doesn't hate people God created because it would be a contradiction to God's omnipotence. God always had the option of not creating what the so-called minister and his misguided minions claim God hates. Within the very definition of the omnipotent, omniscient, benevolent being known as God hate is a contradictory concept. It is as nonsensical as the creation of a website designed to facilitate ill will toward a group of people that God created.

By the so-called minister's assertion, if gays are ill, how do we categorize him and his group who interpret God's messages and contort them to spew venom that frames the so-called minister's victims as victimizers? Somehow, someway, the so-called minister's followers don't see themselves as hate mongers. Do they not realize that hate is a heavy thing to haul around or to use as a vehicle to situate oneself as a hero of some misguided cause? Inward exploration might provide each of the so-called minister's pawns with pause and perspective on the pain they cause many people. There is no upside to the umbrage, upheaval, and unequivocal ugliness unveiled by the so-called minister's organization.

This culprit of the pulpit is the bully that rolls up his sleeves and flexes his muscles when he suspects his strength is greater than the strength of the people he is bullying, but wears both a long sleeve shirt and jacket to cover his muscles when he realizes that his strength may be insufficient against the power of people who see him as he is, if only they decided to roll up their sleeves and collectively demonstrate their strength. Organizations like Plattsburgh for Peace are doing that. We should all seriously consider rolling up our sleeves this upcoming Mayor's Cup weekend and make a statement to all so-called ministers and ourselves. Let's "network" and agree to be "mad as hell and not willing to take it anymore."

I can't hate bullies and you shouldn't either. I am a firm proponent of the fact that as a social justice activist it weakens my efforts if I succumb to the very things I challenge others to avoid, hating the hatemongers, or even too much venom toward highly opinionated, very negative people. They didn't come through the womb hating, and don't have to continue it. But if a hater receives hate back, he or she both won that battle and adversely influenced if not dictated how you manage your energy. Instead, I choose to have a perspective that anyone brandishing hate merits watching, if only for the sheer fascination of that person's socialization defining him or her as dysfunctional.

Considering bullying in a different context, I recall years ago an early mentor of mine sharing with me his philosophy on the different types of people in the world. He claimed that there were three types: energizers, energy stealers, and energy impostors. He said that *energizers* could be spotted from a mile away, because for all intents and purposes they radiate with an intensity that is undeniable and empowering. *Energy stealers* can be seen from a distance as well, except that as they approach, even the most vigilant protectors of their own energy aren't sure they have enough to ward off being dramatically drained. But at least we are able to recognize energy stealers. *Energy impostors,* though, are wolves in sheepskins. They subtly plug into us, and before we know it, like a car that had its lights left on, we are totally drained with little recourse until recharged. Bullies are energy impostors. Sometimes initially, even through no fault of their own, they present this high level of energy that entices us to exchange energy with them. This is done when they entertain us with their charm, posture as a team player, and pretend to be protector of all that is fair and just, only to undermine the larger moment.

While too many people don't see themselves for the bullies they actually are, or the energy stealers they may be, I see bystanders as bullies and energy impostors as well. If for no other reason than their empowering bullies to continue on with their victimizing, bystanders are often as repulsive as those bullies who entertain them and ultimately just as much of a drain upon our emotional energy.

At the end of the day, though, there really are no bullies and bystanders, only victims. Because if our educational systems were really operating as they should be, every child in our educational pipeline would fully understand what bullying is, why we do it, how it feels, the hypocrisy of bullying, and how much better our world would be without it. As it stands now, far too many of our kids grow up with little consideration of the consequences of bullying. Until we understand that to successfully eradicate bullying lessons in diversity and social justice must be implemented, we will all be victims of unpredictable consequences.

> *He doesn't think about the consequences,*
> *Only wants your senses to feel what he does.*
> *So maybe he can build himself up,*
> *Show himself love.*
> *'Cause when he's at home he gets scolded for no reason,*
> *Told he deserves a beatin', cold and has not eatin'.*
> *His parents treat him like he's dirt, so he's a piece of work.*
> *He hits kids on their necks and they tell, call him a chirp.*
> *Believes that he's worth very little, very brittle are his feelings*
> *So he's caught in the middle, like the second of three siblings.*
> *Spreading negativity, deading all the positive.*
> *Causin' kids to also be bullies, 'cause what survival is*
> *Is leading others in a certain way, the curtains stay*
> *Back as the plot unfolds and kids learn the play.*
> *With the meaning being that of discrimination.*
> *Hence becomes the nature of survival in our nation.*

—Vanessa White, "Dissed-Respect: The Impact of Bullying" (2007)

9

OF MISPLACED HATE AND SELF-DEFINITION

I have a dream,
I want to wake up to a revolution,
I have a dream that people will rise up,
Become wiser,
I want to see people united,
After the fighting.
I have a dream.

—Sabac, "I Have a Dream"

A cause that is left sitting is practically admitting
we are quitting our endeavor to capture the light.

—J. W. Wiley

The purpose of this book is to discuss "the nigger in you." It's a conversation that I've had in my head for a while now and felt it was time to get it out. It isn't just a purpose, but as implied by the lyrics and poem above, it's as much a cause as it is a dream and/or a passion. It seems as if everything I do in life finds me on a journey where I not only encounter but actually consider and engage diversity. During my journey it seems I have repeated opportunities to be socially just in my interactions with those I encounter along the way. I have shared some of that journey with you, especially in terms of the type of conversations that occur. Ideally, excellent communication, whatever that context might be for any two or more people, should leave the participants in that conversation more enlightened. As my poem says, I would be "admitting we are quitting our endeavor to capture the light" if I wasn't doing my best to contribute to the ongoing revolution taking place for profound social justice. The light mentioned in the poem amounts to an enlightenment that the proverbial "it" can be better than "it" is. As Sabac's lyrics suggest, my goal is not just to engage/unpack the dysfunctional language we inconsiderately use with one another, but to create a revolution, an army of allies, that will assist *us* in understanding how ridiculous it is for us to be referring to one another by terms with which we wouldn't want to be referred. Am I overemphasizing the significance of our communication with one another? I hardly think so. If a certain person can approach you and say three words—"I hate you," or "I love you"—and completely disrupt your day, mess with your mood, and yes, interrupt your energy, then unfortunately another person can approach you and adversely affect you. Language's power, especially when dysfunctional, can be debilitating.

As a man who has incessantly attempted to engage the *nigger* in him, I have recalled how I began to discover it and shared some of that with you. What you don't know is that before my father's early demise after a six-year absence he introduced me to some concepts I will never forget. He taught me what a **Problem** we as Black males could be seen as within the United States. He showed me how easy the path to **Criminality** could be through his repeated bouts of incarceration. He revealed it to me so well that I narrowly avoided the consequences while so many of my other male family members didn't fare so well. And, unfortunately, my father lived out the stereotypical depiction of "Nigger." As a result, he was somewhat locked in, in terms of how he would be seen in the world. Poorly educated with a history of bad decisions, he had *problem* and *criminal* down pat, so *nigger* was a can't-miss, a lock.

As an educator, an administrator, a presenter, and a consultant I've watched people struggle with a society quite comfortable with some of its citizens being framed as less-than, and all of its citizens being framed as less-than within a possible context. When a society is comfortable with its citizens being ostracized as problems, considered suspects if not criminals, and thought of as niggerlike if not boldly called niggers, where does it turn? It should turn to consciousness and consideration. If we want to eradicate oppression we have to start at a fundamental place. For me, it's about relationships that can grow to ultimately affect positive societal change, especially since I know I can't do it alone, nor would I try.

Throughout this book I started almost every chapter with quotes, or lyrics by rap/hip-hop artists. Many of those artists are our philosophers of the day. The lyrics I chose throughout the book to launch my chapters or serve as significant moments within a chapter were meant to provoke thought about that chapter, and the inherent power of words.

Our artists, by framing and accentuating our reality, contribute to the creation of any and all sociopolitical sentiments that we are conscious, unconscious, or dysconscious about, albeit inadvertently. Those of us seen as or made to feel like problems bordering on criminality are looking for words of encouragement to assist us in transcending discontent, undeserved blame, impatience, hatred, and false bravado. We are looking to grow our perspective, courage, confidence, and consistency. We are looking to always manage our humility, wisdom, and rationality. I learned all these things when at 11 years of age, having not seen my father for two years, I discovered Kipling's "If":

If you can keep your head when all about you
Are losing theirs and blaming it on you;
If you can trust yourself when all men doubt you,
But make allowance for their doubting too:
If you can wait and not be tired by waiting,
Or being lied about, don't deal in lies,
Or being hated don't give way to hating,
And yet don't look too good, nor talk too wise;

If you can dream—and not make dreams your master;
If you can think—and not make thoughts your aim,
If you can meet with Triumph and Disaster
And treat those two impostors just the same:
If you can bear to hear the truth you've spoken
Twisted by knaves to make a trap for fools,
Or watch the things you gave your life to, broken,
And stoop and build 'em up with worn-out tools;

If you can make one heap of all your winnings
And risk it on one turn of pitch-and-toss,
And lose, and start again at your beginnings
And never breathe a word about your loss:
If you can force your heart and nerve and sinew
To serve your turn long after they are gone,
And so hold on when there is nothing in you
Except the Will which says to them: 'Hold on!'

If you can talk with crowds and keep your virtue,
Or walk with Kings—nor lose the common touch,
If neither foes nor loving friends can hurt you,
If all men count with you, but none too much:
If you can fill the unforgiving minute
With sixty seconds' worth of distance run,
Yours is the Earth and everything that's in it,
And—which is more—you'll be a Man, my son!

—Rudyard Kipling, "If" (1910)

Kipling's journey to writing "If" along with its tangential routes is actually an interesting story, but not one for this moment. A part of my journey with "If," however, you already know. It has been such a personal mantra of mine that I doubt if I'd even be in the space I am today without discovering the poem. Each line within "If" literally has its own undeniable merit. I, though, am sharing it with you as I close out my book as one of the gifts I most want you to have. It is invaluable in my intellectual armament for what it has done for my point of view and that of so many others I have shared it with. It is invaluable as a method to ensure high intellectual energy. "If?" is the quintessential conditional question that has us longing for the curious but necessary "then." At the end of Kipling's "If" the "then" is that his son becomes a "man." I shared it with you expecting you to use it one day as a road map to being a better person. "If" you open your mind to its possibilities "If" might also provide you with quite a shift in the way *you* see things.

> "Perspective is the Objective: I was frustrated with the distance I needed to travel until I met a person who couldn't walk."
>
> —J. W. Wiley

Growing up engaging my multiple identities—before I even knew I had them—was an odd thing to somehow be doing. I remember walking home from school, a Catholic school uniform on, all paranoid as to how the public school kids would process me. I stuttered, was very short, and had very light brown eyes. So, all through my adolescence I was plagued with immediate concerns about my ability and social class in my community, and race and privilege in the larger world that I knew awaited me.

> "Most of us hold simultaneous membership in a number of groups based, for example, on our personal and physical characteristics, on our abilities and class backgrounds, and on our cultural, racial, or

religious identifications. We may find ourselves both in groups targeted for oppression and in those dominant groups granted relatively higher degrees of power and prestige. By examining how we are disadvantaged as well as looking at the privileges we have, we can develop empathy for individuals different from ourselves and create a basis for alliances."

—Blumenfeld (2000, p. 268)

I think I was socialized toward developing partnerships with the "empathetic Other." Having been the person throughout my adolescence who could have used an ally, I could sympathize with the person in need of one, be anxious for that person, and generally care about that person.

Nonetheless, once I was introduced to "If" and started to better organize my energy, things started to fall into place. Where I lacked confidence in certain contexts because I was Black, or was more confident because I was male, or was insecure because I wasn't positive that I could do something, I realized that I had gained so much more from being challenged to reflect on how my identity was situated within my society. That is one of the things I gained from "If." It is one of the benefits most people get out of it if they truly take the time to reflect upon its messages. Transcending discontentment is the message of "If." It challenges us to find ways to overcome undeserved blame, implement improvisation during impatience, hate hatred without hating the hater, and appreciate modesty without succumbing to false bravado. The message of "If" is to be more considerate, try to be more courageous, develop and maintain confidence in yourself, and be consistent. Most of us spend our lives looking to grow our perspective, courage, confidence, and consistency. We are always looking to manage our humility, wisdom, and rationality. These are all attributes and approaches, suggestions and strategies that oppressed people often must implement for survival. Even then, the message of "If" isn't enough.

In my discussions with middle school students, I have come to discover how poignantly problematic some of their experiences actually are or have been. It doesn't take much energy to see how angry and/or frustrated many of our youth are within our society. As a result, when disrespected there is a tendency to disrespect back. When someone lies on us, we settle into a comfort zone of knowing we can lie on them with no compunction, just because they did it. We can't hate the hater. It makes us haters, as well as uncool and not as smart as we can be. We must find reasons for respecting, as well as ways to respect, the hater. When we are continuously successful in respecting those who hate us, all of those leadership moments become endless hours exemplified by our courageous defiance in not succumbing to our socialization and moral vision in keeping both hate and the hater in perspective.

> Cornel West in his book *Race Matters* articulated that amongst the many attributes of leadership are courageous defiance and moral vision (1993). It was his articulation of those two ingredients that inspired me to contextualize leadership in relation to diversity & social justice. The crux of the diversity presentations that I have presented at various workshops and student orientations over the years is that people need to embrace leadership on some level or other. I define leadership in a broad enough context where no one can avoid it. Leadership ties into diversity readily enough when you consider that many of our interactions with our peers reveal moments [leadership moments] where we can exhibit courageous defiance or moral vision by challenging a statement about the differences or dysfunctional behavior that exists between us or others outside of our circle or respective crew. This type of leadership action may be the beginning of a phenomenon that continues to occur and simultaneously situates inconsiderate perpetrators to consider their actions and perhaps begin to change their ways.
>
> Challenging students to be leaders must be done in various ways. We know right from wrong. We also know what hypocrisy is. When our knowledge of diversity-considerate/socially-just behavior contradicts our conscious acts, we should face the fact that we cannot have it both ways. A leader should fully understand that if the right thing must be done, then you do it. Perhaps a benefit of such action may be that you will be the inspiration for others to follow. The other side of the coin is the situation where you know what the right thing is, but you do not do it. In that case, it is hard to argue that one is either exemplifying hypocrisy or idiocy. A hypocrite does not practice what she preaches. An idiot is not clear on what the right thing to do may be. The generalized moral of this story is if everyone would really take stock of their actions, considering the consequences of those actions, would not the world be a much better place? The specific moral of the story that we should be challenging our students with is that the reason derogatory terms are often leveled at people is because we do not see the connection we have to, or with them. When we do see ourselves connected, all of a sudden a level of respect is given that often is not available in our interactions with strangers. (Wiley, 2010, p. 100)

Respecting people's ideas, opinions, situations, intelligence, choices, identity, faith, and, whenever possible, the stranger might be just what the doctor ordered.

Respect me, as I respect you
by holding me in esteem.
Don't snicker and scoff
at even my wildest of schemes.

Respect the opinions
you may find so outraging
for every thought that you have
might not be so engaging.

Respect my situation
for I am what I am
at times very sensitive,
at times quite a ham,
at times very moody, sullen or low
at times known to shine very brightly
and glow.

Respect my intelligence
by not trying to test
my ability to relate
to you at your best.
Let me play the role
I feel comfortable in
that may range from clown
to a very good friend.
And by respecting me
don't cavalierly criticize
and don't bellyache.
Allow me the freedom
to make a mistake.
Respect my space
at least for the instant
we all feel the need
to be detached and distant.

Respect my religion
for though our principles may vary,
without faith,
the mere thought of the chaos is scary.

> *And lastly*
> *respect the stranger*
> *whose respect of you is not nice.*
> *Possibly by your actions*
> *he might think twice*
> *and in the process*
> *find a vast treasure of wealth*
> *in the beauty of the feeling*
> *of respecting himself.*
>
> —J. W. Wiley, "Respect" (1983)

Respecting those who disrespect us, not hating the hater, is so critical to our development of a socially just consciousness. The only thing that might surpass extending this type of respect is the need for us to avoid self-hate. Internalized oppression can creep up on us so stealthily that we are responding to its weight without knowing it is present.

I once was so despondent over my socioeconomic class reality that I was homeward bound with the intention of putting a bullet in my brain. As I got closer to entering my neighborhood, the thought of my son and daughters left without me put an end to those thoughts. I'd like to think I could benefit them when my head is in the right place. Years later, in my earlier days at SUNY Plattsburgh, a local suicide prompted me to write my thoughts on the ultimate irreversible act. Ironically, because of the fact that the most dysfunctional dimension of our culture is our inability to talk about death, the one true certainty of our existence, those thoughts were never published. So I wrote a blog about it to get it out there. Now I share those thoughts with you, yours, and anyone who has looked into the abyss and seen nothing. It is possibly all too often the perspective of someone who is unceasingly victimized and feeling as if he or she has no place by which to escape.

On some level, this essay wrote itself when I was very much moved by the death of a very popular local high school student. His death, combined with some of the most provocative/revealing conversations I had had on the topic of suicide in my Moral Problems–Societal Dilemmas course, preoccupied my mind at the time. Perhaps also because an uncle of mine who never fails to often enter my mind took his own life, leaving his 13-year-old son fatherless and without answers. And then there are my own thoughts on ending it all when I went through a traumatic time. All of these I'm sure prompted the essay. However, no motivation loomed larger than the fact that suicide is a conversation we need to find ways to have with each other.

ONE TRULY SERIOUS PHILOSOPHICAL PROBLEM

Sometimes in the quest to examine diversity we fixate too much on the differences and not the commonalities that exist between humans. Perhaps that is why when a truly human moment that transcends some of the social constructions we all succumb to in different contexts occurs, we are mesmerized by the moment, traumatized by the tragedy, spellbound by the spectacle. Suicide is one of these all too common moments that truly demonstrate the vulnerability we all share.

Albert Camus once said "There is but one truly serious philosophical problem, and that is suicide." He didn't relegate this problem to any specific group or type of people, but instead generalized it as a societal problem. The implication I interpret from the article of Camus' "The Myth of Sisyphus" is that in every human culture, society, group, family, etc. at some point humans will entertain a thought about the absurdity of life. Thoughts like, "what is my purpose," "is it worth it all," "why not end my life," permeate all societies once individuals reflect on the mechanical aspects of their lives. The repetition of our daily activities don't necessarily lead us to consideration of the merits of our existence at a specific time in our lives, but Camus asserts if we live long enough, we will have that thought. He says, it is how we facilitate that thought that determines the statement we make to our larger society. More so, Camus states that it is the focus on the quantity of life as opposed to the quality of life that distinguishes whether or not we ultimately have a perspective on life that allows us to continue to bear the burdens of life that we must carry from time to time.

Who doesn't know of a person who opted to exit their earthly bounds earlier than anyone entertained they would? I remember a time in my life where I looked deep into the face of absurdity attempting to find an answer to insurmountable conundrums. The quality of my life at that time was such that running away from life itself was not an unattractive thought. Fortunately, the forfeited life of my uncle eight years earlier who also left behind his 13-year-old son was enough to remind me that I couldn't seriously entertain taking similar action with a three-year-old son needing me, not to mention many others. Additionally, I want to redirect or redefine the quest for quality as not being the only worthwhile venture, but that within the quantity of experiences we encounter, there is quite a bit of quality there as well. Camus asserts that the quantity of life's experiences, collectively, bring about more quality from their individual moments than any experience that we believe is steeped in quality. I embraced this message and earnestly attempt to communicate it to others who may not have considered this enlightening thought.

Every semester, in tribute to my uncle who succumbed to the absurdity of life, as well as that moment that I entertained it myself, I do a lecture on Camus' take on suicide in a philosophy course that I teach. It is the most difficult lecture that I do throughout the semester, as I can never get through it without fighting/ exhibiting emotion in front of the class. Suicide is such a sensitive subject for me that I struggled with my emotions while writing this piece. Nevertheless I lecture on the topic because we need to discuss the subject, not gloss over it. I am a proponent of the fact that we should be discussing suicide more in our general discourse than we do. Camus asserts that a worm exists within all of our hearts that represents the anguish of absurdity. This worm would lose quite a bit of its power if we coerced it out of the abscess of our hearts.

Camus framed his essay with an extremely thought provoking quote: "There is no sun without shadow, and it is essential to know the night." Some level of familiarity with the night enhances our perspective on the day. It is possible that when we reveal to our children and other loved ones our insecurities and struggles with life, and our considerations of whether life is worth living, we may eliminate the mystery of that moment of absurdity or at least enhance the possibility that our loved ones understand that we are capable of relating to them.

It was no accident that two of the middle school students from Peru Central School I featured in chapter 8 insinuated some dimension of bullying contributing to thoughts of suicide:

> "It affects me in life because [I] feel as if I'm not good enough to be here."
>
> —Lindsay A., eighth grade

> "I think bullying is the whole reason people are committing suicide these days."
>
> —Karly Dynko, eighth grade

The sense of inadequacy pressed upon you by someone else's opinion that you don't measure up, don't have the appropriate class standing, is what

Lindsay is speaking to. It sounds as if Karly has some insight into the magnitude of bullying someone. If bullying is the reason, then there is an imbalance of power conjoined with an abuse of power that is contributing to a bully or bullies making people question their very lives.

Warren Blumenfeld (2000) stated, "Although the effects of oppression differ qualitatively for specific target and agent groups, in the end everyone loses" (p. 268). I agree with Blumenfeld that oppression through social injustice adversely affects a community, but everyone doesn't have to lose if we can get communities prepared to engage those bouts of oppression, keeping them from becoming the norm. In the end, the damage can be infinitesimal in contrast to the bonding that can occur during the galvanizing of a neighborhood. This is why a community of individuals must be invested in conversations about diversity and social justice and their relationship to bullying.

Having someone to talk to, to confide in, to turn to is invaluable to people who feel as if they are under siege. Unfortunately, when we are under siege, when we feel overwhelmed with our lives, that is when we struggle to see that we aren't the problem. Even then, that doesn't mean we can't participate in the solution.

> "We may not have polluted the air, but we need to take responsibility, along with others, for cleaning it up."
>
> —Tatum (2004b, p. 80)

So, in conclusion, whether it is a hesitancy to harbor hate, respect that reinvigorates you, considerations of if-then conditionals, an objective of perspective, an understanding of the necessity of embracing leadership moments, finding a way to give someone the benefit of the doubt, or the eradication of nihilism that contributes to suicide, one thing remains as vibrant as it is vital: In our search for self-definition we must find ways to engage and/or unpack dysfunctional language, which necessarily requires action.

> "I'm looking for friends and allies, for communities where the staring, gaping, gawking, finally turns to something else, something true to the bone."
>
> —Clare (2010, p. 498)

> "cripples, queers, gimps, freaks: we are looking for lovers and teachers—teachers to stand with us against the gawking"
>
> —Clare (p. 496)

I've experienced being called a nigger as a child, boy, man, professor and consultant, presenter, and now father. Hence, I've become quite adept at understanding the term and its impact. I also arrived at a state of consciousness whereby I realized that *nigger* is not the worst word in the English language for every person who hears it. *Nigger* aimed at me, a Black man who understands what someone is trying to suggest about me when that person hurls that word my way affectionately or disparagingly, still only carries the weight of its context. *Bitch* aimed at a woman, *retard* directed at someone differently able, *cracker* tossed at Whites, *fag* used to insult people with different sexual orientations are all just as powerful within their uniquely dysfunctional (and affectionate) contexts. If *nigger* is or isn't the quintessential term for disparagement of an "Other," it is probably the most universally known. This is why I have no qualms taking some of its agency away by reframing it as no longer just a racial term, but a term that symbolizes all the many ways we disrespect/bully one another, are inconsiderate of one another, prejudge one another, internalize our demonization, and mistakenly believe that in some sense we are all alone in our despair. We must understand that the feeling of the "nigger in you"—within any given moment and/or context—is apt to visit each and every one of us in its oddly unique way. The nigger in you is the *retard* in you, the *fag* in you, the *bitch* in you, etc. It's that moment when someone in this far too often dysfunctional world is trying to tell you that you are a problem, a criminal, or criminal-like. It is also the moment that we've allowed someone to successfully get into our heads through aiming their dysfunctional language at us often enough and we unfortunately start to believe it. When that does occur and yet we somehow focus on how we feel, it ultimately allows those of us to know that we are not alone in experiencing that dreadful feeling. It also allows us to come together and transcend all the dysfunctional language that is used to oppress us.

There never was an escalator that will help us achieve our pinnacle.
Nor an elevator that will expedite our ascension.
Only an elevation of the mind
Intertwined with a unison in purpose
Will help us achieve our goals.
For in suffering through
degradation, intimidation, and humiliation,
as a whole,
We become whole.

*And therefore, we cannot settle for an exaltation
in the accomplishments
of just the parts.*

—J. W. Wiley

"Every white man in America knows we are Americans, knows we are
Negroes, and some of them know us by our names. So when he calls us a
nigger, he's calling us something we are not, something that exists only in
his mind. So if nigger exists only in his mind, who's the nigger?"

—Gregory (1964, p. 201)

Since we all participate in this name-calling, this disrespect, this inconsideration, this lack of giving *Others* the *benefit of the doubt*, it seems logical that
we should all ask ourselves the same question Dick Gregory asks: "Who's
the nigger?" I am not a proponent, however, of defining a person who has
called me a nigger as a nigger. That's a bit too close to hating the hater for
my taste. As I stated in the introduction of this book, a nigger isn't a person,
but a societal problem created through society's inability to educationally
engage, to successfully integrate our differences. When we label someone a
nigger, beyond referring to him or her as a problem, we also disrespectfully
imply an expectation of behavior that at the very least borders on criminal
activity, both elements of someone whom society deems a societal misfit,
without owning its inability to have better engaged all of its citizens. As a
result, *nigger* is framed this way in our society, a definition that most haven't
considered because we don't discuss the term, or other dysfunctional terms,
enough.

I prefer to exercise insight into why the name-caller is behaving dysfunc-
tionally, perhaps ask the perpetrator to explain his or her word choice, while
I continue on in my efforts to make the world a better place. I arrived at this
serene intellectual space by considering how I've processed the "nigger" in
me, the one society asserts exists within me, and the one I may have internalized and not yet purged. Now when someone shouts "Nigger!" at me from
a passing car, I look at the person and laugh. I know who I am. I understand
my journey. The people screaming epithets from a car window have yet to
begin theirs. Beyond my safety, I am quite concerned about their misguided
minds. That is why I wrote this book and hopefully why you have read it.

So, have you truly stopped recently and reflected upon the "nigger in
you"? If not, isn't it time you started?

REFERENCES

Babyface & Simmons, D. (1993). For the cool in you [Recorded by Babyface]. On *For the cool in you* [CD]. New York: Sony Music Entertainment.

Blumenfeld, W. J. (2000). How homophobia hurts everyone. In M. Adams, W. J. Blumenfeld, R. Castaneda, H. W. Hackman, M. L. Peters, & X. Zuniga (Eds.), *Readings for diversity and social justice: An anthology on racism, antisemitism, sexism, heterosexism, ableism, and classism* (pp. 9–14). New York: Routledge.

Camus, A. (2004)."Life is Absurd." In Louis P. Pojman (Ed.), *The Moral Life* (pp. 616–623). New York: Oxford University Press.

Castaneda, R., & Peters, M. L. (2004). Ableism: Introduction. In M. Adams, W. J. Blumenfeld, R. Castaneda, H. W. Hackman, M. L. Peters, & X. Zuniga (Eds.), *Readings for diversity and social justice: An anthology on racism, antisemitism, sexism, heterosexism, ableism, and classism* (pp. 397–402). New York: Routledge.

Casualties of War. (2001). Dir. Brian DePalma, Perf. Michael J. Fox, Sean Penn, Don Harvey, 1989, DVD, TriStar Home Entertainment.

Churchill, W. (2003). American Indians in film: Thematic contours of colonization. In J. Xing & L. R. Hirabayashi (Eds.), *Reversing the lens: Ethnicity, race, gender, and sexuality through film* (pp. 43–111). Boulder, CO: University Press of Colorado.

Clare, E. (2010). Gawking, gaping, staring. In M. Adams, W. J. Blumenfeld, R. Castaneda, H. W. Hackman, M. L. Peters, & X. Zuniga (Eds.), *Readings for diversity and social justice: Second edition* (pp. 495–498). New York: Routledge.

Corvino, J. (1997). Homosexuality: The nature and harm arguments. In A. Soble (Ed.), *The philosophy of sex: Contemporary readings* (pp. 135–144). Lanham, MD: Rowman & Littlefield.

David, L. (Writer), Seinfeld, J. (Writer), & Cherones, T. (Director). (1993a). The handicap spot [Television series episode]. In L. David (Executive producer), *Seinfeld.* New York: SONY Pictures.

David, L. (Writer), Seinfeld, J. (Writer), & Cherones, T. (Director). (1993b). The outing [Television series episode]. In L. David (Executive producer), *Seinfeld.* New York: SONY Pictures.

Davis, A. (1981). *Women, race, & class.* New York: Vintage.

DePalma, B. (Director). (1989). *Casualties of war* [Motion picture]. United States: TriStar Productions.

Dissed-Respect: The impact of bullying. (2007). Dir. Rich Allen & J. W. Wiley, Perf. J. W. Wiley, Allie Armstrong, DVD, Plattsburgh, NY: Mountain Lake PBS.

Douglass, F. (2001). What to the slave is the Fourth of July. In T. Frazier (Ed.), *Readings in African-American history* (pp. 106–125). Belmont, CA: Wadsworth.

Draper, R. (2012). *Do not ask what good we do: Inside the U.S. house of representatives.* New York. Free Press.

Du Bois, W. E. B. (1986). The name "Negro." In N. I. Huggins (Ed.), *Du Bois: Literary classics of the United States* (pp. 1219–1222). New York: The Library of America.

Du Bois, W. E. B. (1990). *The souls of Black folk.* New York: Vintage Books, Library of America.

Du Bois, W. E. B. (1997). *John Brown: A biography.* Armonk, NY: M.E. Sharpe.

Dyson, M. E. (1996). *Race rules: Navigating the color line.* Boston, MA: Addison-Wesley.

Earth, Wind & Fire. (1974). Fair but so uncool [Song]. On *Open our eyes* [Record]. New York: Columbia/Legacy.

Estevez, E. (Director). (2006). *Bobby* [Motion picture]. United States: The Weinstein Company Home Entertainment.

Eyre, C. (Director and producer) & Alexie, S. (Producer). (1998). *Smoke signals* [Motion picture]. United States: Miramax.

Fine, M., & Asch, A. (2004). Disability beyond stigma: Social interaction, discrimination, and activism. In M. Adams, W. J. Blumenfeld, R. Castaneda, H. W. Hackman, M. L. Peters, & X. Zuniga (Eds.), *Readings for diversity and social justice: An anthology on racism, antisemitism, sexism, heterosexism, ableism, and classism* (pp. 397–402). New York: Routledge.

Frank, T. (1997). *The conquest of cool.* Chicago, IL: University of Chicago Press.

Gilroy, P. (1991). *There ain't no black in the Union Jack: The cultural politics of race and nation.* Chicago, IL: University of Chicago Press.

Gregory, D. (1964). *Nigger: An autobiography.* New York: Pocket Books.

Halpern, B. L., & Lubar, K. (1998). *Leadership presence: Dramatic techniques to reach out, motivate, and inspire.* New York: Gotham Books.

hooks, b. (2004). *We real cool: Black men and masculinity.* New York: Routledge.

Kant, Immanuel. (1991). *Observations on the feeling of the beautiful and sublime,* trans. by John T. Goldthwait. Berkeley: University of California Press.

Katz, J. (2004). Pornography and men's consciousness. In M. Adams, W. J. Blumenfeld, R. Castaneda, H. W. Hackman, M. L. Peters, & X. Zuniga (Eds.), *Readings for diversity and social justice: An anthology on racism, antisemitism, sexism, heterosexism, ableism, and classism* (pp. 247–251). New York: Routledge.

Kennedy, R. (2002). *Nigger: The strange career of a troublesome word.* New York: Vintage.

Kimmel, M. (2000). Masculinity as homophobia: Fear, shame, and silence in the construction of gender identity. In M. Adams, W. J. Blumenfeld, R. Castaneda, H. W. Hackman, M. L. Peters, & X. Zuniga (Eds.), *Readings for diversity and social justice: An anthology on racism, antisemitism, sexism, heterosexism, ableism, and classism* (pp. 213–219). New York: Routledge.

Kipling, R. (1910). If [Poem]. Retrieved from www.poemhunter.com

Langston, D. (2000). Tired of playing Monopoly? In M. Adams, W. J. Blumenfeld, R. Castaneda, H. W. Hackman, M. L. Peters, & X. Zuniga (Eds.), *Readings for diversity and social justice: An anthology on racism, antisemitism, sexism, heterosexism, ableism, and classism* (pp. 397–402). New York: Routledge.

Latifah, Queen. (1993). U.N.I.T.Y. [Song]. On *Black reign* [CD]. New York: Motown.

Leary, J. D. (2005). *Post traumatic slave syndrome: America's legacy of enduring injury and healing.* Milwaukie, OR: Uptone Press.

Leviticus 20:13. Retrieved from http://bible.cc/leviticus/20–13.htm

Lennon, J. (1972). Woman is the nigger of the world [Song]. On *Some time in New York City* [Record]. New York: Apple.

Limbaugh, R. (2007, January 19). *The Rush Limbaugh show* [Radio broadcast]. Transcript available from http://mediamatters.org/video/2009/10/12/matthews-whether-or-not-limbuagh-allowed-to-buy/155606

Limbaugh, R. (2012, May 9). *The Rush Limbaugh show* [Radio broadcast]. Retrieved from http://mediamatters.org/video/2012/05/09/limbaugh-weve-arrived-at-a-point-where-the-pres/184955

Loewen, J. W. (1995). *Lies my teacher told me: Everything your American history textbook got wrong.* New York: Touchstone.

Lorber, J. (2000). "Night to his day": The social construction of gender. In M. Adams, W. J. Blumenfeld, R. Castaneda, H. W. Hackman, M. L. Peters, & X. Zuniga (Eds.), *Readings for diversity and social justice: An anthology on racism, antisemitism, sexism, heterosexism, ableism, and classism* (pp. 203–213). New York: Routledge.

Mailer, N. (2007). The white negro. Retrieved from http://www.dissentmagazine.org/online_articles/the-white-negro-fall-1957

Mill, J. S. (1988). The subjection of women. In S. M. Okin (Ed.), *John Stuart Mill: The Subjection of Women* (p. 23). Indianapolis, IN: Hackett. (Original work published 1869)

Milner, M. (2006). *Freaks, geeks, and cool kids.* New York: Routledge.

Roppolo, K. (2010). Symbolic racism, history, and reality: The real problem with Indian mascots. In M. Adams, W. J. Blumenfeld, R. Castaneda, H. W. Hackman, M. L. Peters, & X. Zuniga (Eds.), *Readings for diversity and social justice: Second edition* (pp. 74–78). New York: Routledge.

Scott, A. P. (2010). *Frequently asked questions about "Indian" mascots.* Retrieved from http://www.aistm.org/1indexpage.htm

Singleton, J. (Director). (1997). *Rosewood* [Motion picture]. United States: Warner Bros.

Solondz, T. (Director). (2002). *Storytelling* [Motion picture]. United States: New Line Cinema.

Spielberg, S. (Director). (1997). *The lost world: Jurassic Park* [Motion picture]. United States: Amblin Entertainment.

Tatum, B. D. (2004a). The complexity of identity: Who am I? In M. Adams, W. J. Blumenfeld, R. Castaneda, H. W. Hackman, M. L. Peters, & X. Zuniga (Eds.), *Readings for diversity and social justice: An anthology on racism, antisemitism, sexism, heterosexism, ableism, and classism* (pp. 9–14). New York: Routledge.

Tatum, B. D. (2004b). Defining racism: Can we talk? In M. Adams, W. J. Blumenfeld, R. Castaneda, H. W. Hackman, M. L. Peters, & X. Zuniga (Eds.), *Readings for diversity and social justice: An anthology on racism, antisemitism, sexism, heterosexism, ableism, and classism* (pp. 79–82). New York: Routledge.

West, C. (1982). *Prophesy deliverance: An Afro-American revolutionary Christianity.* Philadelphia, PA: Westminster Press.

West, C. (1993). *Race matters.* Boston, MA: Beacon Press.

Wiley, J. W. (2009). Affirmative actions at PWIs: Explicating the glass as half full, while pouring something they're more apt to taste. In D. Cleveland (Ed.), *When minorities are strongly encouraged to apply: Diversity and affirmative action in higher education* (pp. 241–278). New York: Peter Lang.

Wiley, J. W. (2010). Dissertation: An evaluation of film for use in developing leadership moments within a context of diversity & social justice. University of Vermont.

Wise, T. (2011). *White like me: Reflections on race from a privileged son.* Berkeley, CA: Soft Skull Press.

ABOUT THE AUTHOR

Dr. J. W. Wiley has served as director of SUNY Plattsburgh's Center for Diversity, Pluralism, and Inclusion for 12 years, with a joint appointment as a lecturer in philosophy and interdisciplinary studies. The courses he teaches are Examining Diversity Through Film; Philosophies on Romance, Sex, Love & Marriage; African American Culture from 1865–Present; Moral Problems–Societal Dilemmas; Examining Dimensions of Cool: A Study of Social Class; and The Philosophy of W. E. B. Du Bois. In these courses he engages the term *nigger* in different contexts with differing consequences with students from an array of backgrounds.

His educational background found him attempting to engage racism in every facet during his pursuit of a doctorate in philosophy and cultural studies at Claremont Graduate University, where he was essentially trying to put a square peg into a round hole. For years, Dr. Wiley has worked side by side with Dr. Eddie Moore Jr. (founder of the White Privilege Conference) presenting "The Nigger Word" in workshops around the country. Dr. Wiley hosted, cowrote, and codirected a film titled *Dissed-Respect: The Impact of Bullying*, while framing bullying as a diversity and social justice concern. He designs and teaches various workshops as needed but always offers Diversity Enlightenment I & II, Examining Diversity Through Film, and Developing Leadership Moments. In these workshops, he has consulted and/or facilitated conversations that included an exploration of diversity and social justice, leadership, workplace and schoolyard bullying, and dysfunctional language with organizations as wide-ranging as Pfizer Pharmaceuticals, New York State Nurses Association, UC San Francisco Medical Center, Princeton Jr. Scholar's Institute, Wyeth Pharmaceuticals, Norwich University, Pace University, SUNY Potsdam, Castleton State College, University of Vermont, Paul Smith's College, and Mount Union College, as well as dozens of high schools and middle schools.

INDEX

ability, 21. *See also* disability
  fragility of, 28
abolitionism, 40, 172
abortion, 149
academic communities, 109–11
accents, 107
acceptance, 11
Acosta, Angel, 146
Adjapong, Edmund, 23
adversity, 15
Affirmative Action, 14
African Americans. *See* Black people
Afro, 151, 155
Allen, Rich, 183
Allen, Woody, 74, 166
  racism of, 167–68
  stereotypical inclusion of, 169–70
  systematic exclusion of, 169–70
Alpha Men, 44
Alpha Phi Alpha, 42, 43
America
  hypocrisy of, 163
  identity hegemony of, 20
  race and, 9
  racism in, 116, 123–31
  Romney on, 148
  socioeconomic class in, 148
American Dream, 17
American History X (film), 8
"American Terrorist" (Lupe Fiasco), 115
anti-Semitism, 52
Any Given Sunday (film), 124
Arabs, 2
Armstrong, Neil, 139
A., Lindsay, 179, 200
Asians, 5, 48, 124–25
  stereotypes of, 131–32
"As Time Goes By" (song), 59
authenticity, 10

Babyface, 101–2
"The Ballad of Reading Gaol" (Wilde), 45
Banks, Russell, 92
beauty privilege, 52
bell hooks, 89
benefit of doubt, 94–96
  of the Other, 203
Beyonce, 91
Beyond Good and Evil (Nietzsche), 69
biraciality, 57
bisexuality, 49
  conformity and, 57
bitch, 4, 59, 202
  categorical imperative and, 64
  Dyson on, 62–63
  engaging, 61–65
  as term of endearment, 72
"Bitch Bad" (Lupe Fiasco), 59, 61
The Black Eyed Peas, 24
Black Muslims, 135
Blackness, 20
Black Panthers, 129, 135
Black people, xiv, 12
  crime and, 13, 18–19
  framing of, 103–4
  Hume on, 115
  institutional power of, 124
  Jefferson on, 116
  Kant on, 115–16
  minority status of, 142–43
  oppression responded to by, 103
  in Plattsburgh, 142–43
  as property, 16
  racism of, 122
  Rock on, 102, 103–4
  snapshot syndrome and, 46
  struggle of, 135
  trustingness of, 122

Morrison, Toni, 92
Mos Def, 92
mothers, 70–71. *See also* women
Mountain Lake PBS, 96
Mousseau, Bryn, 180
moving walkway, 147–48
Mowry, 13
mulattoes, 18
multiple identities, 10, 20–22
    Blumenfeld on, 194–95
    engaging, 194
    Tatum on, 21
"The Myth of Black Sexuality" (Davis), 80
"The Myth of Sisyphus" (Camus), 10,
    199–200
"The Myth of the Black Rapist" (Davis), 80,
    86

NAACP, 17
"The Name Negro" (Du Bois), 17
names, 17
National Conference on Race and Ethnicity,
    62
Native Americans, 2, 5, 124–25
    dehumanization of, 128
    mascots and, 126–27, 129–30
Nazism, 137
Negro, 1, 16, 17, 141–42
    White, 102–3
nerd, 89
"New Day" (West & Jay-Z), 162
New Student Orientations, SUNY Platts-
    burgh, 28
NFL, 164
Nietzsche, Friedrich, 69, 181
Niger, 1
Nigeria, 1
nigger, 16–20, 55, 62, 202. *See also* P = C =
    N
    diversity and, 7
    Du Bois on, 17
    engaging with, 13–14, 192
    as greeting, 141–42
    Gregory on, 203
    identity and, 17
    informal usage of, 141–42
    labeling and, 3

non-Black person use of, 107
    as problem, 19
    pronunciations of, 106
    reputation of, xiii
    Rock on, 102, 103–4
    social class and, 103–4
    socialization to, 7
    social justice and, 14
    societal framing of, 3
    as term of endearment, 72
    using, 71–72
    victims and, 182–83
*Nigger: The Strange Career of a Troublesome
    Word* (Kennedy), xiii, 102
Nin, Anaïs, 167
no homo, 41, 55
nonconformity, 57
normality
    dysfunctional, 61
    overvalued, 12
North Country, 7, 34, 95, 108
North Country (film), 35
Norwich University, 32
noticeable heterogeneity, 4–5
Nugent, Ted, 127
N.W.A, 125
NYSNA retreat, 33

Obama, Barack, 13, 34, 74, 82, 139
    coolness of, 90–91
    devaluing, 161–62
    presidency of, 151–54
    Rock on, 151–52
    on same-sex marriage, 146–47, 164
    stereotypes of, 151–52
    on Tucson murders, 184
    Wiley, J. W., on, 151–54
    "you guys" phrase used by, 165
obesity, 49
O'Brien, Soledad, 82
*Observations on the Feeling of the Beautiful
    and Sublime* (Kant), 115–16
O'Donnell, Lawrence, 82
"Of the Sons of Masters and Man" (Du
    Bois), 18
oppression, 16
    Black people's response to, 103

Also available from Stylus

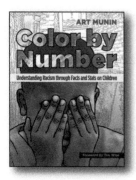

Color by Number
Understanding Racism Through Facts and Stats on Children
Art Munin
Foreword by Tim Wise

For those who haven't given much thought to race matters, this volume could serve as an inoculation against the twisted political siren song of the far-right, providing sufficient knowledge so as to weaken the appeal of those who would manipulate their racial fears, anxieties and insecurities, or try and deny the reality of racial inequality so as to push a colorblind—and therefore, injustice-blind—agenda. And for those already committed to racial equity and justice, the contents herein could be even more important: providing us with the factual information needed to go forth and mobilize others to the cause, not to mention reminding us of just how important is the task which lay ahead.

"I welcome this addition to the literature already extant on race and racism. It is long overdue."—*Tim Wise*, *Author*, White Like Me: Reflections on Race from a Privileged Son, *and* Dear White America: Letter to a New Minority

"This is a powerful social justice tool. The book provides the reader with the necessary numbers and information needed to be a more competent and confident advocate for equity and justice in the 21st century."—*Eddie Moore Jr., Founder/Program Director, The White Privilege Conference*

"The clear and understandable tables help those who are not 'academics' process how our society has not supported the 'have nots.' There is a connection of theory to practice using social justice literature and researchers such as Paulo Freire and Gloria Ladson-Billings. Each chapter has a 'next steps for the reader' section which is ingenious. When I teach my students about social justice, oppression, racism, and sexism they leave the class feeling overwhelmed and helpless. The next steps section gives the reader an opportunity to continue reading, studying, and fighting for social justice. There are no excuses for reading the chapter/book and saying 'this is bigger than me, I cannot be a change agent.' I hope that everyone is willing to be a change agent after reading this book." —*Mary Howard-Hamilton, Holmstedt Distinguished Professor, Higher Education Program, Indiana State University*

22883 Quicksilver Drive
Sterling, VA 20166-2102

Subscribe to our e-mail alerts: www.Styluspub.com